Catherine Fairbrother

Federico García Lorca

GW00498766

'An outstanding and completely contemporary account of Lorca' – *Professor Robert Eaglestone, Royal Holloway, University of London, UK*

'This is a highly innovative study, which will appeal to students and scholars alike' – *Professor David George, University of Wales, UK*

Immortalized in death by The Clash, Pablo Neruda, Salvador Dalí, Dmitri Shostakovich, Carlos Saura, and Lindsay Kemp, Federico García Lorca's spectre haunts both contemporary Spain and the cultural landscape beyond.

This study offers a fresh examination of one of the Spanish language's most resonant voices, exploring how the very factors which led to Lorca's emergence as a cultural icon also shaped his dramatic output.

The works themselves are also awarded the space that they deserve, combining performance histories with incisive textual analysis to restate Lorca's presence as a playwright of extraordinary vision, in works such as

- *Blood Wedding*
- *The Public*
- *The House of Bernarda Alba*
- *Yerma*

Federico García Lorca is an invaluable new resource for those seeking to understand this complex and multifaceted figure: artist, playwright, director, poet, martyr and in the eyes of many, Spain's 'national dramatist'.

Maria M. Delgado is Professor of Theatre and Screen Arts at Queen Mary, University of London, co-editor of *Contemporary Theatre Review*, and author of *'Other' Spanish Theatres* (2003).

ROUTLEDGE MODERN AND
CONTEMPORARY DRAMATISTS
Series editors: Maggie B. Gale and Mary Luckhurst

Routledge Modern and Contemporary Dramatists is a new series of innovative and exciting critical introductions to the work of internationally pioneering playwrights. The series includes recent *and* well-established playwrights and offers primary materials on contemporary dramatists who are under-represented in secondary criticism. Each volume provides detailed cultural, historical and political material, examines selected plays in production, and theorises the playwright's artistic agenda and working methods, as well as their contribution to the development of playwriting and theatre.

Volumes currently available in the series are:

J.B. Priestley by Maggie B. Gale
Federico García Lorca by Maria M. Delgado
Susan Glaspell and Sophie Treadwell by Barbara Ozieblo and Jerry Dickey

Future volumes will include:

Caryl Churchill by Mary Luckhurst
Mark Ravenhill by John Deeney
Jean Genet by David Bradby
August Strindberg by Eszter Szalczer
Anton Chekhov by Rose Whyman

Federico García Lorca

Routledge Modern and
Contemporary Dramatists

Maria M. Delgado

Routledge
Taylor & Francis Group
LONDON AND NEW YORK

First published 2008 by Routledge
2 Park Square, Milton Park, Abingdon, Oxon OX14 4RN

Simultaneously published in the USA and Canada
by Routledge
270 Madison Avenue, New York, NY 10016

Routledge is an imprint of the Taylor & Francis Group, an informa business

© 2008 Maria M. Delgado

Typeset in Sabon and Georgia by
Keystroke, 28 High Street, Tettenhall, Wolverhampton
Printed and bound in Great Britain by
Antony Rowe Ltd, Chippenham, Wiltshire

British Library Cataloguing in Publication Data
A catalogue record for this book is available from the British
Library

Library of Congress Cataloging in Publication Data
Delgado, Maria M.
  Federico García Lorca / Maria M. Delgado.
    p. cm.
    Includes bibliographical references and index.
  1. García Lorca, Federico, 1898–1936. I. Title.
  PQ6613.A763Z6187 2007
  868'.6209—dc22   2007031602

ISBN10: 0–415–36242–3 (hbk)
ISBN10: 0–415–36243–1 (pbk)
ISBN10: 0–203–01271–2 (ebk)

ISBN13: 978–0–415–36242–9 (hbk)
ISBN13: 978–0–415–36243–6 (pbk)
ISBN13: 978–0–203–01271–0 (ebk)

Contents

Illustrations

Acknowledgements

I have accumulated numerous debts of gratitude during the writing of this book. I would like to acknowledge the assistance of the following archives where I conducted research for the volume: the Arxiu Històrico Barcelona (especially Alicia Torres Déniz); the Institut del Teatre, Barcelona; the Centro de Documentación Teatral (CDT), Madrid (especially Berta Muñoz and Gerardo del Barco); the Fundación Juan March, Madrid; the Hemeroteca Nacional, Madrid; the New York Public Library (NYPL). Deep thanks go to the Fundación Federico García Lorca (FFGL), its archivists Sonia González García and Rosa María Illán de Haro, its President, Laura García-Lorca de los Ríos and its former President, Manuel Fernández-Montesinos. I am also grateful to the following organizations that provided information on Lorca stagings and adaptations: the Almeida Theatre, London; the Casa Natal Federico García Lorca, Fuente Vaqueros (especially Inmaculada Hernández and José Rodriguez); the Edinburgh International Festival; the Fundación Rafael Alberti; Kosmas Art/Design (especially William Kosmas); the National Library of Scotland; Oakland Opera Theatre; the National Theatre (NT), London; Opera North (ON); the Peregrine Whittlesey Agency; Schott Music; the Theatre Royal Stratford East (TRSE). During my time in Granada, I benefited from the generosity of Federico García y García del Real and Marta Badía Aparicio at the Huerta de San Vicente and José Pérez Rodríguez at the Valderrubio museum. Mair George was a shrewd companion on the Lorca tourist trail.

x *Acknowledgements*

Thanks are also due to those who shared references with me or answered questions on their own specialist areas: Gordon Anderson, Robert Archer, Phil Auslander, Manuel Aznar Soler, Len Berkman, Jaime Camino, Marvin Carlson, Julia Carnahan, Óscar Cornago Bernal, Trader Faulkner, Joel Fram, Derek Gagen, Víctor García Ruiz, Meli Hatzirysidis, Robert Havard, Sandra Hebron, Kevin Higa, Nadine Holdsworth, Marion Peter Holt, Alan James, François Koltès, Martin Lowe, Michael McCarthy, Joan Matabosch, Marcos Ordóñez, Lourdes Orozco, Patrice Pavis, Paul Preston, Steve Proctor, Víctor Ramírez Ladrón de Guevara, Maribel San Ginés, Alberto Sandoval-Sánchez, Mercè Saumell, Bijan Sheibani, Aleks Sierz, Paul Julian Smith, and Phyllis Zatlin. Frederic Amat, Calixto Bieito, Gael García Bernal, Michael John LaChiusa, Jorge Lavelli, Nicola LeFanu, Alex Morales, Lluís Pasqual, Aribert Reimann, Peter Sellars, and Caridad Svich spoke to me of their experiences 'tackling' Lorca. I owe a debt of thanks to Ira Weitzman and the creative team of Lincoln Center's *The House of Bernarda Alba* for allowing me to attend a private rehearsal of the musical in January 2006. The New York hospitality of Susan Yankowitz and Herb Liebowitz and the Barcelona/Cadaqués hospitality of Ventura Pons and Narciso Fernández Nogales deserve a special mention. I am also grateful to the photographers and production companies who allowed their images to be used in the book.

David Bradby, Robert Eaglestone, David George, and Sarah Wright all provided constructive feedback on the manuscript. Simon Breden, Diana Delgado, and Gabriel Quirós-Alpera were diligent research assistants. The School of English and Drama at Queen Mary, University of London funded a semester's leave and numerous early research trips to Spain. Colleagues and students at Queen Mary, especially Joel Anderson, Una Bauer, Jen Harvie, Paul Heritage, and Gregor Turbyne, supported the project both intellectually and practically. Maggie B. Gale as the lead series editor on the volume was an astute and generous critic. Talia Rodgers and Mary Luckhurst offered apt advice. All deserve a special debt of thanks.

The research visits to New York, Madrid and Granada were funded by an Arts and Humanities' Research Council (AHRC)

Small Grant in the Creative and Performing Arts. The book was completed with assistance from the AHRC's Research Leave Scheme. I am grateful to the AHRC for its support of this project.

This book could not have been completed without the unwavering support of my family, especially the Delgado-Byrnes (Irene, Peter and Daniel), my mother Severina González Pérez, my late father Alfonso Delgado Álava, my partner Henry Little and my son Thomas Delgado-Little. This book is dedicated to them and to the memory of my grandfather, one of the 30,000 who, like Lorca, lies in an unmarked, mass grave.

Referencing

This book uses the Harvard referencing system. Spanish authors tend to have a double surname (the mother's name follows that of the father). While Federico García Lorca is known most commonly as Lorca, he is listed bibliographically as García Lorca, Federico. References to works by Lorca are listed within the text in an abbreviated form. OCI–OCIV refers to his complete works in Spanish, volumes 1–4. GL is used for translated works. While quotations are provided in English, with an English published source noted where available, reference is also made to the Spanish original to ensure that the book can be used by those reading the plays in both languages. Press reviews of productions cited in the manuscript are listed in a separate section of the Bibliography.

Abbreviations of institutions are noted in the acknowledgements section. Dates given in parentheses when discussing Lorca's plays in Chapters 2 and 3 are those of initial composition. It is important to note that Lorca often revised works over numerous years and that these dates do not always concur with those of premiere productions.

Overview

a believable image is the product of a negotiation with an
unverifiable real.

(Phelan 1993: 1)

Spain's institutional body for the international dissemination of
its culture, the Instituto Cervantes, may be named after the early
modern creator of the windmill-conquering knight Don Quixote,
but the dramatist and poet Federico García Lorca (1898–1936)
has now arguably eclipsed him. On the centenary of his birth in
1998, Spain's leading post-dictatorship broadsheet *El País* con-
fidently pronounced him the nation's most translated writer
(Gibson 1998: 28). An exhibition of postcards inaugurated that
same year, featuring an emblematic image of the young photogenic poet 'appropriated' by artists including Joan Brossa, Antoni
Tàpies and Gordillo, remains on tour and is growing with 285
exhibits to date. His verses serve as the title for a prime-time
gardening programme on Spanish television (Smith 1998: 105),
as edifying symbols of Spanish high art on London's underground
system and New York's city-wide buses (Vilches de Frutos 1998:
11). The Resad, Madrid's senior conservatoire, has a performance
space that bears his name. A prominent statue honouring the poet
is situated in Madrid's Santa Ana square. Streets and schools take
his name across Spain and even beyond, in the Americas, where
major venues including Havana's Gran Teatro and Paraguay's
Centro Cultural de la Ciudad in Asunción have auditoria renamed
in his honour. Uruguay boasts a monument in the García Lorca

Park at Piedra Alta in Salto; on the corner of Mexico City's Juárez avenue and Federico García Lorca street stands a prominent bust of the playwright around which annual homages are enacted. Across tourist stands in his native Granada rows of T-shirts carrying his distinctive signature stand alongside those of Arabic insignia, charging bulls and polka dot dresses, pieces of Andalusia that can be transported home for posterity (see Figure 12, p. 194). In London and San Francisco tapas bars and restaurants carry his name, further endorsing his rampant commodification in the decades since Franco's death in 1975.

During his lifetime Lorca may have disapproved of his branding as Lorca (OCIII 773), but it is his mother's surname, the more feminine Lorca to the García of his father, through which he is commonly now referred. Lorca is now a national trademark, a potent icon whose valuable wares are exported across the global cultural marketplace. More so than any other twentieth-century Spanish writer, he remains a paradoxical embodiment of the local, the national and the global. His life and work have become indelibly bound up in a process of mythification that has converted him first into the ultimate countercultural icon – the gay, martyred seer and a taboo topic in Franco's Spain – and now the establishment face of the newly tolerant post-dictatorship Spain.

Authorship and performance

While Lorca was both a poet and dramatist, this study concentrates primarily on his dramatic output for which his poetry was, in the words of one critic, 'a preparation' (Honig 1945: vii). While references are made to his poetic anthologies and their 'afterlives' as theatrical performance, this book deals with the ways in which his dramaturgy has been canonized through modes of performance. The focus is on premiere productions but there are also references to posthumous stagings across Spain, the USA and the UK that have impacted on modes of shaping the Lorca canon.[1] The focus is not on detailed textual analysis of the type provided by critics like Edwards (1980) or Reed Anderson (1984) but on locating the performative indicators encoded into the plays. This is not to say that the 'author-function', as Foucault terms it, does not impact on the readings offered. Rather, following earlier scholarship by Fernández Cifuentes (1986) and Smith (1989), the book argues not for a mythologization of text (replacing that of the author), but rather for a strategy that recognizes the authority of Lorca, not as the measure against which the text is invariably positioned, but as a convergent point for 'projections, in terms always more or less psychological, of our way of handling texts' (Foucault 2001: 1629). Lorca as author-function is a construct of successive generations of readers whose discursive practices have been shaped by the historical, ideological and cultural parameters through which they have received the works. This, in turn, has shaped the modes in which his plays have been read through performance. The performative history of Lorca's dramaturgy cannot be prised apart from his author-function.

Any discussion of the performative strategies through which Lorca's work has been presented necessarily depends on a consideration of his currency as Spain's national dramatist. Crucially, the marketing of Spain through the tropes of Andalusia (sun, flamenco and the gypsies) has fixed Lorca in the popular international imagination as quintessentially Spanish. He is at once 'universal and particular' (Smith 1989: 107), chronicling the lives of the marginalized across national, racial, sexual and gender frontiers while simultaneously presenting socio-cultural documents on the predicaments of inhabitants of a Spanish nation crippled by social inequalities and fierce gender policing. These dualities have informed the modes of reading the texts (see pp. 33–6 of Chapter 1) and shaped a production history that negotiates a sometimes uneasy mix of *españolade* and conceptual abstraction. The discussion of the 'known' plays that takes place in Chapter 2 examines not only the supposed Andalusian iconography of Lorca's best known works – including *Blood Wedding*, *Yerma*, and *The House of Bernarda Alba* – but also the production styles that have reinforced this iconography in Spain and abroad. The emphasis is both on charting the folkloric slant of whitewashed houses, black mantillas and flamenco song and dance embedded in tourist clichés, and its performative 'other'. This latter approach has sought not to 'speak of Spain', dispensing with mimetic referents in favour of an austere stylization whose thematic premise revolves around the socio-sexual encounters negotiated through the text.

While Chapter 2 also examines supposedly 'minor' plays – the puppet plays, *Mariana Pineda* and *The Butterfly's Evil Spell* – habitually perceived as stepping-stones to his later tragedies, these are contextualized in ways that signal their links to local myths and narratives and to broader theatrical movements then finding currency in Europe. The reading of the plays offered here points to the challenges they present to practitioners in negotiating both symbolist drama and subliminal verse (as in the case of *The Butterfly's Evil Spell*), lyricism and dialogue (*Mariana Pineda*) and formulaic *guignol* and the operatic (the puppet plays). If, as I indicate in Chapter 2, dance and opera have embraced Lorca's work so emphatically, it is arguably because his texts oscillate between extremes of language, gesture and emotion that are more easily accommodated by dance and opera's conception of the body and voice *in extremis*.

This study also grants a central place to Lorca's more oblique works that filtered into the public domain much later than his 'known' dramaturgy. While *When Five Years Pass* was first published in 1938, it was not until its initial staging in Spain forty years later, with the productions of *The Public* and *Play Without a Title* that followed in 1986 and 1989 respectively, that focus began to shift to dramatic works that had been hitherto regarded as peripheral or 'impossible'. Both a process of reappropriation and scholarship, the staging of these unfamiliar works re-envisaged Lorca, introducing audiences to a largely unknown section of his repertoire. Critics sought 'to "recover"' the author from the works, proving 'the value' of the texts by 'ascertaining the holiness of its author' (Foucault 2001: 1630), and stressing the palpable presence of recognizable Lorca motifs in the plays (Edwards 1980: 60–124; Higginbotham 1976: 41–69; Soufas 1996: 68–92).

The performative journeys of the plays, however, suggest an alternative view. Indeed, like Smith (1989: 108), I argue that these experimental, and, in the cases of *The Public* and *Play Without a Title* incomplete, works flaunt established rules of dramatic construction. This is not a prescriptive theatre where we identify with characters, judge their actions, and then apply the logic to our own lives. Rather than tell stories, these plays prioritize the theatrical experience itself with its inherent reliance on audience reciprocity and reflection. As with the work of Antoine Artaud and Jean Genet, the emphasis is on a stage practice that reimagines perceptions of time and space as well as the relationship between representation and the real. The directorial process that functions as a trope in both *The Public* and *Play Without a Title* points to a concern with the politics of performance that also informs Lorca's theoretical writings. In charting the performance history of these plays I hope not to homogenize their themes and motifs, but rather to indicate the problematic dialogue between these works and the interpretative discourses through which they are habitually read. As such, I argue for their status as key documents of the European avant-garde.

The book's central premise lies in delineating how performance has affected the ways in which we approach Lorca's life as well as his work. His eventful life has proved an enduring trope in reading his poetic and dramatic output. It has been the performance of his life rather than the performance of his work that has served as the primary prism through which to refract his dramaturgy. The portraits of him by friends and contemporaries were early steps on the road to mythification. His assassination in the early months of the Spanish Civil War conferred martyrdom on him. The conspicuous absence of his dramaturgy on the Spanish stage during the early years of Franco's dictatorship, and the absence of a complete edition of his work until 1953, rendered him the forbidden 'other', more desired in death than in life. Chapter 1 maps the intersections between biography, self and 'other' that have shaped the historiographical mapping of Lorca's life and work. In examining the cult of personality that grew up around Lorca in life and in death it will point towards a necrophilic fascination that has spawned biopics, paintings, poems, operas and rock anthems covered in the final chapter.

Translation and canonization

Even though Lorca has now usurped Ibsen, Chekhov and Brecht as 'the most performed foreign-language playwright on the

English-speaking stage' (Johnston 1993: 21), the perception of his work as a poor second to his life has left him languishing in the shadows of Brecht, born in the same year. Like Brecht, Lorca theorized on the politics and possibilities of theatre, providing a telling commentary in letters, interviews and lectures on the state of Spanish theatre at the time and measures that could be put in place to offer alternatives to staid dramatic writing and antiquated stage practices. Unlike Brecht the production and study of his dramaturgy was hampered by a paucity of translations that contained his influence largely within the Spanish-speaking world.

I have traced elsewhere the canonization of his work that ensued in South America in the aftermath of his death as those who had worked alongside him in Spain went into exile, promoting his dramaturgy and his pedagogy in their own practice (Delgado 2003: 46–52). Dominance in the southern hemisphere, however, does not necessarily mean canonization in the Western world. Spanish may be one of the world's most common languages, with around 400 million native speakers, but it lacks the economic clout of English. The colonialist implications of English-language domination has ensured that theatrical value is conferred on texts that 'make the grade' through the filter of translation. Critics have not been kind to the 'reverential' early translations of the American team James Graham-Luján and Richard O'Connell, first published during the 1940s and remaining in print until Lorca temporarily came out of copyright in 1986. These have been judged as impediments to the dramatist's 'potential for influencing the English-speaking stage' (Johnston 1998b: 55), their 'literalness and frequent clumsiness' (Edwards 1998: 23) giving a stilted impression, as if the plays had 'simply been photocopied into English' (Johnston 1998b: 56). Photocopies always function as a fainter copy of the original and even the most cursory glance at reviews of English-language productions of the plays up to 1986 indicates the problems experienced by critics who were unable to quite see how the rhetorical fabric of the plays might be made to work in a more monosyllabic language.

While copyright laws were soon revised to seventy years, the opportunity granted by this lifting as well as the anniversary commemorations of his death in 1986 that offered a marketing hinge for new productions encouraged a generation of translators to provide alternative linguistic renditions of his plays.[2] Obviously Edwards and Johnston have a vested interest in underlining the 'legitimacy' of their translations, but the plethora of versions of the play now in the public sphere has countered the hesitant views of early critics who followed Lorca's dictum that translation destroys the spirit of a language (OCIII 565; Río 1952: 137). The struggle for ownership of Lorca has been as much played out in the field of theatrical translation as it has in the political or cultural sphere.

While the Graham-Luján and O'Connell translations were not the only ones endorsed by the Lorca estate in the period up to 1986, they were the only translations available in print, sanctioned with an introduction by Lorca's brother Francisco. Tom Stoppard and Langston Hughes were probably the most prominent writers permitted to produce translations of *The House of Bernarda Alba* and *Blood Wedding* respectively prior to 1986, but since then Nilo Cruz, David Hare, Ted Hughes, Pam Gems, Frank McGuinness, Emily Mann, and Caridad Svich have all been commissioned to provide versions of the plays, thus 'endorsing' Lorca through their act of reworking him for the stage and simultaneously gaining credibility through their association with a dramatist increasingly being perceived as one of the 'greats'.

The Lorca 'boom' evident since the mid-1980s has seen most of the dominant players in theatre publishing – Faber, Methuen, Hodder & Stoughton, Bantam Books, Theatre Communications Group, Smith & Kraus – bring out their 'versions' of the plays. It demonstrates that translation is, as much as production, the site of cultural exchange and interaction. Johnston sees the rise of Lorca in Thatcher's Britain as related to the possibilities his plays offer for 'the redefining of community via the formal equivalent of an audience united through the democracy of the emotions rather than the elitism of intellect' (Johnston 1999: 64). Perhaps the integration of Spain into the political and economic structures of the EEC facilitated the 'exportation' of her cultural wares into a climate hungry for the new. The widescale international reverberations of Madrid's *movida* – and its most visible global product Pedro Almodóvar – and Barcelona's design boom – embodied by the 1992 Olympics – served to bring centre-stage a nation that had traditionally been marginalized to the edges of Europe's peripheries.

The printed word and the performative

Lorca was as much part of this sense of discovery as Almodóvar – and it is perhaps no coincidence that Lorca is cited by the latter as a point of origin for his ninth film *High Heels* (1991), with *Blood Wedding* and *The House of Bernarda Alba* referenced in *All About My Mother* (1999) and *Volver* (2006) respectively.[3] The inscription of Lorca into the performative culture of the nation has seen the anniversaries of his birth and death converted into occasions for national soul-searching with politicians, royalty, and cultural icons wading in to appropriate the Lorca *corpus*. Lorca's correspondence and interviews make constant reference to his own horrors at proofing work for publication, accompanied always by 'the inevitable sense of death: that the poem no longer lives' (OCIII 498). Manuscripts were handed to friends or destroyed (Stainton 1999: 119–20). The priority for Lorca was performance (OCIII 438, 572, 606) – of both the poetry and plays – but it has been the publication of his complete letters, edited by Andrew Anderson and Christopher Maurer (1997), and the steady trickle of plays and poems into print through the 1970s, 1980s and 1990s that has facilitated his canonization.

Jorge Guillén (1959: 47–50) locates his importance for contemporaries in his prolific oral recitals. Marcelle Auclair (1968: 87), his friend and early biographer, attributes his reluctance to publish to his status as an itinerant storyteller or *jongleur*. Perhaps J.B. Trend's assertion that 'His poetry is for the ear, not for the eye. . . . The sound may mean more than the sense. The poetry is not in the meaning, but in the evocation' (Trend 1956: 16), can be similarly applied to his theatre. Reducing Lorca to his literary output ignores his own positioning of the plays as performative, 'created to be interpreted . . . to be heard in a theatre. They should last as long as the performance lasts and that's it' (OCIII 572). Lorca celebrates the ephemerality of performance as 'the art of the moment' (OCIII 572), but posterity has sought to preserve that performative moment through its most resonant trace – the play text.

While the printed word may have now 'appropriated' him, his dramaturgy is more theatrical than dramatic (Guardia 1952: 239). Only two of his plays – *Mariana Pineda* and *Blood Wedding* – were published during his lifetime and the errors that litter early editions, as well as the discordant versions of different plays, make it difficult to discuss the 'definitive' text of any one of his works. While it is beyond the remit of this study to discuss the publication history of his *oeuvre*, I am not the first to note that most of his works made it into publication more through the endeavours of family, friends and actors with whom he had left rehearsal drafts, than Lorca's conscious efforts (Fernández Cifuentes 1986: 65). He gave manuscripts away with careless abandon (Alberti 1984: 209). His correspondence is largely undated and thus renders any chronology problematic. The disappearance of letters and drawings from safe deposit boxes during the Civil War (Aub 1985: 247), the wealth of testimony from family and friends referring to Lorca as a compulsive and highly accomplished liar who derived great pleasure from deceits that had something of the art of poetry ultimately means that instability and absence are built into the very fabric of the texts and testaments (García Lorca 1986: 46; Santos Torroella 1995: 33–4).[4] The thousands of Lorcas that float around the public domain (OCIII 745–6) effectively mean that historiographical attempts to 'construct' a biography from the unreliable details that hover between fiction and the parameters of the real can at best only be regarded as a partially possible exercise.

Less than a year before his death Lorca referred to himself as 'an authentic beginner. . . . My work has barely begun' (OCIII 615–16). This sense of an incomplete corpus has certainly governed academic fascination with a writer who left tantalizing trails of plays yet to be written and only partial remains of other projects read to friends and associates. It is this partiality, this sense of unknowability that renders Lorca such an alluring subject of investigation. Much of Lorca's drama revolves around the fallibility of the spoken word, around embellishments and deceits, the fabrication of disguise and illusion. His brother Francisco claims he never trusted the spoken word, meticulously preparing lectures and speeches (García Lorca 1986: 156). Perhaps it is in the gaps between the said and the unsaid, between speech and silence, between the remnants on the page and the scenic vocabularies through which they are embodied that the 'meanings' and pleasures of Lorca's theatre can be teased out. While rejecting authorial intention as a governing matrix for interpretation, this study offers an introduction to Lorca's theatre that recognizes the multiple intersections between persona and product that have shaped the ways in which it is read.

1 Life, politics and mythology

> He [Lorca] was his own masterpiece. . . . He himself, as an
> individual, far surpassed his work.
>
> (Buñuel 1985: 158, 102)

The problems of mapping Lorca's life are as fraught as those of
writing the historiography of his productions – in both cases the
'performance' or signified is resolutely absent. If as Joseph Roach
reminds us, theatre history is a discipline fraught with a sense of
'irretrievable loss', then we should remain alert to the 'desolating
inadequacy' of piecing together a narrative account where so
much remains subject to 'the hallucinationary images of fiction'
(Roach 1992: 293, 297). The problems inherent in attempting any
kind of 'objective' reconstruction of a chronological survey of
Lorca's life when the empirical evidence is anything but neutral,
have been noted by prevous critics (Fernández Cifuentes 1988;
Smith 1998: 2). This chapter does not seek to provide an exhaustive account of his life, rather it draws on historical documents –
existent biographies, testimonies from friends and relatives,
correspondence, interviews and lectures – to examine selective
episodes that illustrate the mythification of Lorca in life and death.

The myth of Lorca

Any discussion of Lorca the playwright and theatremaker is
habitually prefixed by the construction, in death, of a larger-than-
life persona, a 'staggering one-man show' (Gibson 1989: xx) –

pianist, artist, dramatist, poet, actor, director, and raconteur –
preserved forever young in our collective consciousness. From the
studied brooding pose of the cover photograph of Gibson's
biography to the playful, flamboyant portrait adorning Stainton's
account of his life, he gazes out at the reader, both subject and
object, fetishized and preserved in an eternally youthful image of
attractive, elusive allure: a tall, olive-skinned young man with a
round face peppered with moles and a clump of shiny black hair
plastered over his wide forehead (see Figure 1, p. 20).

The portraits painted in death by friends and associates of the
'husky voiced' poet (Cernuda 1970: 157) with 'a magnetism that
few could resist' (Buñuel 1985: 61) have served to construct the
myth of an 'irresistible' (Dalí 1949: 203) 'brilliant and charming'
being (Buñuel 1985: 61), captivating attention when he played
the piano or read from his work (Alberti 1988: 168–70; Cernuda
1970: 158). In the absence of existent recordings of his voice, these
endorsements, from artists, filmmakers and poets who gained
iconic status in their own fields, were legitimized as authoritative
statements. The construct of Lorca as 'performer', introducing
stagings of his plays and holding informal recitals of his work in
his home, in cafés and at parties, has effectively fixed his life within
performative paradigms. Lorca was a celebrity in his own lifetime,
feted at social events in the vein of star bullfighters of the day
(OCIII 529; Martínez Nadal 1974: 11). References to poems
scribbled on the back of photos (Buñuel 1985: 63), habitual
lateness (León 1977: 212) and allegations of parapsychological
powers (Gibson 1989: 385, 391) have positioned him as the
perennial nonconformist, improvising life on the go. In many ways
the legacy of his dramaturgy has been obscured by *lorquismo*; as
his friend Rafael Martínez Nadal was to observe on hearing him
recite a poem in 1923, he couldn't be sure whether the poem was
good or whether it was just well read (Martínez Nadal 1980:
22–3; Stainton 1999: 120–1). While Lorca conceived writing and
directing as a profession rather than an art (García Lorca 1986:
122), the myth of the doomed 'child of the muses' prevails (Gibson
1989: xx).

The Andalusian icon

In many ways one only has to consider Lorca's repeated assertion that he was born alongside the new century and the citation of 1899 as his date of birth by early critics (Campbell 1952: 9; Honig 1945: 11) to realize how slippery and contested much of what is given as 'fact' actually is. Lorca once extravagantly claimed that he had read only two books in his life, *The Bible* and *A Thousand and One Nights*, at other times he boasted of being a voracious reader, devouring at least two works a day (Stainton 1999: 121). Hyperbole, theatrics and storytelling are part of the fabric of Lorca's biography. Pablo Neruda makes reference to happiness as 'as much a part of him as his skin' (Neruda 1977: 115), perhaps unwittingly feeding the image of the happy-go-lucky *torero* bounding through life. Other friends are more revealing in their mapping of his periods of intense self-absorption or *dramones* (Alberti 1984: 200; Aleixandre 1978: 289; Morla Lynch 1957: 14). Lorca's early writings and testaments of his childhood betray an interest in theatrics, game-play, storytelling and disguise that has been much commented on in past surveys of his life and influences (see OCIV 858–61; Edwards 1980: 5; García Lorca 1986: 102; Stainton 1999: 25–6). There are accounts of his dressing up as a priest to recite mass at the back of the house where he insisted the assembled congregation weep during his sermon (Gibson 1989: 15–16), his dolling up of maids and siblings to perform in home entertainments and his breaking of a piggy bank to purchase a toy theatre (García Lorca 1983: 9), his love of church ceremonials and palpable excitement when puppeteers came to town (Higuera Rojas 1980: 98–101, 166). Anecdotes from family servants and the copious relatives with whom he had contact litter his plays (see García Lorca 1986: 47–69).

While he is habitually viewed as the poet of the marginalized – gypsies, women, gay men, African Americans – Federico del Sagrado Corazón de Jesús García Lorca was born into an affluent family. His father, Federico García Rodríguez, was a wealthy landowner and Lorca and his three younger siblings benefited from a comfortable, cultured existence: a well-stocked library, music lessons and paternal patronage. Federico García Rodríguez bankrolled a number of Lorca's publications including his first anthology, *Impressions and Landscapes* (1918). This collection of writings brought together reports of travels across Andalusia, Castile, Léon and Galicia undertaken with fellow Granada University students under the tutelage of the art historian Martín Domínguez Berrueta, contemplations of his native Granada and reflections on artistic endeavour. The cultivation of the Lorca myth has been based, in part, on the rebuttal of a life slavishly in thrall to social conventions, but his perennial student existence was made possible only by his father's lasting economic support. Only when *Blood Wedding*, *Mariana Pineda* and *The Shoe-maker's Wonderful Wife* were presented in Argentina in 1933–4 did Lorca earn any significant financial sums for his writing.

The myth of Lorca as maverick has been fed by a poor academic record, both at school in Granada and later at Granada's university (1914–23), where he struggled to complete his degree. The reassessment of his academic record provided by Andrew Anderson points, however, to the dramatist's possible dyslexia. The evidence that Lorca had difficulty discerning left from right, did not find it easy to follow maps, and suffered problems with telling the time are used by Anderson (1999: 702) to lend weight to his argument. Lorca did not share his younger brother's academic prowess, was a late talker and walker and demonstrated a penchant for music that Anderson notes has been linked by writers on dyslexia to the disability. The manuscripts demonstrate awkward handwriting, misspellings, corrections, variable capitalization, erratic punctuation and a transposition of consonants that also function as indicators of dyslexia (Anderson 1999: 703, 700, 707).

The Granadine landscape in which Lorca spent his early years has been located as a key influence on his writing, providing a context for his plays and poems, a vocabulary of imagery, and a cultural format that drew on the myths, legends and history of the region (see OCIII 523–8; Morris 1997). The family homes in the villages of Fuente Vaqueros and Asquerosa (now renamed Valderrubio), part of the lush plain surrounding the city of Granada where Lorca spent the first ten years of his life, are now museums that further validate the importance of Granada to an understanding of the poet's *oeuvre* (see pp. 192–8). At the University of Granada Lorca cultivated a lasting friendship with Fernando de los Ríos, Professor of Political Law and founder of the city's Socialist Party. He travelled out to New York with Lorca in 1929 and as Minister of Public Instruction during Spain's Second Republic (1931–6) was to play an instrumental part in the establishment of La Barraca, the student theatre company that Lorca directed between 1932 and 1935 (see pp. 26–33). At Granada's Café Alameda, Lorca was part of a *tertulia* or literary gathering named *El Rinconcillo* (The Little Corner) whose members included the journalists José Mora Guarnido (author of an early critical study of Lorca) and Constantino Ruiz Carnero (later to become editor of the local broadsheet *El Defensor de Granada*), the critic Melchor Fernández Almagro, the painter Manuel Ángeles Ortiz, and the guitarist Andrés Segovia. As well as literary activities the group provided tours of the city's hidden corners to visiting artists and writers (like H.G. Wells and Rudyard Kipling) and arranged for plaques to be put up commemorating writers who had visited or lived in the city (Gibson 1989: 60–1). Mora Guarnido (1958: 54) sees the encouragement of the members of *El Rinconcillo* as key to Lorca's decision to write poetry. The exodus to Madrid of a number of the group's regulars may have been one of the factors that precipitated Lorca's move to the Spanish capital in 1919.

Even during his Madrid years Lorca returned regularly to Granada. Summers were generally spent at the Huerta de San Vicente, the summer home purchased by his father in 1926, and now the third Lorca museum in or around Granada (see pp. 195–8). With composer Manuel de Falla, Lorca hatched plans for a travelling theatre company that might preserve local bawdy puppet traditions and realized an Epiphany show with puppets and chamber orchestra for his younger sister Isabel at the family home in 1923 (García Lorca 1986: 142–7). The Festival of *Cante Jondo*, flamenco's deep song, organized with Falla in 1922, celebrated a performance system that was to shape his own literary discourse and the popular conception of him as the gypsy poet. Analysing *cante jondo* as 'a stammer, a wavering emission of the voice, a marvelous buccal undulation . . . a very rare specimen of primitive song, the oldest in all Europe', developed by the gypsies on arriving in Andalusia and a profound influence on musical composition from Felipe Pedrell and Isaac Albéniz to Falla (OCIII 35–6; GL 1991: 25), Lorca deemed the singers or *cantaors* as expressive mediums of the Andalusian people, eschewing affectation for embodiment. If *Gypsy Ballads*, his 1928 anthology, now 'the most widely read, most often recited, most studied and most celebrated book of poems in the whole of Spanish literature' (Gibson 1989: 136), positioned him as the public voice of Andalusia's downtrodden gypsies, then the poems he crafted inspired by *cante jondo*, subsequently published in 1931, consolidated that view.

While flamenco has proved a powerful idiom in the production and reception of Andalusian culture, the careful tracing of its codified ethics and performative languages have all too often been substituted by glib generalizations and a reinforcing of problematic stereotypes that equate the country's cultures with sangría, bullfighting and castanets. The origins of flamenco lie with the gypsies of Spain, who arrived in the Balkans from India and the Far East in medieval times and gradually spread across the breadth of Europe, settling in Spain in the fifteenth century where they were subjected to a wide range of cultural influences – Byzantine, Moorish, Judaic – and evolved the blend of *toque* (guitar), clapping and finger clicking (which offer a percussive rhythm), *cante* (song) and *baile* (dance), commonly referred to as flamenco.

Gypsy culture, as embodied in flamenco, has become 'a paradigm for the exotic' (Fraser 1992: 125). Lorca's correspondence betrays unease at the positioning of his work within gypsy prisms (OCIII 306, 364, 379). Despite protestations that his work was 'antifolklore, anti-local color, and anti-Flamenco', containing 'not one short jacket, suit of lights, wide-brimmed hat or Andalusian tambourine' (OCIII 179; GL 1991: 105), the conceits of flamenco have proved an enduring register through which to read it. Even the ostensibly surrealist anthology *Poet in New York* has been read as a *cantaor*'s lament (Stone 2004: 89–118).

The interweaving of Gypsy and Andalusian in the popular imagination may have played a role in Lorca turning his work away from an ostensibly Andalusian heritage, as evidenced by the erasure on the first page of the manuscript of *The House of Bernarda Alba* of a reference to the action taking place in 'an Andalusian village of dry lands' (Hernández 1984: 20). If Lorca is now viewed as Spain's 'national' poet, this is in part due to the fact that Spain's cultural construction has been indelibly marked by the idioms and myths of Andalusia. Even the cover of the first edition of *Gypsy Ballads*, featuring a blood-red map of Spain, testifies to an interweaving of the national and the regional in ways that draw upon the iconography of both.

The national poet

There is a strong critical consensus that views Lorca as 'the essence of Spain' (Neruda 1984: 60) and 'Spanish to the point of exaggeration' (Cernuda 1970: 162), assessing his work as essentialist in its embodiment of facets of Spanishness (Johnston 1998a: 41; Río 1952: 153, 167–8). As an early critic was to remark, 'Lorca never left Spain' and when he crossed its borders he took the country with him in his suitcase (Sánchez 1950: 154). Lorca's correspondence from New York in 1929–30 indicates the profound disorientation of a poor linguist. Part of the myth of Lorca as the 'universal' poet lies in his supposed recognition of the plight of the oppressed and acknowledged marginalized positions, but his own standardization of African Americans as 'melancholy . . . very good people' (OCIII 1114), betrays more awkward associations. Indeed his oft-cited phrase, 'I don't understand anything' (Adams 1977: 121; Río 1952: 93–4), offers a mode of reading his vision of the city as a surreal concrete jungle that he could access in only the most superficial of ways. Protestantism was dismissed as 'ridiculous' and 'hateful' with Catholicism lauded as superior to all other religions (OCIII 1115, 1122–3). Poems written just over a month after his arrival were classified 'typically North American' (OCIII 1120). The landscape was dismissed as uniformly similar with Coney Island singled out as 'monstrous, like everything in this country' (OCIII 1126, 1109). Wall Street met with particular venom, tainted by a 'vicious Dionysiac worship of money' (OCIII 1125–6). His view of jazz as sharing roots with *cante jondo* (OCIII 1114), both products of persecuted races, fails to take into consideration the particular socio-historical circumstances that engendered each. The exoticization of Harlem is evident in the poems that were to make up the posthumous anthology, *Poet in New York*. In the hostile, dehumanized, concrete metropolis, African American culture stands in stark contrast to a landscape that functions as a displaced object on which Lorca projects his frustration, anger and despair (Havard 2001: 112–41).

Lorca's vision of Cuba, where he spent three months in 1930, was irrevocably shaped by his father's cigar boxes adorned with colourful folkloric labels (Marinello 1965: 18–19). His letters betray the exoticization of the African Cuban population that ran through his documented encounters with African American culture in New York (OCIII 1168–9). That he later described it as the happiest period of his life (Río 1952: 43) has further shaped the conception of him as a pan-Hispanic writer. The praise lavished on Argentine theatre during his time there in 1933–4, his recognition of the importance of Buenos Aires as a theatrical capital (OCIII 446, 532) and the commercial success enjoyed by *Blood Wedding* and *The Shoemaker's Prodigious Wife* in Buenos Aires consolidated his reputation as the Spanish-language's premier dramatist. During the lean years of the Franco dictatorship, when his plays were absent from the Spanish stage, they were frequently staged in Argentina, Chile, Uruguay and Mexico (see Delgado 2003: 46–56).

Referring to himself in his final interview as a 'Spaniard through and through' (OCIII 637), Lorca's murder in the early days of the Civil War further tied him to a nation in whose cause he had suffered martyrdom. More so than Picasso or Dalí, whose trajectories are linked to the Parisian avant-garde, Lorca remains the perennial national emblem – the Andalusian writing of his landscape who also acknowledges his ties to Catholicism, the Catalan avant-garde and Galician poetry (OCIII 1115, 137–49, 1072; OCI 607–14).

The year of his birth, 1898, has acquired a profound symbolic resonance in the Spanish psyche as the year in which the country lost the final vestiges of her empire in the Philippines and Cuba to the USA, prematurely closing a century that had been marked by Napoleonic invasion, three civil conflicts, weak monarchies bound up with political machinations, an antiquated governmental infrastructure, periods of military control, and an emergent working class calling for improved working conditions (see Carr 1980: 1–40). From this climate of despair and profound self-interrogation came the generation of 1898 that included (among others) the poet Antonio Machado, the philosopher Miguel de Unamuno and the novelist Pío Baroja, who all looked to past literary models, like Cervantes's *Don Quixote*, to analyse the calamity of the present and look at ways of providing a reinvigorated future for a country suffering a lamentable sense of self-worth (see Harrison and Hoyle 2000).

Lorca's admiration for the Generation of 1898 has been documented (see Handley 1996). As a member of the Generation of 1927 that congregated in Seville to celebrate the renovating poet of Spain's Golden Age, Luis de Góngora, 'a symbolist three hundred years before his time' (Campbell 1952: 14), he similarly looked to a poetic idiom of considerable syntactical and metaphorical complexity whose verbal elegance and dexterity provided a bold rendering of the experiential through the iconography of the material world. While he has been judged a theatrical innovator, his dramaturgy, like his poetry, draws copiously on the work of his contemporaries. The historical verse of Eduardo Marquina, the expressionistic folklore and farcical bent of Ramón del Valle-Inclán, and the fabricated Andalusia of the Álvarez Quintero brothers have all been located as potent referents (Domenech 1992; Fernández Cifuentes 1986: 25; Río 1952: 152).[1] Jacinto Benavente, the Álvarez Quinteros, Benito Pérez Galdós and José Echegaray similarly created dominant female roles for the dominant actress-impresarios of the day. Unamuno and Galdós attempted to forge a stark theatrical language that debated key social issues. Where Lorca may share with Valle-Inclán the sense of theatre as a sensorial art, appealing to both eye and ear (Sánchez 1950: 152), his theatre is ultimately more *practical* in its articulation of the discourses of performance and in its manipulation of the dramaturgical discourses of the Renaissance dramas of Calderón de la Barca and Lope de Vega

(OCIII 218–21; Guardia 1952: 357–8; Nieva 1996: 124; Sánchez 1950: 102–23).

During his time in Madrid (1919–36) Lorca came into contact with a range of the figures currently shaping the city's literary and cultural scene. These included the poet (and later Nobel Prizewinner) Vicente Aleixandre, the painter and writer José Moreno Villa who was, in 1931, made director of the Royal Library (see Figure 1), and the right-wing poet, José María Hinojosa, who was to be executed by Republicans during the Civil War. The elder statesman of Andalusian letters, Juan Ramón Jiménez, then one of Spain's foremost poets, took a keen interest

Figure 1 The Residencia de Estudiantes as a hub of creative and intellectual activity in Spain: the painter Salvador Dalí, the painter and poet José Moreno Villa, the future filmmaker Luis Buñuel, Lorca, and fellow student José Antonio Rubio Sacristán (later to become a distinguished Law Professor) at the Residencia c. 1924–5. Photo: Archive of Teresa Rubio Tió/Fundación Federico García Lorca

in Lorca's writing and went on to prove a potent mentor and guide. In Madrid Lorca joined the Ateneo, a private members' cultural club, and read in its library (OCIII 672). His first professional production was directed by Gregorio Martínez Sierra who ran one of the city's most adventurous venues, the Eslava. At *tertulias* held at the city's cafés he fraternized with the polemical dramatists Valle-Inclán and Ramón Gómez de la Serna, the Uruguayan painter and scenographer Rafael Pérez Barradas and the Nobel Prizewinning neurologist Santiago Ramón y Cajal. Buñuel (1985: 62) was to refer to him as knowing 'everyone who counted'. And those 'who counted' promoted the myth of Lorca in their own writings.

The Dalí–Lorca axis

Lorca and Dalí met at Madrid's Residencia de Estudiantes, a student boarding-house to the north of the city modelled on Oxbridge's college system. Lorca entered the Residencia in 1920, and its progressive ethos and celebration of the edifying potential of culture is strongly reflected in his own writings (OCIII 204). At a lecture given in 1933 on the 'Play and Theory of the Duende', Lorca made reference to attending close to a thousand lectures at the Residencia in the period up to 1928, for he was a regular visitor to the institution even after officially moving out in 1925 (OCIII 150; GL 1991: 42). The range of speakers across the cultural and scientific spectrum included composers and musicians like Stravinsky and Ravel, writers and architects like H.G. Wells, Louis Aragon, Le Corbusier, Valéry, and G.K. Chesterton, and philosophers and physicists like Walter Gropius, Henri Bergson, and Albert Einstein. Lorca delivered a number of his best-known lectures there: 'The Poetic Image of Don Luis de Góngora' in 1927 and 'On Lullabies' in 1928 (OCIII 53–77, 113–31; GL 1991: 59–85, 7–22). The Residencia's staff included the Nobel Prizewinner Severo Ochoa and Madrid University's physiology professor, later the Republic's final prime minister, Juan Negrín, who supervised its laboratories, and Juan Ramón Jiménez, who ran its in-house editions. A potent emblem of a forward-looking Spain open to new influences and the promotion of cross-disciplinary practices during the pre-Civil War years, the Residencia remains a commanding symbol of the progressive educational frameworks dismantled by the ideological agenda of Francoism.

The mythology of the Residencia is bound up with Lorca, Dalí and Buñuel, whose time there was to prove so seminal to the genesis and evolution of their artistic vocabularies (see Figure 1).[2] Buñuel arrived at the institution in 1917, Dalí in 1922 and both have delineated the concerts, film projections, play readings, and productions that marked the institution's 'hands on' approach to culture (Buñuel 1985: 51–77; Sánchez Vidal 1996: 35–63). The Residencia's role as a hub of surrealism in Spain is due, in no small part, to the fact that while based there all three came into contact with, and were to be radically shaped by, the probing dictums, creations, attitudes and manifestos emanating from the French capital (see Morris 1972: 12–21).

While the Buñuel–Dalí–Lorca axis has remained a popular prism through which to refract the *oeuvre* of all three, Buñuel's observations that the friendship was misrepresented – 'He [Dalí] was much closer to Federico than I was. I was more a friend of Dalí's than Federico's' (Aub 1985: 104) – is borne out in Morris's observation that Lorca's 'dedication of eleven poems to Buñuel in 1921 suggests a warmth and admiration that were not recip- rocated wholeheartedly' (Morris 1972: 49), at least not until after Lorca's death. While Dalí was to refer to himself as 'little son' in his correspondence with Lorca, Lorca in turn, described the painter as his 'inseparable companion', 'little Salvador . . . the ineffable Dalí' whose paintings live 'close to my heart' (OCIII 869, 849–50). Lorca stayed with Dalí and his family in the remote Catalan town of Cadaqués on two separate occasions in 1925 and 1927 and their cross-fertilization of each other's work moves beyond shared interests in the unconscious as a governing principle of artistic creation.

Rafael Santos Torroella (1984: 19) labels the period between 1926 and 1929 Dalí's Lorca years. Already in 1924 Dalí had painted a triple portrait of Lorca at the Café Oriente, his face semi- shaded as if decomposing. A 1923 'Cubist Self-Portrait' bears traces of Lorca's physiognomy, similarly the subject of the 1923–4

'Portrait'. References to the dramatist and his musical abilities are discernible in both 'Pierrot with Guitar' (1923) and 'Pierrot Playing the Guitar' (1925) – the year Dalí was to confess in a letter to Lorca that he was the only interesting man he had ever known, accompanying the remarks with an inscribed sketch of a picador and bull (Dalí 1987: 24). A sketch of Lorca feigning death in Cadaqués was completed a year later as 'Still Life (Invitation to Dream)' (1926) where the dramatist's head is prominent in the central sphere of the painting threatened by an approaching triangular shape perhaps indicative of the danger of the female 'other'. 'Still Life by Moonlight' (1926) fuses the heads of Dalí and Lorca against the backdrop of Cadaqués in an image of wholeness undermined by the severed limbs-cum-dead fish that surround it. 'Composition with Three Figures (Neo-Cubist Academy)' (1926), 'Harlequin' (1926), 'Barcelona Mannequin' (1926), 'Still Life by Mauvre Midnight' (1926), 'Table in Front of the Sea' (1926), 'Self-Portrait Splitting into Three' (1926–7), and 'Little Ashes' (1927–8) all feature references to Lorca as a silhouette, shadow, super-imposed mask or floating decapitated head.[3] Dalí illustrated the poem 'Gypsy Feud', published by Lorca in the Sitges-based magazine *L'Amic de les Arts*, of which Dalí was one of the leading lights (GL 1927). The drawing, 'The Poet at the Empúries Beach seen by Salvador Dalí', uses motifs of severed heads and scattered body parts that feature conspicuously in Lorca's own drawings of this period. One of Dalí's most celebrated paintings from this period, 'Honey is Sweeter than Blood' (1927), positions Lorca's head, between two rotting donkeys, in a mode that anticipates the visual referencing of *Un Chien andalou* (1929).

The imagery of Dalí's canvasses permeates Lorca's 1927 prose poems (OCI 487–507). Lorca drew prodigiously during the period post 1922 and the sketches, doodles and drawings all provide evidence of a shared iconography and register of motifs. The Cubist dimensions of Lorca's work can be seen in the amputated hands, melancholy androgynous figures from *commedia dell'arte*, maimed or disfigured faces, shadowy masquerades, masks that mutilate, split or disgure the human face, and rotting corpses that consistently probe the relationship of self and other. The split face technique visible in 'Clown with a Double Face' (1927) is one shared with Dalí, and Lorca's five Harlequin drawings rendered between 1927 and 1928 all refer back to Dalí's 1926 'Harlequin', distinguished by a 'juxtaposition between playfulness and restrictiveness in relation to the mask' (Wright 2000: 7). These are figures as much haunted by the spectres of death and fragility of creativity (denoted by the dismembered hands) as those populating Dalí's 'Honey is Sweeter than Blood'.

The collection of drawings exhibited by Lorca in 1927 at Barcelona's Dalmau Gallery has served as a canvas on which to project desires and fantasies that surround the unknowable details of Lorca and Dalí's relationship.[4] 'The Kiss' (1927) superimposes the more angular face of Dalí on Lorca's broader visage (see Figure 2). 'East Wind' (1927) allegedly captures Dalí's face in miniature on an open fan (see Gibson 2003: 183). A portrait of Dalí reproduces characteristics evident in Lorca's earlier 1925 study of 'Slavdor Adil', his playful anagram for the painter. Dalí is cited by Lorca in his lecture 'Thoughts on Modern Art'. Lorca is appreciatively analysed by Dalí in his review of the Dalmau exhibition and Dalí forms the subject of one of Lorca's most celebrated poems, 'Ode to Salvador Dalí', first published in 1926 (Dalí 1927b).

Dalí provided the high modernist scenography for Lorca's *Mariana Pineda*, staged by Margarita Xirgu's company in Barcelona in 1927 (see Figure 4, p. 56). Saint Sebastian proves a shared referent in essays published in magazines, drawings and correspondence during this period. A figure of identification for both, he is simultaneously the ideal artist, serene before the arrows that would perforate the flesh and a homoerotic symbol whose wound-orifices are open to receive anticipated penetration. A reminder of other parts of the body that remain unseen, the wound-orifice also serves as a metaphor for the eye, further pointing to the drawings as dramas of seeing and touching (OCIII 1019–20; Dalí 1987: 42–8).[5] Motifs of perspective and representation are also evident in Lorca's 1925 dramaturgical sketches, like *The Maiden, the Sailor and the Student* and *Buster Keaton Takes a Walk* which embrace the surrealist vein that he was to turn to post 1929; the latter's manuscript features scrawled references to 'Dalilaitita /Daliminita/Dalipuruta/Damitira/Demeter/Dalí'.

Figure 2 Lorca's Dalí years: 'The Kiss' (1927) © Fundación Federico
García Lorca, Madrid/DACS, London 2007

The rupture in the relationship between Lorca and Dalí has
been subject to much conjecture. Dalí has provided graphic
descriptions of Lorca's attempts to sodomize him (Aub 1985: 549;
Bosquet 1966: 52); Buñuel's homophobic correspondence sought

to lure Dalí away from Lorca and towards Paris (Sánchez Vidal 1996: 158–67). Both Dalí and Buñuel bemoaned *Gypsy Ballads'* excessive artifice, sentiment and cliché (Dalí 1987: 88–94; Sánchez Vidal 1996: 178). Lorca perceived Dalí and Buñuel's *Un Chien andalou* as a spiteful affront (Buñuel 1985: 157). Lorca and Dalí met only again in 1935 and, while plans were hatched for a possible opera on sexual 'deviants' (Dalí 1987: 96), the collaboration was never realized. A late interview with the elderly Dalí testifies to the importance of their friendship (Dalí 1986; Gibson 1986a); covered in Carlos Saura's *Buñuel and King Solomon's Table* (2001), Paul Morrison's *Little Ashes* (2008) and Roger Avary's proposed *Gala Dalí* (c. 2009), it remains a creative axis suspended in the sphere of the speculative.

Politics and martyrdom

The life, times and death of Lorca have served to position him as a martyr of the left. He enjoyed a secular education and a liberal father who did not share the right-of-centre affiliations of Granada's bourgeoisie. *Don Perlimplín* was closed during Miguel Primo de Rivera's censorious dictatorship (1923–30). *Gypsy Ballads'* representation of the Civil Guard as an oppressive, rural police force, flogging gypsies and filling the populace with fear perhaps served, during the panic and confusion of early stages of the Civil War, to position Lorca as transgressive 'other' threatening the forces of law and order. His homosexuality was undoubtedly a prominent factor in alienating him from a conservative culture that he had publicly denigrated in his last published interview (OCIII 637; Gibson 1986b: 40). Family vendettas may have also come into play as the Roldáns, powerful landowners in Granada, took offence at Lorca's portrayal of their relatives, the Albas, in his final play, *The House of Bernarda Alba*.[6]

It is perhaps his association with the student theatre company, La Barraca, an organization embedded in the culture of Spain's Second Republic, that most served to mark Lorca as a writer of the left. The general elections of 1931 were conducted against growing civil unrest and the victory of the liberal left – at a time when prominent European nations were turning to authoritarianism – saw King Alfonso XIII flee the country. The new political order was distinguished by a significant number of intellectuals. A quarter of the Cortes, the law-making lower house, was made up of academics, pedagogues, writers and journalists who looked beyond Spain for models that linked cultural dissemination to social regeneration (Holguín 2002: 51–5).

Lorca's friend Fernando de los Ríos, first as Minister of Justice and then as Minister of Public Instruction, was at the forefront of a social agenda addressing the prising apart of the relationship between Church and State, an inefficient and antiquated military, a largely illiterate peasantry blighted by economic penury and exploited by prohibitive rents, urban discontent in the new industrial centres and nationalist demands in Catalonia (Holguín 2002: 4–5). In 1931, with 32.4 per cent of the 25 million population of Spain thought to be illiterate (Holguín 2002: 227–8), decrees were issued to stop landowners employing workers from outside the municipality to keep wages low. Eight-hour days were introduced with accompanying sick benefit and paid holiday. Divorce was legalized, and reforms introduced to purge the army of its overly high proportion of officers (see Carr 1980: 119–26; Preston 1983: 26–91). A mass literacy programme was conceived to remove education from the clutches of the Church with the planned creation of 27,150 schools over five years and one hundred municipal libraries a year (with libraries established where possible within village schools) as part of a mass literacy programme. By December 1933 3,151 libraries and 6,570 schools had been established across rural Spain (Holguín 2002: 145–52).

One of these libraries was in Fuente Vaqueros, formally opened by Lorca in September 1931 with a speech that celebrated the signature of the Second Republic as 'culture' (OCIII 201–14). At a time when Lorca was increasingly in demand as a public speaker,[7] this lecture provides a solid indication of his affiliation with the hegemonic aspirations of the Second Republic in creating 'a nation of republican citizens from the shards of a shattered body politic' (Holguín 2002: 5). In extolling books as 'humanity's greatest work' and positioning the fathers of the Russian revolution not as politicians but as writers like Dostoyevsky and Marx, Lorca promoted a vision of culture as life affirming and life changing (OCIII 204–5). His statement that 'Man doesn't live by bread alone' (OCIII 203) demonstates how profoundly the progressive ethos of the Residencia – where learning functioned as an ongoing activity with benefits visible outside the confines of the classroom – had shaped his understanding of culture.

One of the most distinctive cultural initiatives of these years, the Misiones Pedagógicas (Teaching Missions), offered a mobile school in the form of a combination of travelling libraries, theatres, concerts, films, and museums with replicas of works from the Prado. At the 495 villages visited between 1931 and 1934, lectures on civic duty were provided, promoting democratic structures as models of social organization. Sections of plays were read aloud and contextualized and gramophone records played a range of works aloud in village squares.

La Barraca (The Hut) was created as an extension of the Misiones Pedagógicas. Lorca was named artistic director working with an associate, fellow playwright and screenwriter Eduardo Ugarte. The company was created under the auspices of the students' union at the Philosophy and Arts faculty at the University of Madrid. Auditions were carried out to create a company of around thirty students with a mission not just to educate but to renovate the theatre to act as a catalyst for further experimentation.[8] Lorca's original plans envisaged one company based in Madrid and another which performed outside the city in the locality, going further afield during the summer (OCIII 383). While these were not to materialize, in part because state subsidy for the company was effectively halved in its second year (OCIII 394; Sáenz de la Calzada 1976: 154), the company allowed Lorca to put into operation his thoughts on a socially engaged theatre (OCIII 532, 607, 615). The boilersuit uniform which all male members wore,[9] embroidered with the company's logo of two superimposed actors' masks positioned on a wheel (designed by artist Benjamín Palencia and emblematic of the company's itinerant status), was part of the new ethos of a democratic workers' state and had echoes in similar experiments carried out in the Soviet Union that also envisaged culture as a means of shaping national identity.

While Lorca was to naively deny that the company had an explicitly political agenda (OCIII 393), its missionary zeal is evident in interviews given during his time as its titular head when he refers to 'the great ideal of educating the people of our beloved Republic by means of restoring to them their own theatre' (Adams 1932: 239). La Barraca's agenda lay in removing works 'from the back of libraries' and placing them in the public arena where theatre could function 'as one of the most expressive and useful instruments for the education of a country' (OCIII 397, 255). While Lorca envisaged an eventual international repertoire for La Barraca, the decision was made to focus initially on the 'national theatre' of the Golden Age canon (OCIII 386, 251). The seventeenth-century playhouses, *corrales*, had brought audiences from across the social spectrum. In aiming to capture something of the populism of a form that had emerged from travelling players on makeshift portable stages (the *farándula*), Lorca attempted to provide theatrical fare that might bridge the schisms of the two Spains that were set to implode in 1936.

The first tour in July 1932 brought together three interludes by Cervantes and Calderón's *auto sacramental*, *Life is a Dream*, supplying the unadorned populism of Cervantes with the sacred divinity of Calderón. Silent film footage remains of Lorca, masked by black veils against the backdrop of Palencia's celestial design, in the role of the Shadow in *Life is a Dream* – a play that he saw as the prototype for *The Tempest* and Goethe's *Faust* (OCIII 218–21).

La Barraca travelled light with a portable stage and simple, largely conceptual sets, designed mainly by Palencia, Santiago Ontañón and José Caballero, transported in a lorry that accompanied the bus in which the performers and crew toured. Lorca's original plans had involved the presentation of the same play on two consecutive nights with the first offering a historical reconstruction of sorts and the second a more modern, simplified reading. He was to dispense with the former but promoted a scenographic and performance style that referenced Max Reinhardt's aesthetic and never tried to erase the anachronism of staging a historically distant work in contemporary dress (OCIII 252–3; Adams 1932: 238–9). Although he did not have a methodology *per se*, the professionialism that he had witnessed first hand with Xirgu's company imbued his working relationship with La Barraca. While the early performances demonstrated the need for longer rehearsal periods, they also pointed to Lorca's attention to the mechanics of production. Actors were expected to undertake preparatory research and learn their roles early. Dispensing with the prompter's box, Lorca blocked work with actors, acted out roles to indicate particular performative styles, and paid close attention to rhythm and pacing, avoiding declamation in a prioritization of diction and intonation. Performers were encouraged to recognize the audience's presence and observe its responses. Sets and costumes were recycled from production to production, the uniforms adapted into costumes. Lighting was used to create mood and special effects as well as to illuminate the actors. Music was perceived as integral in shaping both the movement and the vocal inflection of the performers.[10] The effect for the audience should be that of seeing a new play (OCIII 563).

Lorca's input also involved the dramaturgical reshaping of plays in ways that recognized how viewing conditions, dramatic conventions and theatrical spaces had shifted in the 300 years since the works were first staged. Lope de Vega's 1619 play, *Fuenteovejuna*, staged by La Barraca in 1933, was set during the 1930s rather than the reign of Ferdinand and Isabel. The subplot of the Catholic monarchs was cut, perhaps as a way of commenting on the irrelevance of the monarchy. The black suit of the Commander, with the crest of the Order of Calatrava positioned on the left of his jacket, transformed him into a wealthy rural landowner or *cacique* abusing those who worked on his land. This is not to say that historical research had no place, rather the research was used to provide a context for the play that would allow for the translation of elements into a contemporary landscape.

While the company was ostensibly organized around democratic principles and eschewed a star system (OCIII 398), Lorca's presence served in many ways to undermine this ideal. His introductory speeches, announcing the title of the play(s) and the company's mandate in lieu of a programme (OCIII 571–2), veered towards the pompous and after a particularly long effort, he was dragged offstage by a technician (Stainton 1999: 304). He was quick to sack those who disagreed with him and avoided manual labour while celebrating the physical toil undertaken by the workers La Barraca supposedly served (Sáenz de la Calzada 1976: 44, 131; OCIII 397). In early performances he appeared unprepared for the heckling or the complications that ensued when audiences were erroneously charged for tickets (Gibson 1989: 331–2). Other commitments gradually intruded on time spent rehearsing, and the 1934 production of Tirso de Molina's *The Trickster of Seville* was only partly rehearsed by Lorca before leaving for Argentina (Sáenz de la Calzada 1976: 146–7).

Lorca's association with the company fuelled criticisms in the right-wing press. His comments on cultural nourishment, cited earlier and qualified in a 1936 interview (OCIII 632), were picked up by hostile critics, who questioned the sufficiency of addressing the 'spiritual' at times of substantial material deprivation. The company was criticized for taking away jobs from professional actors even though this was never part of its mandate (Byrd 1975: 59; Holguín 2002: 113–14). Lorca's assertions of the company's secular agenda, while hijacking the vocabulary of the right in stressing the high theatrics of the mass and the aspiration to 'take Good and Evil, God and Faith into the towns of Spain again' (Adams 1932: 239), incurred the wrath of the Church.

The fascist magazine *Gracia y Justicia* was particularly vituperative in its homophobic slurs on Lorca – pointedly referred to as 'Loca' (madwoman) – and its decrying of the alleged homosexual slant and improprieties of the company (Anon 1932). The November 1933 elections saw the CEDA conservative alliance secure the largest number of votes and the following years, known as the *bienio negro*, were marked by political infighting as the various feuding factions of the left tried to stop the rise of fascism within Spain. The death penalty was reintroduced and agrarian reforms that had made it difficult for landlords to undercut wages and import cheap migrant labour were repealed. As well as worsening labour relations, there was increased tension between Catalan nationalists and a central government that appeared no longer willing to recognize political autonomy for Catalonia (see Carr 1980: 123–34; Preston 1983: 92–150).

If Lorca had worked to promote a nationalist discourse that fostered civic agency and education for all, the right-wing coalition turned to a nationalism, criticized by Lorca (OCIII 637), that looked back to Ferdinand and Isabel's forging of a Castilian state bound by *Hispanidad*, where identification with the nation was irrevocably tied up with the Catholic religion, the Castilian language and mythologies constructed to promote a particular world view that looked inwards rather than outwards to Europe. It is not therefore surprising that the centre-right government chose to halve and then withdraw La Barraca's grant (OCIII 571). And while Lorca was adamant that the company would continue to perform with or without subsidy (OCIII 578), his own involvement with the company waned during 1934 and early 1935 and by April 1936 he had formally been replaced as artistic director.

Lorca's association with the left, however, continued. The liberal intelligentsia mobilized in support of *Yerma* in 1934, a play whose polarized reception was as contentious and polemical as that of Synge's *Playboy of the Western World* in 1907. In 1935 he took part in readings to commemorate the first anniversary of the Asturian miners' revolt and accompanied Xirgu to a performance of *Fuenteovejuna* where the proceeds were targeted to assist political prisoners (Stainton 1999: 406–7). In 1936, he drafted a manifesto signed by over 300 figures from the cultural sphere that was published in the communist newspaper *Mundo Obrero* on the day prior to elections that saw the left's Popular Front alliance double their seats in the Cortes. Escalating unemployment and civil unrest – with the right turning increasingly to violence as the primary weapon to destabilize the Republic – generated threats of revolution, counter-revolution and military coups by factions of both the left and right. Lorca left for Granada on 13 July; the Civil War broke out on 17 July when General Franco launched a military uprising in Morocco; Lorca was assassinated on either 18 or 19 August under Nationalist orders, ten days after seeking refuge at the home of the Falangist family of the poet Luis Rosales.

Jorge Luis Borges attributes Lorca's idealization in Argentina to having 'the good luck to be executed' (Burgín 1973: 110), and the high rhetoric of martyrdom shaped early reports of his death (Anon 1936b; 1936c; 1936d). While his sister Isabel, then studying in Madrid, initially assured friends he was in hiding but not dead (Alberti 1987: 268–9; León 1977: 214), rumours circulated that he had escaped to the Sierra Nevada Mountains, an unnamed consulate or Switzerland (Alberti 1984: 133). In 1938 Cernuda (1970: 160) warned that the Civil War had transformed Lorca into a 'messianic bard'; criticizing his work was thought to be in bad taste (Sánchez 1950: 163). By the mid 1960s even the right-wing's flagship daily *ABC* marked the thirtieth anniversary of his death with a commemorative edition set to exhonerate the regime of any implication in his murder, presented as a lone act carried out by thugs without prior authorization (Cano 1966). While filmmaker Edgar Neville (1966) may have pushed for a reading of Lorca as a dramatist who 'lay above political parties' with a body of work that 'has brought glory to Spain throughout the world', his legacy remains a potent political weapon, opportunistically appropriated by both left and right and indelibly associated with the Nationalists' illegitimate seizure of power in 1936.

Lorca and the critics

Even the most cursory glance at the swathes of Lorca scholarship indicates the expansive metaphoric terrain through which his work has been read. From satirical humorist (Higginbotham 1976) to grand tragedian (Gaskell 1972: 106–16), his plays have allegedly denounced the corrupting influence of financial transactions and parental abuse (Fernández Cifuentes 1992: 97); contemplated the operations of time (García Lorca 1986: 189) and Christian theatrics (Newberry 1976: 806), and articulated the anguish of the gypsy race and his own psychological torment through an appropriation of flamenco's *cante jondo* or deep song (Stone 2004). Any critic approaching Lorca's *oeuvre* necessarily needs to acknowledge a trajectory of past scholarship that has played a decisive role in shaping how his theatre has been read and produced and the ways in which this has been bound up with the Lorca myth. In the cases of *The Public* and *Trip to the Moon* critical studies appeared in print even before works had been circulated through production or publication, feeding the universalizing tendency that obliterates the particulars of the textual remains in favour of general thematics that conveniently encompass the whole *ouevre*.

Early critical studies were realized by those who had known him as a friend (Guillén 1959; Mora Guarnido 1958; Morla Lynch 1957; Río 1952) and/or translators of his work (Auclair 1968; Campbell 1952) and supposes 'the author as originating subject' (Smith 1989: 110). The emphasis is elegiac, eulogizing him as an almost extra-worldly being (Guillén 1959: 13) who carried poetry in the blood (Mora Guarnido 1958: 146), and whose 'genius' was somehow incompatible with such mundane tasks as the learning of another language (Río 1952: 38). The battle for ownership of the dramatist that I trace elsewhere in the book (pp. 101, 173–201) is evident in agendas that see critics all arguing for the validity of 'their' Lorca. The Argentine Guardia (1952: 90) thus negates the influence of Lorca's time in New York, instead inscribing the importance of his period in Argentina in 1933–4. Mora Guarnido (1958: 146), as a fellow Granadine, underlines the consequence of the region's agricultural landscape, imagery and myths in shaping Lorca's cultural formation, an approach followed by Morris (1997).

Paul Julian Smith (1989) reads the elegiac approach as one of the dominant modes of Lorca criticism. Here the text is viewed as 'an unfinished monument to a life cut short, as a theatre in which future death is at once anticipated and commemorated' (Smith 1989: 109, 110). Certainly an inordinate number of studies dwell on death as the primary motif of his writing (Barea 1944: 53–76; Cernuda 1970: 162; Guardia 1952: 162–73; López Castellón 1981; Martínez Nadal 1974; Sánchez 1950: 79). Lorca's 1934 statement 'I live surrounded by death!' (OCIII 514) and his concept of *duende* as the death muse (OCIII 150–62; GL 1991: 42–53), as well as the copious anecdotes surrounding his repeated posing as a corpse (Dalí 1976: 15), and Dalí's frequent depiction of a decapitated or mutilated Lorca in artworks realized between 1924 and 1930, are cited to substantiate this reading. I am not suggesting that 'the theatrics of death' (Stainton 1999: 12) are not visible in his work, simply that they are inextricably and often unwittingly bound up with the high theatrics of the circumstances of his death reconstructed by Gibson (1974).[11]

The humanist approach to Lorca's work perceives the dramatist as a social critic (Anderson 1984; Edwards 1980) whose plays provide key insights for comprehending the society in which he lived and worked. The plays are often read as veiled auto-biography commenting on his predicament. As such unsatisfied passion and thwarted desire are repeatedly located as dominant motifs (Honig 1945: 177; Mora Guarnido 1958: 166; Río 1952: 62, 140); the crafting of strong female roles assumed to be a veiled portrait of displaced homosexual desire (Binding 1985: 173; Gibson 1989: 356). Such readings, however, simply fail to consider the material conditions in which Lorca crafted his works, dominated by powerful actress-managers like Margarita Xirgu and Lola Membrives. Lorca himself recognized that Spain lacked good male actors (OCIII 502) and his moulding of copious female roles can be viewed as a direct response to the times in which he was writing.

Lorca's positioning of the social and the sexual as the twin prisms of his theatre (OCIII 612) has served as a compelling guide to critics on the organization of their own readings of his theatre. The tension between instinct and social conformity played out across the realms of the sexual is a dominant organizing concept (Johnston 1999: 57–8; Lima 1963: 188–287). Frustration, 'particularly for women, but also for men' is viewed as both 'the theme and keynote' of his drama (Adams 1977: 194, 195) and it ties into the repeated evocation of his supposedly progressive treatments of gender and sexuality as indications of his contem-poraneity (Edwards 2003). The urge for social transformation attributed to Lorca's dramaturgy may be more of an indication of the role critics have wanted Lorca to assume: part of a critical strategy that seeks to find redemptive potential in his death.

While early studies conspicuously avoided any references to his homosexuality (Mora Guarnido 1958: 216–31; Río 1952: 36),[12] subcultural readings have followed 'claiming' Lorca as a gay dramatist. Binding's 1985 opus, Feal Deibe's (1989) study and Smith's (1989, 1998) highly sophisticated deconstructions of the Lorca 'cult' draw heavily on psychoanalysis in constructing their treatments of discourses of homosexuality. Smith's concentration on the more marginal or 'impossible' works indicates a trend increasingly pursued by Lorca scholars. Fernández Cifuentes (1986), Wright (2000), Harretche (2000), and Jerez Farrán (2004) all provide close readings of texts that have either habitually been judged minor works (like *The Butterfly's Evil Spell* or *Mariana Pineda*) or positioned within the realms of the surreal or the unstageable (like *The Public* and *When Five Years Pass*). Both Harretche and Jerez Farrán's conclusions travel along the well-established tract of seeing the life as irrevocably linked to the works.

There is a potent wave of criticism that negotiates theatrical paradigms in reading Lorca's dramaturgy. George (1995) and Wright (2000) have provided extensive treatments of the iconography of *commedia dell'arte* in the writing. Soufas (1996) places his dramas within European modernist currents, moving against tendency to see his work primarily within a national context of Spanish stage renovation, like Edwards (1980) and Higginbotham (1976). Like Cao (1984), he positions the dramatist within avant-garde paradigms that recognize the role of performance and reception as organizing motifs of the works. This study builds on the earlier scholarship, expanding on the approaches of Bonaddio (2007), Edwards (2003), Fernández Cifuentes (1986), McDermid (2007), and Smith (1998) while drawing on a broader range of productions from variant media. The focus is not simply on showing the multiple intertextual resonances in the plays that demonstrate his acknowledged debt to Spanish dramaturgy (OCIII 612–13), but on indicating how these tie in to wider international debates on the function and role of theatre conducted during the 1920s and 1930s. If Lorca has been classified as the 'Picasso of the theatre' (Nieva 1996: 125), this is in part because the sense of spectacle and juggling of discordant theatrical genres from lyrical melodrama to popular operetta lend his theatre something of the air of a Cubist collage. Like Brecht, Lorca can be viewed as a theatrical magpie reworking elements overtly 'poached' from different literary, theatrical and pictorial sources. It is for this reason that he is perhaps judged, more than his contemporary Valle-Inclán or the Nobel Prize-winners José Echegaray and Jacinto Benavente, as the dramatist responsible for 'printing the stamp of modernity on tradition' (Vilches de Frutos 1998: 12).

2 The 'known' Lorcas

During the half-century that followed his death, a particular vision of Lorca's *oeuvre* prevailed that was based on the limited number of works then in the public domain. This is what I refer to as the 'known' Lorcas, plays ostensibly located in or around Granada. Some like *Mariana Pineda*, *Yerma*, and *Doña Rosita* make explicit reference to specific locations in Granada and its surrounding countryside. Others, like *Blood Wedding* and *Yerma*, have been positioned within an Andalusian context by association, with productions using both mimetic and conceptual scenographies that reinforce the interweaving of Andalusia and gypsies in the popular imagination.

All of these plays provide commentaries on the predicament of women trapped within rural communities in early twentieth-century Spain. *Mariana Pineda* explores allegorical uses of the female as an emblematic image of liberty. *Blood Wedding* foregrounds the isolation faced by rural women drawn into arranged marriages. *Yerma* explores marital incompatibility and the problems of childlessness in a society where women are defined by their ability to procreate. *Doña Rosita* maps out the emotional geography of middle-class women who are unable, or choose not to, marry. Lorca's characterizations demonstrate the way in which the roles we play are all shaped and conditioned by the dominant ideologies of the societies we inhabit. Even *The House of Bernarda Alba*, the only one of these plays unstaged during his lifetime, has at its centre a domestic environment – habitually the terrain of the female – marked by the internal strife and jealous rivalries caused by enforced imprisonment.

These plays and their production histories have effectively canonized Lorca and the exploration of them offered in this chapter provides a reading of their iconography while examining how this iconography has been reinforced through production styles both in Spain and abroad. While one production strategy has involved reading the texts through particular symbols of Andalusia – whitewashed houses, fans, mantillas, flamenco, and *duende* – another has seen directors dispense with mimetic referents in favour of conceptual approaches that emphasize the more musical or ritualistic aspects of the works. *Yerma*, *Blood Wedding* and *The House of Bernarda Alba* have been the sites for some of the most exciting theatrical experiments of recent times.

Peter Brook has referred to the canvas membrane set that Fabià Puigserver created for Victor García's 1971 production of *Yerma* as one of the definitive moments of twentieth-century stage design (Delgado 1998: 101). Antonio Gades and Carlos Saura's dis- membering of *Blood Wedding* (1981) for the screen as ballet and the rough, raw physicality of Calixto Bieito's *The House of Bernarda Alba* (1998) have presented alternative configurations of the works, showing how they have been appropriated for the demands of the postmodernist age. For those who would see *The House of Bernarda Alba*, his final and perhaps most resonant play, as a study of dictatorial oppression and intimidation, the view of stage director Pedro Álvarez-Ossorio (1998), that the first initials of the daughters' names spell out a dedication 'a *mamá*' – to mother – suggests the ambiguity both of a persona and a play which consistently resists easy categorization. For a writer whose correspondence, plays and poems revolve around the presentation of a series of complex coexisting identities, is it perhaps not surprising that his final testament to his beloved mother should be a dark, claustrophobic and elusive domestic drama in whose interplay of silence and malicious accusations lie a bitter micro- cosm of the larger conflicts played out on the country's political stages which were to erupt in a fratricidal civil war, scars of which still haunt the national psyche.

The Lorca canon has effectively been constructed through international stagings of the plays. While the focus here is largely on performances in the English-speaking world, references are also made to seminal productions in Spain that have shifted the performance vocabularies of the texts. While David Johnston has argued that British actors, like their contemporaries in the USA, are trained largely within the Stanislavsky tradition and thus 'experience difficulties with the emotional pitch of Lorca's theatre' (Johnston 1998a: 44), even in his own lifetime Lorca recognized the problems experienced by Spanish actors in locating a stage language for modernist works that, veering uncomfortably between realist and symbolist paradigms, easily accommodate facile folkloric clichés (García Lorca 1986: 201–2).

The Butterfly's Evil Spell (1920)

> The theatre that always lasts is that by poets.
>
> (OCIII 563)

Any contemplation of Lorca's dramatic output necessitates a consideration of the conditions that generated it. *The Butterfly's Evil Spell* is indelibly bound up with Gregorio Martínez Sierra's attempts towards an art theatre modelled on the francophone experiments of André Antoine, Paul Fort and Aurélien Lugné-Poë, to whom he was frequently compared (Borrás 1926: 10). At the Eslava working within the limitations of a twelve-foot deep stage, Martínez Sierra built on the initiative of Adrià Gual's Barcelona-based Teatre Íntim, cultivating a theatre that eschewed the machinery of the proscenium arch stage while providing more fluid scenic environments that might comment on subjective, psychological states rather than aspire to any kind of assumed fidelity to nature. The Eslava was a theatre that used lighting as a sculpting instrument and celebrated imaginary landscapes. It looked to a revolving stage and different stage levels that questioned linearity and conventional horizontal modes of organizing space and narrative. The focus was more on vertical compositions and layered contexts, extended rehearsal periods, the use of music to enhance the onstage environment, a cutting-edge repertoire, and conspicuous directorial interventions. With its 'in-house' post-impressionist designers – Manuel Fontanals, Rafael Pérez Barradas and Siegfried Burmann (see Abril 1926: 19–36) – Martínez Sierra's laboratory theatre pointed to a protected environment where the actor might investigate his/her relationship to the audience in more complicit and flexible ways (Borrás 1926: 9, 16).

We know that Lorca met Martínez Sierra on arriving in Madrid in 1919 and that the latter encouraged him to expand a poem, now lost, about a cockroach who aids an injured butterfly and then falls in love with her, into a play with promises of staging it (Gibson 1989: 88; Stainton 1999: 60–1). Naive as to the workings of professional theatre, however, Lorca struggled to meet Martínez Sierra's deadlines for completion. Rehearsals were marred by disagreements over the play's title – imposed by Martínez Sierra who rejected Lorca's suggestion, *The Lowest of Comedies* (García Lorca 1986: 136) – and discrepancies over a performance register that veered between melodrama and ballet. Lorca sought to get the play withdrawn in the days prior to its opening (Mora Guarnido 1958: 126).

Crafted in verse, *The Butterfly's Evil Spell* is conceived around symbolist paradigms, with evident links to Maeterlinck's *The Intruder* (1890) and Rostand's *Chantecler* (1910), seen in Madrid a year earlier (Sánchez 1950: 38). Lorca's intoxication with *A Midsummer Night's Dream*, whose traces similarly haunt *The Public*, *Play Without a Title* and Act 3, Scene 1 of *Blood Wedding*, can be observed in *The Butterfly's Evil Spell*'s treatment of an enchanted space in which transformations are fashioned by that which passes as love.[1]

The play concerns the adventures and misadventures in love of Boybeetle. Silvia, a fellow cockroach, is infatuated with him but he cannot return the sentiments, despite the protestations of his mother who covets Silvia's financial assets. His affections come to rest on a wounded butterfly, an 'otherworldly' being to whom he confesses undying love. She, however, fails to reciprocate, abandoning the lovelorn suitor at the end of the play.

Beyond mimeticism: the play in performance

Readings of *The Butterfly's Evil Spell* have been decisively shaped by the contentious reception of the first performance, on 22 March 1920, marked by jeers, heckling and calls for insecticide to be poured on the scorpion woodcutter (Gibson 1989: 97–8; Vilches de Frutos and Dougherty 1992b: 23–31). Critics, however, noted that the piece, despite monotone verse patterns and negligible dramatic development, demonstrated potential in its poetic vocabulary (Alsina 1920; Floridor 1920; Machado 1920). The harshest review found the play defied the attempts of the cast to locate a performance language for it (Andrenio 1920).

It is perhaps worth noting here that Martínez Sierra's initial idea had been to stage *The Butterfly's Evil Spell* with puppets instead of actors (Gibson 1989: 96). The text's play on difference and lyrical language may have been more palatable when delivered through the mechanics of the grotesque fictive body of the puppet that does not allow for easy identification between performer and role. The production appears to have been distinguished by an uncomfortable dependence on mimeticism – exemplified through the use of the human performer – with a costume aesthetic marked by antennae, feathers and wide capes evoking the wings of a cockroach and an abstracted set design more suggestive of the entrails of a human body than a rural woodland.

Pérez Barradas, who designed the costumes, had also been responsible for the initial scenography for the production, conceived as a plethora of giant daisies: a forest perceived through the retina of an insect. This vision had been rejected by Martínez Sierra, who then entrusted the task to Fernando Mignoni (García Lorca 1986: 136–7). Set, costumes and performance aesthetic all seemed to suggest three conflicting aesthetics. Dancer Encarnación López Júlvez, also known as 'La Argentinita', in the role of the butterfly, was trapped within a transparent sequined costume, with pink tights and 'ridiculous wings' that gave her the air of a fairground tightrope walker (Mora Guarnido 1958: 128).

The play provides variations on a theme, with the characters little more than a chorus of undifferentiated voices and stock types – the interfering mother, the suffering artist, the prying neighbours. This is a poetic oratorio for the voice rather than a dramatic vehicle with narrative pulse. The arias delivered by Silvia and Boybeetle echo each other in their articulation of predicaments shaped by rejection. While most critics view it as a minor work (see Edwards 1980: 27–30; Soufas 1996: 235), Fernández Cifuentes (1986: 29–44) argues for its status as a score, dependent on a performance idiom that draws on maligned forms of spectacle for effective realization. The importance of Edvard Greig's music and La Argentinita's dances in further reinforcing the lyric tones of the play suggests aural and gestural languages as key components of the piece's aesthetic. Although subsequent productions have enveloped the textual remains – the ending has been lost in the extant manuscript – in constant musical accompaniment, the dramatic awkwardness of the play defies camouflage.[2]

Nonetheless, the allegorical formation of the piece as well as its curiosity value as Lorca's first staged play has proved alluring. The butterfly, emblematic of the trickery, deception and illusion of the stage serves as reminder of the most basic practices of masquerade that shape the theatrical act. The poet Boybeetle's fascination with the butterfly exemplifies the illusions/delusions conjured both in love and on stage. Love is shown to be dependent on the representations we create of our objects of desire and the ways in which they exist primarily in our consciousness. Boybeetle may be conceived as a veiled metaphor for Lorca's own unhappiness at the time (Gibson 1989: 97), or a prototype for his later protagonists confronting public opinion in the pursuit of a love that cannot be contained within social expectations or protocol (Edwards 1980: 30), but it was a play that Lorca viewed as peripheral to his development as a playwright.

The changes, modifications and erasings on the surviving script do, however, indicate the ways in which Lorca reshaped the play throughout the rehearsal process, recognizing the collaborative processes of theatremaking that were to impact on his future dramaturgy. While it is probably now seen as one of the Eslava's most resonant productions, as early as 1926 its four performances barely get a mention in a book edited by Martínez Sierra on the aspirations, achievements and legacy of the theatre.

The Basil-Watering Girl and the Prying Prince (1922), The Billy-Club Puppets (1922) and The Puppet Play of Don Cristóbal (1930–1)

> You are the support structure for theatre, Don Cristóbal. All theatre comes from you.
>
> (OCII 707)

Lorca's puppet plays have, habitually, been allocated only perfunctory attention by critics who view them primarily as experimental steps towards the tragedies. *The Basil-Watering Girl and the Prying Prince*, first staged on 6 January 1923 at the family home in Granada, briefly features a shoemaker often seen as the prototype for the husband in *The Shoemaker's Wonderful Wife*. The play's structural division into 'prints' links it to the similar dramaturgical shaping of *Mariana Pineda*. The thematics of adultery, deception and the enactment of a socially inscribed role in *The Billy-Club Puppets* is regarded as an early treatment for that in *The Love of Don Perlimplín for Belisa in the Garden*.

These plays, however, function within an alternative framework that acknowledges the stylistic considerations and carnivalesque origins of the puppet theatre (see Astles 1999). All juggle meta-theatrical devices that foreground the storytelling process, presenting the characters as types brought in by the narrator to enact the tale. In *The Basil-Watering Girl*, the Negro evokes the function of theatre as he opens the play by announcing 'Stories for sale!' (GL 1984a: 296; GL 1996b: 32). This is a tale put together before our eyes with characters brought on stage according to the demands of the narrative.

As with *The Billy-Club Puppets* and *The Puppet Play of Don Cristóbal*, the play makes reference to bodily functions – the Prince, we are initially told, cannot appear because he is 'having a pee' (296; 32). The pleasure and punishment of the body feature heavily in these pieces. All take place in a metaphorical, carnivalesque space distant from existing social and cultural frameworks. All are populated with characters that come from varied economic fields. The point of origin for the plays lies in the *cristobicas*, travelling Andalusian *guignol* puppet shows featuring the Spanish manifestation of Punch or Pulcinella, Don Cristóbal de Polichinela, that Lorca hoped to build on in plans conceived with Manuel de Falla for an itinerant theatre company, 'Los títeres de Cachiporra de Granada' (The Billy-Club Puppets of Granada). The puppeteer is at once part of the action (speaking with the puppets) and outside of it (manipulating them), and personifies the dualities inherent on reversals and pairings that shape the narrative's form and content.

> The openings and orifices of this carnival body are empha-
> sized, not its closure and finish. It is an image of impure
> corporeal bulk with its orifices (mouth, flared nostrils, anus)
> yawning wide and its lower regions (belly, legs, feet, buttocks
> and genitals) given priority over its upper regions (head,
> 'spirit', reason).
>
> (Stallybrass and White 1986: 9)

The leaden wooden heads, mechanized movements and abrasive gestures of the *cristobicas* refuse to work within mimetic paradigms. Tapping into uncertainties generated by disguise and masquerade, they point to the imitative nature of identity. Lorca's puppet plays defy authorial imposition. They are based on folk tales and recognized generic plots, promote double-edged humour and rely on ritualistic repetition, alliteration and colloquialisms. Their bawdy language and sexual innuendo has flagrant points of contact with Fernando de Rojas's *La Celestina* (1499) and Valle-Inclán's farces. All are anti-hierarchical, undermining legitimized forms of power and authority. All feature characters performing 'other' identities and are consciously self-referential. In *The Basil-Watering Girl*, the Prince disguises himself as a grapeseller to win over Irene's affections. Irene takes on the role of a magician to cure the lovesick Prince. The Prince is as obsessive a character as Don Cristóbal in *The Billy-Club Puppets*, the first draft of which predates *The Basil-Watering Girl*. While the protagonist of *The Billy-Club Puppets*, Don Cristóbal, functioned as a master of ceremonies of sorts for the Epiphany entertainment staged at the García Lorca house in 1923, the play, consistently revised by Lorca during his lifetime, was staged in Madrid only in 1937 and first published twelve years later in Buenos Aires. Its numerous treatments between 1922 and 1936 all feature an ensemble of characters who function without inner histories or psychological reasoning in texts that move across unfixed variations (Fernández Cifuentes 1986: 85–92).[3]

The earlier version referred to as *The Billy-Club Puppets* opens with a narrator-cum-compère who introduces the performance that is about to begin: the 'Tragicomedy of Don Cristóbal and Miss Rosita'. As with the prologue of *The Butterfly's Evil Spell* and *The Shoemaker's Wonderful Wife*, this is a metatheatrical framing device that comments on a bourgeois theatre that sends its audience to sleep in an environment of 'gold and crystal' (OCII 40; GL 1983b: 23). The theatre presented here is an outdoor theatre – interestingly much of the action takes place in the public sphere – affiliated not to 'the counts and the marquises' but 'the plain people' (40; 23).

The tale owes much to Cervantes's interludes or *entremeses* both in structure and plot. According to Lorca's brother Francisco, Rosita's shoe scenario in the final scene is lifted directly from Cervantes' *The Hawk-Eyed Sentinel* (García Lorca 1986: 151). Rosita is in love with Cocoliche but her father sells her in marriage to Don Cristóbal, here referred to as the diminutive Cristobita. Cocoliche drowns his sorrows on hearing of the impending marriage and the appearance of a mysterious Young Man, later revealed as Currito, suggests an earlier amorous liaison with Rosita that further questions the stability of the Cristobita–Rosita partnership. On the wedding day farce ensues as Cocoliche and Currito – the latter disguised as a shoemaker – enter Rosita's quarters. As Cristobita arrives in search of his bride-to-be, Currito stabs Cristobita and his loud demise leaves Cocoliche and Rosita embracing amorously at the play's end.

Cristobita agrees to marry Rosita because she is attractive, poised and small, 'a woman should be just that tall, no more, no less' (45; 28). There is something of the perfect mail-order Bride in his conception of her as an object of consumption. Significantly both Mosquito and Cocoliche also refer to Rosita through material paradigms: as an overripe fruit, a mother of pearl boat, a tasty morsel. She is either a consumable or a mannequin onto which they drape precious artifacts, later mapping her responses to the trinkets with which they have adorned her.

The men in the play are weak-willed braggarts, fortified by alcohol but largely incapable of action. Cristobita may boast of a capacity to split Fígaro in two (66; 46), but his avarice and gluttony mark him out as a largely inactive entity whose pleasures come primarily through scopophilia. Currito is hesitant and wary and can only act when disguised as another. Cocoliche cries like a petulant child. All three men suggest clear parallels between spectating and voyeurism. Masculine prowess, as Cristobita's fate indicates, is a construct that needs deflating.

The men's passivity is contrasted with Rosita's artistic engagement with her embroidery (Soufas 1996: 38–9). While Rosita's craft can't protect her from the public world that Cristobita represents or his attempts to direct the action, it functions, not as an image of 'daily drudgery which speaks of freedoms denied' (Johnston 1998a: 84) but as a representation of creative labour within the private sphere of the home and agency in a society that denies women a sense of self-worth outside the roles of wife and mother (Soufas 1996: 43).

While *The Billy-Club Puppets* was conceived for puppets, there is an ambiguity in the text as to whether these performers are puppets or actors performing as if they were puppets. The jubilation of Rosita and Cocoliche in the play's final moments seems to be based, in part, on a realization that Cristobita is a puppet and therefore not in a position to possess Rosita. Cristobita is a prototype Punch with an ample belly, a hump and a wooden head. He wishes he were made of wine – a sly jibe at his *machismo* – with cake for a belly (75; 56). As he bursts the sound of grinding springs is heard. His insides are not flesh and blood but sawdust (78–9; 58–60).

Repeated references are also made to the other characters' non-human status. Rosita's father wears a pink wig and has a face to match. Fígaro the barber who appears in Scene 5 is a variation on the roguish barber of Beaumarchais, Mozart and Rossini. The village of whitewashed houses in which the action takes place appears almost as if in miniature. Rosita is referred to as 'about three feet high' (45; 28), a diminutive puppet on a stage of castanets, smugglers, lemons, orange groves and other populist referents of Andalusia. References made in the play to *Mariana Pineda*, the heroine of his subsequent full-length play, and Don Juan Tenorio, the eponymous womanizing anti-hero of Tirso de Molina's *The Trickster of Seville* (68, 74; 49, 55), subsequently appropriated by Mozart and Da Ponte in *Don Giovanni*, suggest a self-consciously artificial universe where the everyday is lyricized.

Interestingly the musical references serve to position the play within a pseudo-operatic register that further reinforces its textuality. As in opera, musical elements are used repeatedly to echo and comment on the predicaments of the characters. Flutes accompany Currito's stabbing of Cristobita (77; 57), Mosquito blasts from his trumpet as the coffin is carried onstage (78; 59) and a bassoon and piccolo sound as Cristobita is pushed into the coffin in the play's final moments (79; 60). The play's evolution involved plans to score it and Lorca met in late 1935 with the Philippino composer Federico Elizalde to plan the musical and choreographic accompaniment (García Lorca 1986: 148).[4] While unstaged in his lifetime, abortive attempts towards a production litter his correspondence (OCIII 624, 1062, 1155), providing a strong indication of the importance of representational visibility in any potential reading. This is a play clearly crafted on the premise of direct contact between performer and spectator: its opening acknowledges the audience's presence as Mosquito asks them to hush in anticipation of what is to come (40; 23). Mosquito is positioned both outside the action – commenting on stage events – and inside it – irritating the slumbering characters. His name may even be a self-referential nod to the insect-characters of *The Butterfly's Evil Spell*.

These metatheatrical elements are perhaps more pronounced in *The Puppet Play of Don Cristóbal*. Written in 1930–1, this is a play about the rites of theatregoing that opens with a reference to the puppet-show as 'the expression of the people's imagination'

(OCII 398; GL 1990: 67); i.e. that which cannot be fixed within the text. The prologue is delivered by a Poet conversing with a Director who is 'shaping' the action. This more succinct verse variation on the earlier prose play conceives Don Cristóbal as a doctor involved in malpractice who has murdered a patient to get hold of his money. The Rosita he pursues is more sexually vigorous. Their marriage, brokered by her mother, sees the defiant Rosita bring her lovers to the marital home where, in the fullness of time, she gives birth to quadruplets. A fifth addition to the family emerges in the play's final sequence to the wrath of Don Cristóbal, who kills Rosita's interfering mother when she insists the children are his.

The play is cruder than *The Billy-Club Puppets*. Cristóbal's first entrance is delayed because he's peeing offstage; his club is perceived as a blatantly phallic symbol; equations are made between sexual and oral pleasures. Cause and effect structuring is dispensed with as time is condensed to the point where the action resembles a farcical cartoon, lending it something of the dramatic pitch of Alfred Jarry's *Ubu* plays. At the end the Director appears and picks up the puppets, severing Cristóbal from the continued beating of his mother-in-law, and reinforcing the contrived status of the piece. The puppet is shown to be an incomplete body whose existence is dependent on the '"growing out of" another body or other bodies' without which 'it does not exist (at least in terms of performance)' (Astles 1999: 114).

In tracing Cristóbal's family tree as 'cousin to the Galician Bululú and brother-in-law to Aunt Norica from Cádiz; brother of Monsieur Guiñol from Paris, and uncle to Don Arlechino from Bergamo', a theatrical lineage is sketched that puts on the stage 'vulgarities that overwhelm the tedious triviality to which it is condemned' (411; 79). These are puppets taken out of the theatrical museum. Whereas the Poet argues for Cristóbal's status as an evil stereotype, the play defies such authorial intention. The Poet's prologue, championing the authority of the text, is undermined by an ending where it is the director who is seen as the triumphant theatre artist orchestrating and controlling the action of the puppets – a veritable contrast to Jacinto Grau's *Mr*

Pygmalion, written in 1921, where the author is destroyed by his puppet creations.

Lorca played the role of the Poet in the first production of the play at Buenos Aires's Avenida Theatre on 25 March 1934. Modifications were made to the play that involved Lorca engaging in dialogue with Don Cristóbal at the opening (OCII 707–8). Subsequent performances at Madrid's Florida Hotel on 12 October 1934, at the Lyceum Club on 26 January 1935 and at the Book Fair at the Paseo de Recoletos on 11 May 1935 included changes that suggested an ongoing evolution and engagement with a formula capable of endless revision.

These plays have not enjoyed the copious stagings of *Blood Wedding*, *Yerma* or *The House of Bernarda Alba*. Luis Olmos teamed up with Amelia Ochandiano for a dance version of *The Billy-Club Puppets* in 1998 but arguably the most resonant staging remains José Luis Alonso's 1986 production of *The Puppet Play of Don Cristóbal* at Madrid's Centro Dramático Nacional (CDN). Alonso's production suggested a parallel between Lorca and the Poet by having the latter played by an actor with a striking resemblance to the former. On Gerardo Vera's puppet-stage, doll-like human performers were manipulated by stagehands dressed, like the Poet, in the boilersuit of La Barraca – pointing to an implicit association between La Barraca and the recently established CDN. The acting was emphatically front-on, challenging any sense of the characters as three-dimensional beings (see Figure 3), with a burlesque score by Carmelo Bernaola providing a running commentary on the action and accenting what Alonso saw as Lorca's parody of Federico Moreno Torroba's *zarzuela* (or popular operetta) *Luisa Fernanda* (1991: 355). Alonso's fast-moving reading was loud, rude, lewd and political, with the human puppets brought onto the stage as the narrative required. Their fixed facial expressions and mechanized movements, as well as a costume register that moved from eighteenth-century farce to 1930s agit-prop, suggested an ongoing manipulation of human agency that moved from the historical and theatrical past into the present of a socialist, democratic Spain supposedly laying to rest the demons of the country's recent history.

Figure 3 Human performers as mechanized puppets: Alfonso del
Real as Don Cristóbal and Chari Moreno as Rosita's
Mother in *The Puppet Play of Don Cristóbal*, at Madrid's
CDN, directed by José Luis Alonso, 1988. Photo
Chicho/CDT

Mariana Pineda (1923–5)

If Andalusian folk tales and colloquialisms provide a point of
reference for the puppet plays, the city of Granada serves as a
manifest presence in *Mariana Pineda*. The piece revolves around
a city martyr garroted in 1831 for her role in the conspiracy to
overthrow King Fernando VII, the reactionary Bourbon monarch
placed on the Spanish throne following the Napoleonic occupation. Lorca had grown up around the mythology of Mariana
Pineda, her statue stood across from his bedroom window in
central Granada: 'a Juliet without Romeo . . . closer to the
madrigal than the ode . . . dressed in white, with her hair loose
and a melodramatic expression verging on the sublime' (OCIII
785; GL 1983a: 45, 44).

For Lorca 'the elegant, brave, terribly beautiful' Mariana was 'the symbol of an ideal revolutionary' (OCIII 499). He conceived the play as a fitting theatrical testament, 'a grand theatrical ballad' of her final days (OCIII 768). This is a play inspired by the strained verse dramas of Eduardo Marquina: *The Cid's Daughters* (1908) and *The Sun has Set in Flanders* (1909). The opening and closing verses that frame the action are taken from a well-known ballad formulated from her myth (García Lorca 1986: 157). Possible textual influences, however, go beyond Spain. *Mariana Pineda*'s thematics suggest parallels with *Tosca* (Mora Guarnido 1958: 135), and there are structural echoes of *Antigone* in a female protagonist who breaks the law, and is faced with an ultimatum from the representative of that law: retract your actions or die. Self-knowledge comes from the decision-making process (Fernández Cifuentes 1986: 56).

Lorca's treatment of the myth involves an overt falsification of the historical knowns of Mariana's life (OCIII 491). This process of invention conceives the widowed mother of two as passionately in love with Pedro de Sotomayor, one of leaders of the liberal conspiracy against Fernando VII. Pedro is able to escape the tower in which he is imprisoned when Mariana smuggles in a monk's habit. She is involved in embroidering a flag for the rebels that falls into the hands of Pedrosa, the Police Chief of Granada. She is arrested and transferred to a convent, Santa María Egypcíaca, where Pedrosa offers her freedom in exchange for the names of her co-conspirators. Confident that Pedro will find a way to save her she refuses to comply with Pedrosa. The former, however, escapes to England and Mariana is led out to her execution as the play ends.

Mariana's link to the liberal cause is conceived through romantic prisms. The stitching of the word 'liberty' on the flag is presented as a means of pleasing her lover. Perhaps the timing of the play, drafted and redrafted as Primo de Rivera's military dictatorship tightened its grip on the country, may have rendered it too contentious to have Mariana sacrifice herself for political ideals. Here we are offered a fine needlewoman, embarking on women's work, who happens to be caught in a political crossfire. Her domain is the private sphere, a home violated both by Pedro and his co-agitators and then by Pedrosa. The 'flag-text' she creates at the demand of another renders her vulnerable and ultimately leads to her destruction (Soufas 1996: 43). The identification of Mariana 'with the production of a type of script, the rebel flag using writing rather than colors or other symbols to communicate its message', allows for the play to be read as a dramatization of the 'conflict between the private and public aspects of playmaking' (Soufas 1996: 45, 42–3): with meaning imposed by a discerning audience for which 'authorial intentions' are a largely irrelevant entity.

Lorca re-envisages the public narrative of Mariana Pineda through a reshaping that positions the tale as artifice, a construct of the imagination of the girl who pauses to listen to the ballad at the play's opening. Recognizing that he 'couldn't "do" all of' the 'thousands of distinct Marianas' that float in the public consciousness (OCIII 361), Lorca opts for a pining, lovelorn Mariana. The character of Pedro de Sotomayor is a fictive amalgamation of her cousin Fernando Álvarez de Sotomayor and her lover and father of her illegitimate child, Casimiro Brodett. Both were affiliated with the liberal cause. Álvarez de Sotomayor spent time in prison in 1828, escaping with Mariana's aid. Brodett was forced to leave Spain in 1830. Pedrosa is a suitably malevolent conception of Ramón Pedrosa y Andrade who, as Chief of Police in the city, was responsible for stamping out political dissent (Guardia 1952: 269). He is referred to in the first two acts as an omniscient presence, consistently linked with surveillance and spies. Predictably he offers Mariana freedom for the price of sexual favours. While Lorca provided stage directions requesting that he not be played in a caricatured fashion (OCII 140; GL 1994: 36), his language fixes him within the register of the stage villain: a sexual predator, consistently linked with surveillance and spies and ominously clad in black.

Fernando, the teenage brother of Mariana's friends, is similarly conceived within limited constraints as an infatuated and naive young man who flies off the handle at regular intervals to reinforce the passion of his sentiments. Mariana may manufacture Pedro as a romantic hero and worthy object of her affections, but his own actions (and crucially inactions), render him a largely passive figure, putting Mariana in danger as he meets with his comrades at her home and then abandoning her to the gallows for the safety of foreign soil. He is a constant void in the play, absent from both the first and third acts. Even when present his language functions almost constantly in the past and future tenses (Fernández Cifuentes 1986: 54). He is trapped in an in-between space that does not recognize or accept the demands of the present.

Mariana exists in counterpoint, dominating the play as a physical presence moving between effusive lyricism and silence. She stands in emphatic contrast to Pedro's flat boasts, Fernando's protesting rhetoric and Pedrosa's sexual bullying. This is a play that announces 'what is left unsaid' as 'more important than what is said' (OCII 140; GL 1994: 36). Fernández Cifuentes (1986: 60) reads the play as a duologue between lyric poetry and dialogue represented respectively by Mariana and by the conversations with those who visit her at the house. Lorca viewed Mariana as a character from the Golden Age stage and the play effectively draws on its verse forms (OCIII 491). Her six intermezzos serve as poetic interludes that reflect her sentiments, moods and tones, a 'diversity of poetic strains' unified into 'one sustained chord' (García Lorca 1986: 167).

> Mariana is more than a poetic vision. She is poetry itself as Lorca has conceived it in relation to his theater, besieged by the exigencies of time and space, and the even more pressing need to make it palatable for the theater public.
>
> (Soufas 1996: 46)

Reviews of the opening production located the protagonist of the piece not as Mariana but as poetry that flutters across the stage (Fernández Almagro 1927). In referring to the work as 'the *intentional stylization* of a Romantic play', Francisco García Lorca (1986: 161) maps out the 'interpretative ground' of the staging. Lorca had originally hoped that Martínez Sierra would direct the play with Catalina Bárcena in the title role (OCIII 792, 799–800), boasting that the director claimed the work could rival Zorrilla's *Don Juan Tenorio* (OCIII 818). His correspondence also acknowledges that the current political climate was unlikely to tolerate a production (OCIII 799, 817, 819; GL 1983a: 57–8). Martínez Sierra withdrew from any intention to stage the work in early 1926 (OCIII 882; GL 1983a: 71), and Lorca asked the established dramatist Eduardo Marquina to pass a copy of the work to Margarita Xirgu, the Catalan actress who had usurped the ageing María Guerrero as Spain's most powerful actress-manager. Securing a staging for the work runs as an obsessive concern through his letters at this time (OCIII 889–90, 893, 896, 906, 923–4; GL 1983a: 81, 89–90). Continued parental bank-rolling of his literary ambitions depended on evidence of artistic activity and Lorca's back-up plans included a further list of actresses including Josefina Díaz de Artigas, Carmen Moragas and Lola Membrives to approach with a view to staging the work.

Xirgu's agreement to stage the play was a huge boost to his theatrical aspirations. Xirgu's status as a major celebrity and influential impresario was a considerable endorsement of a fledgling dramatist. The play was to initiate a fertile nine-year collaboration with Xirgu that generated four further stagings in his lifetime as well as her posthumous presentation of *The House of Bernarda Alba*. *Mariana Pineda* is tellingly dedicated to Xirgu and eulogies to her craft, professionalism, visionary programming and imaginative versatility as an actress litter his writings and interviews (OCIII 194–6, 363, 548–9, 561, 576, 617–18). Lorca was to state in 1935 that 'I owe to Margarita Xirgu everything I have achieved in the theatre' (Rodrigo 2005: 284). This statement provides some indication of the significance her collaborative input was to exert on the development of his dramaturgy.

From Lorca's 1927 staging to Mariana as flamenco (2003)

Lorca is credited as director of the premiere production (which opened at Barcelona's Goya Theatre on 24 June 1927, and later began a brief run in Madrid on 12 October of that same year). The play's subtitle, 'a popular ballad in three prints', provides an indication of the 'look' Lorca envisaged for the piece.[5] All three acts are composed to recall nineteenth-century prints and refer-

ences are made to characters positioned in poses that evoke
illustrations of the period (OCII 106; GL 1994: 15). Costume
too is presented through noticeably intertextual means. For her
Act 2 appearance Mariana wears a pale yellow dress, 'the yellow
of an old book' (117; 22). In the final act, dressed in white, she
is referred to in terms that accord her deified qualities like a
radiant Madonna in a religious painting (149; 41). Lighting effects
too are conceived beyond naturalism in highly precise synthetic
terms as with 'the topaz and amethyst light of the candles' that
'make the room tremble poetically' as Fernando reads Pedro's
letter to Mariana in Act 1 (108; 17). The constant interruption
of striking clocks functions further as a sonic pulse to the action,
an aural soundtrack that adds momentum to a work often viewed
as hampered by its 'lack of theatrical dynamism' (Alberti 1984:
200). Lorca contracted Dalí to provide the set design for the
production, from his own initial rough drawings (García Lorca
1980: 432). The latter's scenography eschewed mimetic detail in
favour of a suggestive modernism that drew on cubist perspectives
in providing an imagined rather than a folkloric Andalusia (OCIII
1007).

The conception of a 'private dramatic-imaginative space' that
'overlaps the entire performance' (Soufas 1996: 42) was rendered
through a small set that seemed to fit within the frame of the larger
proscenium stage like a lithograph (see Figure 4). The coordina-
tion between costumes and décor allowed each to pick up on the
curves, stripes, colours and textures of the other (see Anderson
1984: 72). Period detail was jettisoned in favour of stark contrasts
of colour and shape in three backdrops – a receiving-room,
drawing-room and the convent garden – that commented on the
discourses of pictorial representation that had shaped the habitual
representations of historical verse dramas without reproducing
them. Certain critics did recognize the painterly look of the production as both invoking an etching and indicative of an interior
world (Bernat i Durán 1927; Madrid 1927), but wondered as to
whether the period costumes rested easily within the avant-garde
set (R.C. 1927).

Characters were viewed as evocations of mood rather than
psychologically credible individual entities (Machado 1927;

Figure 4 A metatheatrical lithograph: Salvador Dalí's ornate design
for the opening act of *Mariana Pineda*, at Madrid's
Fontalba Theatre, 1927. Photo: Fundación Federico García
Lorca

Madrid 1927; R.C. 1927; Vicuña 1927). While critics commended
Xirgu's 'realistic' juggling of the different Marianas (see Ayala
1927; G.C. 1927; Moragas 1927; R.S. 1927), parallels with the
contemporary political situation of Spain, in the grip of a military
dictatorship, remained unstated. Díez-Canedo (1927) refuted any
possibility of seeing her as a revolutionary symbol, judging her
the victim of a lover infatuated only with a political cause. The
uncertainty surrounding the Madrid opening, which many feared
the authorities would not allow to go ahead, converted Mariana
into a 'civic heroine', robustly applauded by the audience as,
condemned to death and abandoned by her lover, she exalted
freedom's praises (Alberti 1988: 255).

   Lorca's view of the play, articulated during the production's
Granada run in 1929 as the 'frail work of a beginner' (OCIII 195),

indicates his oft-cited dictum that the chronological gap between composition (it was initially drafted in 1923) and performance had rendered it 'at the *margins* of my work' (OCIII 957). In an interview given on the play's opening, Lorca recognizes the piece's faults and anachronisms (OCIII 360–3). Its subsequent checkered production history points to a play that is viewed in many ways as a curious prelude to his later *Doña Rosita*. English-language productions have favoured the folkloric approach of white-washed houses and Moorish apertures (as with Kate Wild's 2002 production at London's Gate Theatre) or a look that provides some sense of period detail in the costumes while opting for a more abstract spatial environment (as with Tessa Schneiderman's 1987 UK premiere and Max Key's revival for London's Arcola Theatre's 2006 Lorca season). The overwrought language has proved challenging – significantly Gwynne Edwards' translation recognizes the verse structure but controls and contains its more lyrical flourishes within a prose version peppered by judiciously chosen rhyming couplets. Even Spanish-language stagings, however, as with José Díez's 1982 production, have struggled with the verse structure, providing a naturalistic set steeped in historical detail that often jars with the unnaturalistic language (Álvaro 1983: 201–4).

Perhaps it is not surprising then to note that the most celebrated production of recent years has proved Lluís Pasqual's flamenco rendition for Sara Baras, which enjoyed a five-month run at Madrid's Calderón Theatre in 2003. Pasqual's reworking put aside the chronological structure in favour of a series of flashbacks rendered primarily through duet encounters with the three men who shape Mariana's sense of self. The stage space was dominated by a metallic grille of pseudo-Moorish design that opened up to allow passage in and out of Mariana's physical and psychological space. Behind it a wall of mirrors provided reflections of the action and camouflaged a site of surveillance and counterpoint through which Mariana was observed, courted and abandoned. As with Carlos Saura's *Blood Wedding* – referenced through the mirrored bare set – the adaptation made visible the gaps and silences in the play. Here we saw Mariana's garroting rendered through a black ribbon pulling her through to the grille. Historical representation was discarded in favour of transcendent imagery and a black and white costume palette offering a photographic analogy for the print. Significantly Baras created *Mariana Pineda* in 2002, the year she was named 'The Face of Andalusia' by the Andalusian Government's tourism board. The association of Baras – flamenco's photogenic star eschewing frilly frocks for classy evening wear – with Granada's emblematic heroine, served to position Lorca's play beyond the realms of the folkloric. The Pasqual-Baras *Mariana Pineda* transformed traditional forms into a hip global product. This was Lorca's text envisaged as celebrity-endorsed fusion flamenco: the appearance of a Lorca lookalike singing an elegy to freedom at the production's end further reinforcing the associations between Lorca's *Mariana Pineda* and a contemporary artist forging new discourses of dance-theatre for the international market.

The Shoemaker's Wonderful Wife (1924–6)

Like *Mariana Pineda*, *The Shoemaker's Wonderful Wife* enjoyed an extensive period of genesis and development. While working on it during the summer of 1924, Lorca acknowledged the influence of the *cristobicas* puppet theatre on its style (OCIII 809). There are evident echoes of *commedia dell'arte*'s stock characters, Cervantes' interludes, and Falla's takes on Alarcón and Cervantes, *The Three-Cornered Hat* (1919) and *Master Peter's Puppet Show* (1923) (García Lorca 1986: 175–80). The play's subtitle, 'a violent farce in two acts', alludes to Valle-Inclán's satirical farces, *The Marquise Rosalinde* (1912), *The Italian Farce of the Girl in Love with the King* (1920) and *The Licentious Farce of the Chaste Queen* (1920), which similarly cast a discerning critical eye over contemporary mores, hypocrisies and conventions. Plot echoes of *The Taming of the Shrew* and *Hamlet*'s play-within-a-play can also be traced. The play's title references both Calderón's 1637 play *The Wonder-working Magician* and Santiago Rusiñol's *The Prodigious Puppet* (1911), with the Author envisaged as a showman conjuring tricks with far-reaching implications.

Crafted in prose but peppered with verse ballads and ditties, the play, initially completed in the summer of 1926, appears to have been conceived with Catalina Bárcena in mind for the title role (OCIII 819, 1061; GL 1983a: 57–8), although by 1928 he was already casting around for other possibilities. Xirgu's plans to stage it were postponed by the bout of pneumonia she suffered in 1929 and the play finally opened, following further development during that year, on 24 December 1930 at the Español Theatre under the direction of Cipriano Rivas Cherif.

The Shoemaker's Wonderful Wife is the only one of his completed works to have a single location across the course of the action. The plot is a take on the familiar tale of a young girl married to an older man that similarly shapes *The Billy-Club Puppets*, *The Puppet Play of Don Cristóbal* and *Don Perlimplín*. The unhappy 18-year-old girl, pushed into marriage with a meek, socially observant cobbler, cannot adapt to life in the public eye, warily watched by the various townspeople who pass by her window. Her husband, hurried into marriage by his more forceful sister's wishes, is similarly dejected as the randy Mayor and three further suitors regularly pop by to 'admire' his young wife. Finally, in frustration and despair he leaves for pastures new at the end of the first act. The second act sees the enterprising Shoemaker's Wife now at work in the workshop she's transformed into a bar, frequented by her four admirers. Locals, classifying her as a fallen woman, pass by in horror and her only companion is a young boy, who informs her of the local tittle-tattle. The Shoemaker returns disguised as a puppeteer, with a tale of an older man cheated by his juvenile Bride that has evident parallels with his own predicament. The show is halted by a knife fight involving two of the Wife's young suitors and the situation allows the Shoemaker to gauge the degree, if any, of her deception. As neighbours begin to descend in anger at the tavern, the Shoemaker reveals himself and both are reconciled, vowing to stand together against the small-minded town's wrath.

The prologue to the play, delivered by Lorca in the opening production, appears to have been crafted during rehearsals. Appearing in a cape adorned with stars – a reference to the Author who opens Calderón's *Great Theatre of the World* (1640–1) – this was Lorca as showman, both a master of ceremonies and a purveyor of the magical who sets the scene for a theatre of self-conscious illusion. His prologue directly addresses (perhaps even teases) an audience who may want more simplistic fare. He asks for their 'attention' not 'kindness' in an era where the stage is 'often simply a business'. His is a plea for a theatre of poetry in an age where poetry has retreated from the stage 'in search of other places where audiences will not be shocked, for instance, when a tree becomes a puff of smoke, or three small fishes, obeying a command, become three million to satisfy the hunger of the multitude' (OCII 196; GL 1990: 3). This is the theatre as a space of fantasy and wonder where, as the prologue ends, the Author's top hat, initially a marker of his social prestige, lights up with a green light and then shoots out water. The letter he tantalizingly waves in his hand but never opens serves as an image of information as yet undivulged and of the promise of what is to come. It may also be an amusing nod to the favoured device of revelation in nineteenth-century melodrama, also much favoured by Ibsen.

The Wife's opening pleas to the Author to be allowed onstage further reinforce the play's metatheatrical underpinnings. Just prior to its opening, Lorca was to position *The Shoemaker's Wonderful Wife* within his literary past, classifying *The Public* as a more current indication of this theatrical thinking (OCIII 375). Nevertheless, the prologue's vision of a poetic register for theatre that allows for a stage world of transformation and trickery points to concerns that embrace these later 'impossible' works. The play is grounded in a popular vocabulary infused with Andalusian syntax and sayings but its iconography indicates a broader performative register. The set and costumes provided by Salvador Bartolozzi from drawings initially supplied by Lorca afforded allusions to Picasso's designs for *The Three-Cornered Hat* (1919). This was the stage as spectacle, a construct with echoes of a burlesque *guignol* set conceived in gaudy colours that recall popular prints of the day (Díez-Canedo 1930; Fernández Almagro 1930). The audience were invited into an enchanted space, where they could leave aside their dreary lives and fall for the magic of a puppeteer's tale that charms both the audience and its onstage surrogate, the Shoemaker's Wife.

The Shoemaker's return and the fiction he crafts shows history to be as much of a construct as the set on which he performs. His rewriting of the past allows for the retelling of events anew. In his version, the wife walks out on her husband; in hers, the husband is a dashing hero on a white horse dressed in a tight black suit and red tie (OCII 231, 219; GL 1990: 35, 23–4). Each converts the other into what they need to believe. Disguise proves liberating for, in listening to his ballad of the flirtatious wife entertaining suitors, the Shoemaker's Wife is able to experience 'the resonances that art can have in the everyday reality of those who experience it' (Anderson 1984: 54).

In *The Shoemaker's Wonderful Wife*, we are shown theatre's capacity for reinvention. The ending that supposedly reunites the couple actually leaves little resolved. The Shoemaker has now returned and stands determinedly by his wife's side as they face the rowdy band of neighbours. We are not left convinced, however, that he can overcome those who stand against them. Act 1 saw him cower regularly when pushed or probed. The townspeople may not take kindly to his deceit. Chaos, as *commedia dell'arte* often reminds us, returns to the stage when disguise is abandoned. Perhaps the fact that in *Don Perlimplín*, which Lorca was writing concurrently, he makes reference to a Shoemaker being strangled by his wife (OCII 242–3; GL 1990: 46), further suggests that the omens for a happy ending don't look too good.

From abstraction to Andalusia: stagings of the play

While the play has been read as a 'comedy of local customs and manners' (Vilches de Frutos 1998: 13), holding with Lorca's observations on its Andalusian ambience (OCIII 375), the first production eschewed explicit Andalusianisms in favour of a stage environment of austere abstraction. In viewing the play as a comment on the poverty and vulgarity of reality and the merits of our re-envisaging its possibilities (OCIII 375), Lorca alludes to its self-consciously textual framing – commented on by reviewers who evoked Goldoni and Valle-Inclán as prevailing referents (Díez-Canedo 1930; Olmedilla 1930). In classifying it as both a 'Harlequinesque pantomime' and a 'sainete', *ABC*'s critic pointed to the broad range of stylistic influences that had shaped this work (Floridor 1930), 'almost a ballet, simultaneously a mime and a play' (OCIII 468).

While Lorca was to use the costumes and blocking of Rivas Cherif's staging for the single performance of the play presented with Pura Ucelay for her Club Teatral Anfistora on 5 April 1933 (Ucelay 1990: 164), revisions to the play were made during this time that are evident in the reworked staging Lorca provided for Lola Membrives's company at Buenos Aires's Avenida Theatre in December of that year. Extending the opening prologue, which he again delivered for the Buenos Aires opening, he refers to the action as a 'pantomime' (OCIII 646), indicating the tone of the changes wrought on the play. The presence of Membrives, a more physically pliable actress, in the title role allowed him to add five songs and dances that further reinforced the musicality of the earlier draft. The 1930 draft features references to an exaggerated polka played by flute and guitar as the Shoemaker's Wife dances with an imaginary suitor in Act 1 and a trumpet used by the disguised Shoemaker for attracting attention in Act 2 (OCII 208, 223; GL 1990: 14, 27). The later version adds musical numbers from the eighteenth- and nineteenth-century repertoire that underline the choral importance of the villagers who watch over the Shoemaker's Wife.[6]

Already in 1930 Lorca had argued for the importance of the chorus in the work, 'irreplaceable . . . the voice of conscience, of religion, of remorse' (OCIII 374) but the chorus function was to be enlarged in the subsequent rewrite. By 1933 he was referring to it as a 'pantoplay' structured to the rhythm of a ballet (OCIII 468). The idea of inscribing discourse through and around the body was crucial to the design concept formulated by Fontanals for the staging: a white-walled room with stairs to the back and only three chairs so as to assist easy movement. Costumes were florid, with a more exaggerated cut than in the opening production. The overall effect seemed to be more in line with a Falla ballet than an acerbic Valle-Inclanesque farce.

Lorca saw the 1930 staging as a chamber version, a prelude to a play whose 'definitive' draft was premiered in Buenos Aires (OCIII 471, 469). That Madrid critics located references to Serge Diaghilev when Membrives's production toured there in 1935 reinforces the piece's status as a composite work where décor, music and choreography are all brought together as a means of commenting on the libretto-text (Fernández Cifuentes 1986: 113). The play functions as a fable on the commodification of the female body. The Shoemaker's Wife's body is the object in demand. She marries for economic security but refuses to be 'tamed' by a husband who lavishes trinkets on her (OCII 201, 206; GL 1990: 8, 12). The Mayor's advice on keeping women in their place involves hugging them, stamping on them and shouting at them and, if all three fail, taking a stick to them, perhaps ominously indicating how he has already got through four wives (206; 11). The Young Man with a Sash doesn't advocate domestic violence but instead longs to place the Shoemaker's Wife on display, contained within the confines of a painting (210; 15). Theirs is a culture that conceives the female as an object of appropriation.

In eschewing the position of dishrag, nun or decorative vehicle for male contemplation, the Shoemaker's Wife offers agency and pro-action. Her movements may be conceived in doll-like terms (Ojeda 1935), but she refuses to remain imprisoned within the male psyche as a passive mannequin. As the play's central character, the object over which the men compete, the action is perceived through her eyes (OCIII 472). In citing Lorca's view of the play as 'the feast of the body' (OCIII 485), Fernández Cifuentes (1986: 115) locates the body as the dominant overlay character of the piece. The stage directions call for exaggerated, abrasive movements that should have comic reverberations and are likened to those of a puppet. The stagings of *The Shoemaker's Wonderful Wife* with which Lorca was involved in a directorial capacity expose the cultural shaping of the body: human behaviour presented in artificial moves and gestures that function as a commentary on the constructed nature of all social conduct and regulations.

When Membrives's production was seen in Madrid reviewers located the influence of ballet on the choreography and the strong choral elements (Espina 1935; Mori 1935) with hopes that the piece would be transformed into a ballet with La Argentinita in the title role (Ojeda 1935). Views of the piece as a ballet without music have shaped its subsequent afterlife (Díaz-Plaja 1954: 185). Luis Olmos's hugely successful version realized during the mid 1990s and subsequently filmed for television in 1995 punctuated the text with extended dance routines that enacted the characters' sentiments and predicaments. The cartoonish painted backdrop suggested a pastiche Andalusia with something of the distended perspectives of Alice in Wonderland but the performers oscillated between the high artifice of the dance and a largely naturalistic Castilian-inflected delivery of the text. Juan José Castro's opera, premiered in 1949, has palpable echoes of Falla's *Three-Cornered Hat* in the kind of musical motif allocated to the wife and the incorporation of popular dance and Andalusian motifs (exemplified by enormous fans). While Lorca may have seen any further addition of music to the piece as a travesty in undermining the musicality of the dialogue (OCIII 478) musical accompaniment has been a standard feature of subsequent productions that have recognized the ways in which music serves to 'denaturalize the scene' (OCIII 472–3)

Stagings have often followed a strategy of providing recognizable icons of Andalusia while incorporating masks and puppets as a means of conjuring a performance magic that echoes the Author's opening pleas. Max Ferra's 1998 production for New York's INTAR turned to both Falla's *Love the Magician* and flamenco, and dressed one of the suitors as a bullfighter as a means of underscoring the fabricated Andalusia in which he'd chosen to locate the action. Here the unmasked actress in the role of the Shoemaker's Wife was evidently significantly older than 18, but constructed a coquettish image of innocence and virtue that built on the motifs around disguise and camouflage that distinguish the work. Puppets sat alongside male performers in drag enacting interfering village gossips. The lascivious snuff-taking Don Mirlo was presented as a version of the Ratcatcher in *Chitty Chitty Bang Bang* (1968). These were actors in the mould of puppets on a set evocative of a doll's house, a strategy also employed in the US premiere of the play directed by John Stix in 1949 which presented living puppets enacting the play-within-a-play with strings pulled by the disguised Shoemaker-narrator.

English-language productions, almost exclusively using the shorter, less physically demanding 1930 draft despite Lorca's preferences for the later version, have tended to be within small-scale fringe venues. Here, on restricted stages, providing a diminutive world, almost in miniature, the performers appear grotesquely out of proportion to their constrained environments. Both the 1990 and the 1998 stagings, by Robert Delamere and Andrew Pratt respectively at London's Battersea Arts Centre, presented a shrewish Wife entrapped within a surreal milieu of slanting distorted proportions that appeared more the projection of her anguished mind than a concrete home. Both utilized visual signifiers of Andalusia (fans, dance shoes, brash, showy dresses) in exaggerated forms as destructive codified weapons. Both offered a chorus moving in ominous synchronicity, with music providing a mode of punctuation rather than mere illustration.

Despite Lorca's claims that Max Reinhardt intended to stage it (OCIII 408), this has not been a play favoured by auteurist directors. Perhaps the most politically contentious reading was seen not in Franco's Spain but in communist Poland where Tadeusz Kantor's 1955 staging at Katowice's Teatr Slaski conceived an absurdist Chaplinesque Shoemaker who flew in the face of the ethos of socialist realism. Two years later, a further production at Krakow's Stary theatre brought in a more overt Bakhtinian aesthetic of circus slapstick and playful vaudeville on a set dominated by a giant shoehammer (Aszyk 1986: 275–7), an ironic visual comment on the hammer and sickle, and a site of symbolic struggle. While the 1933 draft was judged a move towards popular operetta or *zarzuela* (Vilches de Frutos and Dougherty 1992b: 69), endorsing a reading of the piece as a fluffy fable, Kantor's stagings indicate its potential for articulating concerns around the prescriptive containment of both artistic and social practices.

The Love of Don Perlimplín and Belisa in the Garden (1925)

While *Don Perlimplín* was not produced until after *Blood Wedding*, its presentation in a double bill with *The Shoemaker's Wonderful Wife* has served to associate it with a play that shares its generic plot of a young woman married off to a much older man for blatant economic reasons. The 50-year-old bookish Perlimplín is a coy virgin, persuaded by his motherly servant Marcolfa to enter into marriage with a woman half his age, his neighbour Belisa. Belisa's mother, aware of the old man's financial assets, agrees to the wedding. On their wedding night, however, fearful of what Belisa represents, he is wary of consummating the union. As the light is switched off, two sprite-*duendes* pull a curtain over the couple and discuss the situation. When they pull back the curtain Perlimplín can be seen in bed with two golden horns protruding from his head – the sign of a cuckold. He is ecstatic but the five male hats positioned on the floor and the five opened doors with ladders leading down to the garden suggest he may not have been alone in enjoying Belisa's favours. Perlimplín's realization of this leads him to create a new identity for himself as a young suitor who captivates Belisa with his romantic letters. The final scene sees Perlimplín observing Belisa in the garden preparing to meet her young lover. When Belisa stumbles on the body of her supposed red-caped love-interest, however, she discovers it to be Perlimplín. By masterminding his suicide, he eradicates both lover and self. It is both a cruel gesture that frustrates Belisa's sexual drive and a move towards her possible transcendence of physical needs in favour of a more spiritual attachment that wipes out the need for erotic satisfaction.

Lorca's conception of the play as an 'erotic *aleluya*' (OCIII 870) points to its self-consciously theatrical idiom. *Aleluyas* were originally illustrated pamphlets celebrating the Resurrection thrown to crowds during Holy Week processions. Developing beyond their original religious function they became popular comic strips presenting short cartoons of generic character types with firm roots in *commedia dell'arte* (Ucelay 1990: 13–17). The two-dimensional, pseudo-cartoonish world of the *aleluya* forms the determining register for the action.

The play is set in a patently synthetic world, fitting for a pro-tagonist as trapped in the world of books as his fictional prototype, Don Quixote. Belisa's mother is adorned in a wig 'full of birds, ribbons, and glass beads' (OCII 244; GL 1990: 47). Belisa appears in the play's penultimate scene dressed in an eighteenth-century red dress with a hat trimmed with ostrich feathers and large earrings. This is a fictive space of 'delightfully wrong' perspectives (254; 55). Green walls and black furniture frame the prologue's balcony. The great canopy bed dominating the bedroom in Scene 1 is draped with plumes. Six doors promise concealment and revelation in farcical fashion. The dining-room of Scene 2 has food painted on the table. The presence of cypress trees of Scene 3 denotes impending death. At the end of the prologue, as the marriage deal is negotiated, a flock of black paper birds fly past: an ominous sign created through visibly theatrical means. The *duende* sprite-goblins that appear in Scene 1 tantalize the audience with what may be happening behind the curtain they have pulled across Belisa and Perlimplín, playing on the curiosity of the spectator. Curtains, wigs, headdresses and capes all feature conspicuously in the play, signalling a fascination with the mechanics of disguise and deception. In *Don Perlimplín*, Perlimplín, Belisa and the audience become predictably prey to allure of the visual.

This is a play about stage creation and spectatorship, with the theatrical act shown to have a palpable scopophilic drive (see Feldman 1991; Wright 2000: 39–61). Perlimplín and Belisa are both orchestrators and witnesses of the theatrical action. Both construct a 'reality' of the desired other from the imagination. Perlimplín scripts a lover as ephemeral as performance itself. Prompted by the wily Marcolfa he performs the role of a keen suitor that he adapts to suit the demands of the situation in which he finds himself. He transforms Belisa into an object of trepidation and betrayal, a *femme fatale* who represents that which he fears. She first appears half-naked, an enticing presence whose state of partial undress masks and reveals what lies hidden within. She is an image of the masquerade that is femininity and that cannot be trusted. His love for her is conceived only through the realm of his imaginary. He is content only when he can frame her through a keyhole or a balcony window, or wrap her within an expansive red cape. Only when she is contained within the realms of the two-dimensional, as fitting with the play's origins as *aleluya*, does the 'pathetic stick-doll of a man' Perlimplín feel safe (263; 63).

His is a love that belies physical contact. The voluptuous sexuality Belisa represents threatens to usurp his sense of order and self. She is an ever-present reminder of the risk of castration.

He allows fiction to take over and turns his frustration in on himself. Perlimplín may perceive the final act of violence as 'the triumph of my imagination' (261; 62), but even the imagination has limitations. Perlimplín's comments that 'Belisa now has a soul' (263; 63) fail to comprehend that her soul mourns the red-cloaked lover (or imaginary), not Perlimplín the imaginer, and that it is the former who lives on in her imagination.

Copious referents have been drawn on in mapping the play's theatrical discourses. Lorca saw Perlimplín as a Calderonian (anti-)hero who doesn't want to avenge his wife's cuckolding in habitual vengeful fashion (OCIII 406). In its charting of the rituals of courtship beset by disguise and scheming servants, there are echoes of Rojas's *La Celestina*. Debts to Fernand Crommelynck's *The Magnificent Cuckold* (1921), Carlo Goldoni's *Arlecchino, Servant of Two Masters* (1745), and Valle-Inclán's *The Horns of Don Friolera* (1921) have also been located by critics in the parody-laden plot (see García Lorca 1986: 187; Guardia 1952: 282; Higginbotham 1976: 38–9; Sánchez 1950: 43). The schisms between love and desire have proved a popular prism through which to view the play (Edwards 1980: 47; Lima 1963: 141–56), but more recent readings have presented it as a fable on an emergent sexuality that is both seductive and terrifying. Sarah Wright, for example, discusses the play as an inverted 'Beauty and the Beast' tale where the focus on adultery and revenge functions merely as a 'seductive charade' for Perlimplín's rising awareness of his own mortality (Wright 2000: 49, 56).

Staging Lorca's 'chamber opera'

Lorca's view of *Don Perlimplín* as a preliminary sketch to a longer work (OCIII 408) has often led critics to see it as a minor work. Although rejected as 'hopelessly contrived' by Buñuel and *una mierda* by Dalí (Buñuel 1985: 101–2), Rivas Cherif planned to stage it with his experimental theatre group El Caracol in 1929, but the production was banned and the rehearsal script confiscated following a supposed contravening of the official suspension of all theatrical activity in the wake of the Queen Mother's death (Aguilera Sastre and Aznar Soler 1999: 131–2). The tense political climate may have left the authorities unwilling to allow the go ahead of a play with a lewd subtitle and a retired military officer in the role of the cuckolded Perlimplín (Ucelay 1990: 145–53). The play was eventually rescued from the pornographic section of the State Security Office by Pura Ucelay, the enterprising director of the Club Teatral Anfistora, who first presented it with *The Shoemaker's Wonderful Wife*, in a production co-directed with Lorca, on 5 April 1933 (Ucelay 1992: 454).

Santiago Ontañón took responsibility for the 'delicious' décor of pastel colours (Nuñez de Arenas 1933), giving the sense of an abode made of sugared confectionery. Ucelay's period costumes and wigs signalled historical pastiche, underlining the contrast between the lyric and the grotesque that Lorca endeavoured to fuse in the play (OCIII 409). This was a world far removed from folklore or fans (Fernández Almagro 1933), and Perlimplín's exaggeratedly naïve childishness found a complement in a set of awkward perspectives. The mannered performance style was judged to contribute to the crudity of the spectacle by a number of critics, leading to an uneasy fusion of sentimentalism and rakishness (Cueva 1933; Vilches de Frutos and Dougherty 1992b: 85–6). The presence of Boccacio's *Decameron*, the sexual game-play of Marivaux and the sensual fervour of Musset were evoked as strengths by the more liberal critical establishment (Chabás 1933; Marín Alcalde 1933; Ucelay 1990: 172–6). The satirical treatment of marriage and adultery, however, generated both the premature departure of outraged punters and critical concern (Ucelay 1990: 174–6).

While Lorca was to refer to it as his favourite work (OCIII 566), the play's language defied Mildred Adams (1977: 146), Lorca's early choice as English translator, as not making 'theater sense'. Joan Littlewood's 1945 Theatre Workshop production divided audiences with its sexual explicitly language. Seen at the Edinburgh Festival in 1949 with Ewan McColl in the title role, it offered a bawdy farce enveloped in lighting effects that were seen to outdo 'the achievement of Technicolor on the screen' (Anon 1949).

Lorca described the play as configured through music, using Scarlatti's sonatas to link the different scenes and the dialogue 'cut by chords and musical underscoring' (OCIII 409). The live pianist that accompanied the opening production functioned almost as a metronome, proferring the play a more human dimension than the puppet aesthetic may have initially suggested (Chabás 1933). Littlewood's staging used strains of Falla instead of Scarlatti between the scenes. Andrew Platt's 1998 production at London's Battersea Arts Centre offered percussive scrapings of violin bows against cymbals to underscore the action.

Lorca's brother Francisco classifies *Don Perlimplín* as written for four instruments with dialogue commencing on a single note that is then repeated with variations on the tonality (García Lorca 1986: 183–5). This is evident in the play's opening section where the repetition of segments of dialogue serves as a *leitmotif*. Opening as a kind of musical quartet, the play then moves into numerous duos – what García Lorca (1986: 185) sees as further evidence of the simplicity of the deployed *aleluya* form. It may be this structural debt to musical form that has proved so attractive to composers. Lorca classified *Don Perlimplín* as 'a chamber opera' (OCIII 409) and its conspicuous musical reworkings demonstrate the appeal of this compact play to post-Second World War composers searching for pastiche texts on which to hang their post-modern dissection of harmonic motion. While theatre has struggled to find a way of realizing a farcical discourse that dispenses with buffoonery and a prose register that veers from the lyrical to the absurd, opera has embraced both these facets as well as the cinematic and musical qualities of the piece.

Wolfgang Fortner (1962), Bruno Maderna (1962), Karel Goeyvaerts (1972) and more recently Conrad Susa (1984), Miro Belamaric (1994) and Simon Holt (1998) have all provided readings that exploited the play's parodic realms and melancholy pathos.[7] Maderna's Italian-language radio opera, first heard in 1962, fuses operatic orchestration with traditions of melodrama and music theatre that rely on instruments to take on roles in the way that a puppet might. Perlimplín is conjured by a flute and Belisa's mother by a sax quartet; Belisa is a soprano and Marcolfa a declamatory rather than sung presence.

Ten years later, in *Bélise dans un jardin*, Karel Goeyvaerts used the play as a structural framework on which to hang a sound experiment that negotiated different vocal registers including hissing, humming, and speaking, as well as singing. Conrad Susa's *The Love of Don Perlimplín* was conceived around the super-imposition of different melodic idioms. The collection of instruments prominent in the orchestration provided a neo-classical timbre. Puccini, Rossini, Mozart, Stravinsky were all referenced in a musical pastiche that found its visual counterpoint in the pop-up storybook set provided by Douglas W. Schmidt for David Alden's New York's Pepsico Summerfare 1984 staging. Parallels were drawn with Sondheim's *Sweeney Todd* in Alden's 'use of elaborate props built against a shabby backdrop, with the characters acting out different scenes in different corners of the stage' (Page 1984). Perlimplín's desk was an all-engulfing structure built of giant books that pointed to his academic reclusion. David Malis's Perlimplín was a wizened Don Bartolo-like figure with straggly long hair and a prominent bald patch. Ruth-Ann Swenson's Belisa was a buxom Rapunzel, part-Barbie doll, part-wily seductress. Nancy Gustafson's Mother was a stick insect in a crinoline and obscenely ostentatious wig.

In 1998 Simon Holt's titled his operatic rendition of the play, *The Nightingale's to Blame* as a reference to the nightingale heard as Perlimplín confronts Belisa with the imminent murder of her supposed suitor in the play's final scene. Here again both opera and production highlighted the piece's referents. Perlimplín's opening appearance, struggling to render a Scarlatti sonata on an onstage piano, linked the piece to Lorca's own musical undertows. Monteverdi was a conspicuous operatic model with the ensemble there to enhance the drama and 'to "cushion" the voices' but Berg's *Wozzeck* and Janáček's *The Makropulos Case* were also traceable in the musical enactment of psychological positions and the design of the music 'like a film score to carry the words along' (Holt, cited in Clements: 1998: 14).

Neil Irish's pantomime-like set, based on Lorca's sketches, offered the sense of watching the action through a distorting concave mirror like that advocated by Valle-Inclán in his 1920 *esperpento, Bohemian Lights*. Donald Maxwell's Perlimplín, both shy adolescent and lascivious old man, was rendered 'a mix of Don Quixote, Falstaff and Sir Andrew Aguecheek rolled into one' (Maddocks 1998). Patricia Rozario's coquettish Belisa was all broad plumed hats, pastel coordinated frocks and coy movements. Frances McCafferty's Mother, bird's nest resting on her head, was a relentless gossip, rarely pausing for breath. Again, here, the instrumentation – dominated by bass clarinet and alto flute with appropriate sound effects provided by bells, harp and piccolo – was sparse and harsh, with no violins to provide romantic reassurance. Perlimplín's curt, stuttering phrasing and yawning motifs were contrasted with Belisa's more effusive vocal lines. Here there was no chorus of crones hovering around the action, as in Susa's version, just the 'extreme leaps and wild melismas of the vocal writing' for six voices, 'close tuned to the pungent palette of the 17 instrumentalists' in 'a canny recreation of the sound of Lorca's verbal fusion of the lyrical and the grotesque' (Finch 1999).

Blood Wedding (1932)

Critical approaches to *Blood Wedding* can be summarized as pivoting around 'language, reference and genre' (Smith 1998: 44), all of which will be touched on in the reading of the play and its performance history offered here. Like *Mariana Pineda*, *Blood Wedding* is based on a historical episode from Lorca's native Andalusia, elaborated and reconceived as codified fiction. A brief newspaper item in July 1928 commented on the elopement of two cousins on the day before the Bride-to-be was due to marry a local farmhand. The escaping couple was hunted down by the Bride-to-be's family, who shot dead the male cousin and left the female cousin for dead at the side of the road.

Lorca's plotting presents a tale that uses only the bare bones of the story at once removed from the specificity of its Almerían location or its character names. These are characters presented through the roles they play in the narrative (Bride, Bridegroom, Mother, Servant). Only the supposed 'outsider' Leonardo is given a name but it is one imbued with allegorical significance, for Saint Leonard is the patron saint of slaves and Leo the zodiac sign of the sun. The breakdown of his name from *león* (lion) and the verb *arder* (to burn) thus positions him, not outside the social framework of the play but at its very heart, as a danger contained within. The Mother may agree to her son, the Bridegroom's, marriage to the woman known simply as the Bride but the Bride's past association with Leonardo perturbs her. Leonardo is a member of the Félix family whom she holds responsible for the deaths of her husband and elder son. As the wedding day approaches we are made aware of the fact that Leonardo, now married to the Bride's cousin, and the Bride are still in touch and that he is unhappy at her impending nuptials. Leonardo visits the Bride on the morning of the wedding but is unable to make her agree to halt the proceedings. The wedding celebrations are later arrested as Leonardo's wife realizes that her husband and the Bride have eloped. The Bridegroom and his clan run off in pursuit of them. The portentous landscape that greets them in Act 3 is inhabited by Three Woodcutters poised to sever the family trees represented by Leonardo and the Bridegroom, a Moon that lights the way for both pursuer and pursued, and Death disguised as a Beggar Woman. The men's off-stage deaths are mourned in the play's final scene where the Mother leads the surviving women in a wake for the absent phallus, culminating in the orgasm of the 'dark root of a scream' (OCII 475; GL 1987: 93).

Subtitled 'a tragedy in three acts and seven scenes', *Blood Wedding* is embedded in a cultural understanding of blood feuds and vendettas that bears the imprint of classical Greek tragedy. The play's title announces the *denouement* and carries within it the collision of what appear to be opposing dynamics. Blood is, according to the First Woodcutter, a 'path' to be followed (455; 74) but it is linked to the wedding with which it is juxtaposed through the shedding of blood that accompanies the marriage festivities. Both terms represent the contrary impulses that drive the action forward.

The play's cyclical structure further serves to underlie the prescriptive nature of the action and the enclosed world that constrains the Bride. The Mother is conceived like an avenging Clytemnestra commanding revenge once she realizes the lovers have fled. The Three Woodcutters are a chorus commenting on the predicament of the lovers and their course of action. The Three Girls that appear in the final scene weaving wool have been compared to the Three Fates handling the strings of life. As with

Sophocles's *Oedipus Rex* the play revolves around the break-up of a family unit that is supposedly predetermined before the commencement of the opening scene. Characters seek to define themselves within a seemingly endless history of blood discourses. They speak of being dragged by forces beyond their control or a destiny ordained by 'greater' powers. In the final scene, the Mother and Bride both speak of the men killing each other 'On a day appointed, between two and three' (474; 92). The play's opening scene establishes the house as a womb sheltering the phallus from the danger contained without. A proliferation of weapons – knives, pistols, pitchforks, axes – further reinforces the threat. References to the knife frame the action; the Bridegroom views it as a benign instrument for cutting grapes, the mother as a weapon of mutilation and an agent of death (416, 475; 33, 93).

Each character is defined in terms of heredity. The Mother perceives Leonardo as tainted because of his blood-link to the Félixes (421; 39). The Bride is associated with her mother, who didn't love her husband, entering into marriage out of a sense of duty. Even Leonardo speaks of her in Act 1, Scene 2 as needing to be watched (425; 43). This is the role she is expected to play: an unreliable presence in need of surveillance. Leonardo and the Bride explain their relationship in Act 3, Scene 1 in terms of the four elements shaping and controlling who they are and what they do. Against such elements preventative action is perceived as futile. As Leonardo informs the Bride 'And I put a wall of stone / Between your house and mine . . . I threw sand in my eyes. / But I'd get on the horse / And the horse would go to your door' (463; 82) As with Oedipus's attempts to escape the premonition of the oracle, the prophesies of the opening scene must come to pass.

The play's negotiation of tragic motifs links it to Synge's *Riders to the Sea*, first published in Spain in 1920. Both works are set in a rural world of rigid expectations where mothers lose their sons to forces they judge beyond their control; both chronicle a world where men are expected to follow the fate of their fathers, women that of their mothers; both close with lamentations conducted within the confines of an environment conceived as a place of worship. The whitewashed room in which the final scene of *Blood Wedding* takes place is described as having 'the monumental quality of a church' (466; 85); a solid intransient space that casts no shadows, a mausoleum where the women will remain buried for life.

Valle-Inclán's *Tragedy of Illusion* (1901) and *The Bewitched* (1913) have also been evoked in the public mourning of a younger generation of men whose deaths challenge an established biological order that anticipates children burying their elders. Ibsen's *Peer Gynt* (1867) is another cited referent with Peer's abduction of the bride Ingrid seen as a possible precedent for the elopement. Ibsen's fusion of the mythical (the Trolls) within a vernacular of poetic naturalism may also have proved a stylistic prototype. The Golden Age drama of Lope de Vega that Lorca was then adapting and staging with La Barraca is also demonstrably present in the play. The wedding scene reworks those of Lope de Vega's seventeenth-century dramas, *Peribañez* and *Fuenteovejuna* and the woodcutters may be a reimagining of the death-foretelling stranger met by the knight in *The Knight from Olmedo* (c. 1620).

Parallels have also been drawn with Gabriele D'Annunzio's peasant verse tragedies and Maeterlinck's treatment of character as subject to the malevolent control of external forces. The play's fusion of classicism and expressionism has been compared to that of Eugene O'Neill's *Desire Under the Elms* (1925) and *Strange Interlude* (1928). And the character of Death has been traced to the peasant in Lenormand's *The Man and his Phantoms* (1924), which similarly juggles Freudian references to subconscious forces and impulses. Benavente's *The Passion Flower* (1913) and Guimerà's *Marta of the Lowlands* (1897) too present a rural society of suffocating conservatism where female agency is controlled and subverted. Lorca's poetic output is even judged to have left its imprint on the drama.[8] The mythical forest of *When Five Year's Pass* where time is similarly suspended may also be a precursor for the landscape of 'great moist tree trunks' of Act 3, Scene 1 (455; 74).

Lorca was to locate this scene firmly in the Bach cantata ('Wachet auf, ruft uns die Stimme', BWV 140) he listened to repeatedly during the weeks in August 1932 when completing the play (OCIII 511). The seven movements of Lorca's play parallel those of Bach's cantata with both pieces ending with a *chorale*. Andrew Anderson (1987: 25) reads the Bride and Leonardo as archetypal figures with unconcealed biblical references, and the cantata correspondingly juggles extensive biblical quotations. Both feature Bridegrooms for whom the rites of marriage remain eternally deferred. Both use the recitative and duet, interweaving harmonies and a layering of sound. Both use song lyrics to comment on the predicament of the characters. In view of this the play's prominent operatic afterlife is perhaps not so surprising.

While the final act is executed in verse as a build-up to the denouement, the selective use of verse in the first two acts of the play – the brooding lullaby and the wedding song – comments on the surrounding action. The former is an example of the cradle-song that Lorca was to lecture on in 1928, a nocturnal ballad whose horse protagonist serves as potent metaphor for the errant Leonardo. The latter establishes the ritualistic coda of the ceremony – the Bride at once presented as an archetypal Bride but similarly demarcated from those who have gone before her in being sung of in white and appearing in black. The bridal song also reiterates the play's strong gender divide with the Bride described in terms of possession – a treasure to be claimed by the Bridegroom accompanied by oxen. The financial implications of the marriage are suggested in the play's organization of colour with the Groom's association with yellow and gold and the Bride's with silver and white emphasizing the economic aspects of the union. The financial imperatives that propel the marriage-transaction serve to counter the determinist impulses that would see the characters as 'victims' of fatalist forces. The commercial prerogative cannot endorse a desire that does not fit the wider economic priorities.

The Bride may have been read by critics as a desiring subject arguing for a channeling of a desire society expects her to deny (see Edwards 1980: 133–56; Lima 1963: 188–216), but, as Paul Julian Smith (1989: 115–25) has similarly noted with respect to Adela in *The House of Bernarda Alba*, she perceives herself as a hole that needs to be filled, a lack seeking a supplement. In both plays references abound to an unmitigating heat associated with sexual cravings. The Bride does not appear opposed to the institution of marriage as presented in the play – an economic arrangement. Her opposition is based on a perception that her husband cannot satisfy her desires. The Bridegroom is in many ways a contrast to Leonardo and the inflexible male values celebrated in the text. We are told that he is a virgin and abstains from wine (429–31; 48–9), a symbol of fertility and virility. He embodies the domestic in ways that Leonardo, ill at ease within the family home and irrevocably linked to his horse, does not. Both physically and psychologically the Bride functions within a terrain of barren lands filled with weeds, stones and thistles tellingly described by the Bridegroom as 'dry'. The Mother's reply that his father would have covered them in trees references the nourishing potential of the phallus as primary signifier of a rural world of male hunter-gatherers (428; 46). Leonardo is the 'dark river' operating in contrast to the 'tiny drop of water' represented by the Bridegroom that cannot possibly alleviate the stifling heat and burning thirst that serves as a metaphor for the Bride's sexual desires (472; 90). The impassioned exchanges between the Bride and Leonardo in Act 3, Scene 1 reveal that both are prepared for a *liebestod* – an ecstasy and union in death – but it is in fact Leonardo and the Bridegroom who achieve this *liebestod*, a consummation in death of 'two rushing streams / Still at last amongst the great stones' (470; 87). The two men 'killed each other for love', the Mother states in the final eulogy, mourned in images associated with lost virginity (474; 92).

As with others of his 'known' plays, such as *Doña Rosita* and *The House of Bernarda Alba*, spinsterhood or 'singledom' is presented as a lamentable prospect. All these plays map a society where expectations are passed on from generation to generation. Women are expected to remain in the home together embroidering 'edgings and little woollen dogs' (417; 34), men to leave a son on every street corner as the Bridegroom's grand-father did (417; 35). At the play's end, having lost her remaining son, the Mother classifies herself as 'poor'. Without a 'single son she can hold to her lips' a woman has no significant existence (471; 89). Motherhood is ultimately marked by loss in the play. It is one of the reasons why Almodóvar has referred to Lorca as 'one of the few writers to have expressed . . . the pain of mother-hood . . . in a truly heartbreaking and touching way' (Adamson 2007b).

Finding a stage language for the play: early productions

Critical opinions on the play have opted for 'social-existential realism' or 'the interplay of mythic-archetypal forces' (Soufas 1996: 93) and this serves equally well as a comment on performative strategies that have often struggled to find a gestural and decorative language that embraces both the symbolic realism of the first two acts and the impressionist conceptualism of Act 3, Scene 1. In many ways, overt stylization is present from the opening, in a stage environment conceived in minimalist terms primarily through the colour schemes of the different abodes. For the first production at Madrid's Beatriz Theatre, opening on 8 March 1933, Lorca struggled in rehearsals with performers who were unable to come to terms with the musical rhythms of the language. Manuel Collado (in the role of the Bridegroom) and Josefina Díaz de Artigas (in the role of the Bride) ran a company specializing in light comedy. Casting against type may have seemed a canny decision in attempting to attract a more expansive audience, but rehearsals proved fraught with Lorca pushing for mathematical precision and an attention to voice, inflection, and rhythm that challenged their assumed modes of acting (García Lorca 1986: 201; Sáenz de la Calzada 1976: 110). Reviews noted the declamatory style and mannered gestures of Díaz de Artigas and Josefina Tàpies in the role of the Mother (Fernández Almagro 1933; Nuñez de Arenas 1933).

The modernist décor of Fontanals and Santiago Ontañón followed the colour schemes laid out in the play's stage directions. Playful nods to Andalusian iconography were evident in the large fans and cut of the costumes. The company's association with the folklore-infused comedies of the Álvarez Quintero brothers served further to position the play firmly alongside the *Gypsy Ballads* (Fernández Almagro 1933), establishing an association with the poetic anthology that has definitively marked the stage languages through which the play is frequently presented. This cave-like setting of the Bride's house had critics wondering whether it was a gypsy world (Fernández Cifuentes 1986: 138). This was, however, an onstage Andalusia reduced to its most prominent signifiers and bereft of linguistic intonation markers (Agustí 1933; Mori 1933).

Lorca was not involved in rehearsals for Lola Membrives's staging of the piece that opened at Buenos Aires's Maipo Theatre on 29 July 1933; he did, however, assist Rivas Cherif on the third Spanish-language production presented during his lifetime in 1935. José Caballero's sets were grounded in the evocation of an austere whitewashed environment of different levels that allowed for different pockets of action, especially during the wedding scene. Strident geometric lines against a cold light enclosed the action. A rugged backdrop was put in place for the forest landscape of Act 3, Scene 1 that allowed for ominous shadow play and conveyed a sense of entrapment. The performance of Xirgu as the Mother, like that of Membrives before her, served to shift attention away from the Bride, perceived to be the protagonist of the opening production, and led Lorca to refer to it as the play's real premiere (OCIII 617).

While Lorca's reputation in the English-speaking world has been built posthumously, *Blood Wedding* was one of the few plays to be translated and staged in North America during his lifetime. Its presentation on 11 February 1935 as *Bitter Oleander* in José Weissberger's translation at New York's Neighbourhood Playhouse was saturated in Andalusian affectations. Production photos show Nance O'Neil's Mother and Eugenie Leontovich's Bride in high mantilla, ornate black and prominent decorative crucifix. Reviews refer to precious postering, 'poetic awkwardness', loud laments, excessively affective acting and a staging 'so fretted with studio attitudes . . . it has been removed from the soil and clapped into the straight-jacket of style' (Anon 1935a; Atkinson 1935). It was, according to one critic, as if Lorca's characters, 'great ones for talking . . . had eaten whole libraries full of seed catalogues' (Brown 1935); 'when one monosyllable won't do, they use only two; and when these fail, the castanets click and the bystanders sing, lament or dance' (Sobel 1935).

Critics were unsure as to whether the piece was a masque, short story, or ballet (Adams 1977: 172; Sobel 1935).

As Smith has effectively delineated in his excellent analysis of the production, the staging's excesses were perceived as concurrent with the affectations of the play's assumed referent and have shaped Anglo-American responses to both the work and the playwright's wider dramaturgy (Smith 1998: 46–53). Even the most cursory glance at reviews of Peter Hall's staging at London's Arts Theatre in 1954 lamented a 'gloomy impressionistic opus' that fails to travel well and is best kept to an 'intimate' fringe venue that 'mainly attracts the intelligentsia' (Clem 1954).

Folk settings, cultural tourism and canonization

Productions have been plentiful across fringe venues but the presence of the play across the established sector since the fiftieth anniversary of Lorca's death testifies to its now canonized status. Productions have habitually opted either for picturesque *español* or defiantly rejected it in favour of more expressionist mannerisms. Julia Bardsley located the action in a sandy bullring (in a 1992 production at the Leicester Haymarket) complete with a thirty-strong chorus of Holy Week penitents and an imported *cante jondo* singer. Nigel Jamieson's 1993 reading contracted musical troupe Cumbre Flamenca to provide 'authentic' choreography and Spanish-sung refrains that pulled against a mutating scenic backdrop and mythical forest evoked through hourglass-like sand waterfalls. Jamieson's staging, as is so often the case with English-language productions of Lorca, problematically equated dance with flamenco: it is an association that has proved hard to dislodge.

Other productions have displaced the peasant setting into similar folk surroundings, as with Boris Tumarin's 1949 staging for New York's New Stages presented across a sloping rural plain with a country music score, or the Mexican Laboratorio de Teatro Campesino e Indígena de Tabasco touring production, brought to New York by Joseph Papp in 1986. Presented in an outdoor park by a 150-strong cast the tale was framed by farming activities, children's games and a frantic movement of horsemen negotiating the rural terrain that presented a detailed context for the action. Both the Act 2 wedding and the final scene's lament were accompanied by extensive processions that created a sense of the concrete world ravaged in the production's final scenes – the onstage machete duel between Leonardo and the Bridegroom and the drawn out funeral lament.

Increasingly, however, directors have eschewed cultural tourism as a way of inscribing the play's supposed universality. Yuval Zamir's 1992 staging at London's Bridge Lane Theatre and Lawrence Till's 1994 production for Bolton's Octagon Theatre opted respectively for an almost medieval monasticism of black-costumed tribes, atonal chants and amplified dripping sounds and a Lancashire setting where Henry Livings' dialect-laden translation evoked a dour pre-First World War rural world that rested somewhat anachronistically with the references to vine-yards, heat and sun. Gerry Mulgrew's 1988 staging for the Edinburgh Fringe Festival dispensed with received pronunciation in favour of a Scots chorality, stark harmonies and percussive clapping to underscore the action. Jonathan Martin's 1989 production for the Asian Theatre Cooperative transported the play to a pseudo-Asian location of imposing burnished terracotta walls and proved a potent antecedent to Uzma Hameed's Asian-refracted adaptation, *A Dark River* (1998). Anthony Clark's 1987 staging for Manchester's Contact Theatre used a diagonally slit cloth as a prominent scenographic signifier, separating the antagonistic lovers across a racial divide.

Melia Bensussen's 1992 production of Langston Hughes's translation for New York's Joseph Papp Public Theatre used an African American and Latino cast in a jazz- and *cante jondo*-scored fictive plain that fused 1920s Harlem with 'stuccoed walls and cycloramic strips of sky simulating the Spanish landscape' (Gussow 1992). Rufus Norris's 2005 reading at London's Almeida Theatre cast rising Mexican star Gael García Bernal as the brooding Leonardo heading a multicultural cast working largely in English as a second-language (see cover image). If there was a decorative referent it was Mexico's day of the dead, here evoked by an ever-present Death prowling the stage like a *Cabaret*-style master of ceremonies. The mélange of accents – from Icelandic to Irish – uneven performance styles and the conversational tone of the truncated translation offered a patently surrealist colouring that fell, at times, into the trap of replacing one type of cliché with another. Played out on a red cave of a set and a moveable curtain-screen on which silhouettes danced, hovered and imploded as reflections of the lovers' fevered states, this was a parable of a love that cannot survive even the post-modern melting pot of contemporary society.[9]

The play's truncated production history in Spain has similarly been marked by performative incongruities. While Caballero provided an emblematic set of truncated rocks and all-engulfing thorns for José Tamayo's 1962 production at Madrid's Bellas Artes Theatre, Tamayo's mannered actoral work led to the impression that the cast had been transferred from a rustic *zarzuela*. José Luis Gómez's 1986 production, seen at the Edinburgh International Festival, negotiated naturalistic props and costumes and onstage musical instruments against a simple setting of far-off hills. For the forest scene the pace of the action shifted, with a shimmering female moon moving almost as an extraterrestrial being with her voice inflected as if through mechanized amplification and Three Woodcutters trapped in eerie slow motion. Souhel Ben Barka's 1976 film translated the action to the Moroccan desert, crafting an introductory section that showed the back history of the Bride and Leonardo. Its Franco/Greek/Arabic cast, dubbed into Spanish (including Irene Papas in the role of the Mother), created a dislocation between the visual and verbal spheres and negated the legitimacy of the Arabic language through a linguistic control that recognized that the mechanisms of obligatory dubbing imposed in 1941 by Franco still resonated.

Saura's celluloid ballet (1981)

The most celebrated celluloid production of the play, Carlos Saura's 1981 adaptation of Antonio Gades and Alfredo Mañas's 1974 ballet, dispenses with all dialogue, crafting a six-episode narrative that favours gesture and rhythm as forms of storytelling. Movement is controlled and contained as it is in the play, but here it is music and not dialogue that acts as a metronome, marking the performers' steps. While, on one level, the adaptation dispenses with Act 3, Scene 1, its supernatural characters are inflected through décor and costume. The white walls of the rehearsal room and the Bride's white dress can be envisioned as a reflection of the Moon (see Figure 5). Tellingly the Bride's stretching out of her arms as the men fall recalls the Beggar Woman's dramatic gesture at the end of Act 3, Scene 1 as the lovers depart. The wedding's *pasodoble* dance is enacted by pairings whose eyes move in contrary directions, testifying to the different patterns of attraction at play in the scene.

The camera contains and encloses the dancers in a 'floating fourth wall', even forming 'the missing ceiling' in an enacted love-making encounter between Leonardo and the Bride (Stone 2004: 171). The Mother contains the Bridegroom within a *fajín* belt that she binds firmly around his waist. The compatibility between the Bride and Leonardo is suggested by Saura's cutting from one to the other, creating a sense of harmony and balance. With Leonardo and his Wife, on the other hand, the camera captures the physical gulf between them. The telling prologue to the performance shows Gades with a photo of La Barraca, thus setting up an analogy between their respective aims and, in turn, Saura's in reinterpreting Lorca's play.

The Gades/Mañas/Saura adaptation presents the offstage deaths of Leonardo and the Bridegroom as the drama's climax. An enthralled camera tentatively follows the two men as they hypnotically encircle each other (see Figure 5). It traces the contours of each body as it falls to the ground. The impression is of action captured in slow-motion, only the sound of the men's breathing and the release of the knife blades punctuating the silence provides an indication as to its legitimate tempo. The Bride rises from the dead bodies of the two men, pulling bloodstains down her white dress before moving to the mirror where she faces the viewer. This *Blood Wedding* is enacted through a body that creates the sounds of the drama – the horses are evoked through the dragging of feet on the floor, the *zapateado* conveys each

Figure 5 The Bride/Moon (Cristina Hoyos) hovers over the
Bridegroom (Juan Antonio Jiménez) and Leonardo (Antonio
Gades) just prior to the moment of death: *Blood Wedding*,
dir. Carlos Saura, 1981. Photo: Suevia Films

man's possessive intentions towards the Bride. The body is both
the site of conflict and the regimentalized object over which the
feuding families do battle. 'If the desirable male body is the lost
object' of the play, 'exiled off stage' (Smith 1998: 70), the Gades/
Mañas/Saura reading returns it centre stage.

While this is not the only ballet reworking of the play, it is
arguably the most resonant. The Royal Ballet version, first
produced at Sadler's Wells in 1953 with a serialist score by Denis
ApIvor and choreography by Alfred Rodrigues, is now rarely
revived. The Dance Theatre of Harlem's *Passion of the Blood*
(2001), set to music by Jesús Villa-Rojo, Francisco Tárrega and
Isaac Albéniz, followed the Gades/Mañas/Saura conceit of staging
the confrontation between the Bridegroom and Leonardo –

here renamed Rafael. This served as the narrative climax, with the Bride pushed away from Leonardo's corpse to occupy her socially endorsed place alongside the Bridegroom. Augustus van Heerden's choreography often positioned the female dancers in positions where they appeared like dolls trapped in a music box. The whitewashed buildings set against a translucent blue sky reinforced the staging's pictorial qualities, contrasted with modern dress costumes that articulated the play's topicality.

Blood Wedding *as opera*

Titled an 'opera without music' when first staged in English in 1935 (Anon 1935b), *Blood Wedding*'s operatic outings testify to a text whose musical structuring has proved an alluring pro-position. From Juan José Castro's 1943 diatonic rendition to Wolfgang Fortner's 1957 'fine-grained weaving of song and speech, folk-tune and 12-note, brightness and dark' (Porter 1992), from Sándor Szokolay's melodic 1968 take, avoiding both serial structures and explicitly folkloric elements and using large orchestral and choral forces to striking dramatic effect, to Nicola LeFanu's 1992 version drawing on modal influences, a chromatic language and the microtonal structures of non-Western traditions (LeFanu 1994), the tale's erotically charged language has been reworked as musical theatre that dramatizes the challenges of miscegenation negotiated in the narrative through varied (and at times discordant) musical registers. The play's cacophony of textual discourses serves as an ongoing challenge to academics and directors alike who locate dramatic merit in homogeneous structures that deny difference or discord as organizing principles of theatrical creation.

Yerma (1933–4)

Lorca referred to *Yerma* as the central component of a 'dramatic trilogy of the Spanish land' (OCIII 418) that he had commenced with *Blood Wedding*. While initially viewing the play through the thematics of female sterility (OCIII 419), by the time it opened in Barcelona, he classified it as a tragedy based on honour, acknowledging its relationship to the revenge plays of Calderón in both content and form and its shift from an ostensibly realist register to overt symbolism (OCIII 612). Described by Lorca as 'plotless' (OCIII 582, 583), it centres on the predicament of its named protagonist, Yerma, whose name tellingly signifies barrenness. Yerma's longing for a child is not matched by that of her husband who is more concerned with the material gains of his farming activities. While Yerma is attracted to a childhood sweetheart, Víctor, her own sense of social propriety won't allow her to leave Juan whom she wed through a marriage arranged by her father. She seeks fertility assistance through Dolores and the Pagan Woman who offer pantheistic and herbal remedies. This serves only to alienate her further from Juan whom she eventually kills at the close of the play.

plot / lack of!

Yerma has been compared to Ibsen's *Ghosts* in its presentation of 'the barrenness of a society in thrall to dead ideas and the stranglehold of the past' (Billington 1987). Juan labours on the land but he is presented (in contrast to the more imposing Víctor) as pale, 'sadder and skinnier' by the day, as if 'growing backwards' (OCII 480; GL 1987: 160). He positions Yerma as homemaker with his sisters watching over her: 'The place for the sheep is the sheep-fold and the place for the woman is the home' (503; 182), he states in terms similar to those used by Bernarda in *The House of Bernarda Alba*. Víctor too articulates the view of the house needing a child (486; 165). While critics argue for a compatibility between Víctor and Yerma based on their shared song in Act 1, Scene 2, Víctor, perhaps more even than Juan, represents the values of the society that defines and confines Yerma. Yerma longs for the endorsement of children but the play positions her occupation of the public sphere – her footsteps like those of a man, her escaping to feed the oxon at night – as impediments to the realization of her womanhood (506; 186).

Paul Binding (1985: 173) argues that the play demonstrates 'a fixity of purpose proper to the classical drama'. Lorca viewed the choral function as more developed than that of *Blood Wedding* with the chorus displacing the protagonists across three scenes where they intervene in the manner of a Greek tragedy (OCIII 548). The sense of movement from day to night in the play's use of light across the five years that the six scenes encompass also serves to impart a classical unity on the action. Yerma's predicament is associated by María with that of the suffering Messiah (507; 187), but the Pagan Woman argues not for passive belief in a distant god but for agency and pro-action (489–90; 169–70).

Yerma's desire for a child serves unquestioningly as the text's main drive, informing and motivating its dialogue and imagery. In a society where women have little economic freedom, children, it is implied, provide social purpose, security and, importantly, pleasure. Smith's perceptive reading of the play links 'the image repertoire of Yerma's hymns to motherhood (of swollen rivers and well-tilled fields)' to 'the more lyrical pages of conservative doctors contemporary with García Lorca. . . . [E]choes of contemporary debates over feminism and reproductive rights can be glimpsed in the words of the Second Girl and the Old Woman' (Smith 1998: 24–6). The former advocates a free love that depends not on contractual matrimony (491–2; 171); the latter an equation of conception with sexual pleasure (489; 169). Even Juan, often perceived as a reactionary element within the play, refuses to see children as the intrinsic third piece of the nuclear family jigsaw but his is an opinion firmly rejected by Yerma, and his own lack of libido, alluded to through references to his weak will and reticence, positions him as an inappropriate partner for the more spirited Yerma.

Smith (1998: 26–33) turns to the writings of the celebrated medic Gregorio Marañón, a friend of both Lorca's and Xirgu's, in arguing for the text's articulation of a view of motherhood incompatible with sexual pleasure. Yerma's childlessness positions her as a suspicious 'unhealthy' being. The Washerwomen equate her with the *macho* childless women who are 'all painted faces, carnations in the hair and other women's men' (496; 176). Yerma explains the pain children bring as fresh and necessary for health (485; 164–5): the implication being that childlessness is a distinctly unhealthy state. Yerma describes herself in similar terms to *Blood Wedding*'s Bride and *The House of Bernarda Alba*'s Adela, as brittle, thirsty and in need of irrigation (504, 506; 183, 185). References abound in the play to crops and animals, to streams, water and wells. Yerma's thirst for a child is presented as a physical need: her unborn child like the salt of the sea, the fruit of the earth and the rain held within a cloud (505; 185). Hers is a libido channelled exclusively towards procreation but her failure to conceive positions her as an outsider, much like the reticent Juan. In both characters Smith (1998: 32–3) sees traits of what Marañón classifies as 'intersexuality' with the inverted male acting and virilized female each struggling to annihilate the other sex carried within.[10]

Ángel del Río (1952: 13) saw phantoms of Unamuno's stark dramaturgy in the play and the schematic use of character and setting echoes that of *The Other* (1926) with an austere narrative that similarly juxtaposes murder of 'the other' within the family with destruction of self. The play's first act, for example, is conceived around Yerma's encounters with Juan, María, Víctor, the Pagan Woman and the Second Girl, who each provide a different perspective on her predicament. Rivas Cherif's production set a precedent for stagings of the play that, whether bereft of metonymous detail or not, have been organized around typological motifs. The concept of the land as a fertile plain engulfing Yerma was evoked through the rolling hills of Fontanals's set: a landscape from which Yerma is at once removed by the imposing structure of the marital home. The pilgrimage to Moclín, by the Sierra Nevada, is often cited as a point of origin for the pagan ritual of Act 3, Scene 2 (García Lorca 1986: 217–18; Mora Guarnido 1958: 31–4), but both Lorca and Rivas Cherif's embryonic involvement with Gustavo Pittaluga's ballet *The Cuckold's Pilgrimage*, premiered in 1933 by La Argentinita, suggests *Yerma*'s visual realms may also have been shaped by this earlier work.

The play as polemic: Yerma's 1934 premiere

The controversy that greeted the opening at Madrid's Español Theatre on 29 December 1934 marked the play as a potent statement on oppression and social discontent. The political context in which it was presented provided an especially fraught receptive base that grouped reviews around predictably partisan lines. The left mobilized its support for a text that showed Spain now finally standing alongside the rest of Europe in the pioneering spirit of its dramaturgy (Bargas 1935; Díez-Canedo 1934; Fernández Almagro 1934; Hernández 1979: 299–308). The right called on readers not to see it, castigating it as a vulgar, blasphemous affront to decent people and a monotone chant of carnal motherhood that blatantly falsified peasant speech (Araujo Costa 1934; Cueva 1934; Escalpelroff 1935; Hernández 1979: 299–308). Lorca cites an Italian journalist who had seen the work claiming its notoriety matched that of Ibsen's *A Doll's House* (OCIII 616). Tellingly, for the Barcelona opening on 17 September of the following year, Xirgu inserted a programme note stressing its Catholic credentials (Vilches de Frutos and Dougherty 1992b: 103). Even before the play's opening its moral merit was debated in the press (Anon 1935).

Reviews here also identified actress and role, and by association author and play (Cortés 1935; Moragas 1935; Sánchez-Boxa 1935), with one critic going as far as to state that 'Yerma is Margarita Xirgu' (Morales 1935). Her contribution to the work, acknowledged by Lorca (OCIII 548–9), is evident in narratives of the rehearsal process that stress her willingness to address his tardiness in arriving late for rehearsals (Caballero 1984). The equation between protagonist and author that views the play as a direct statement on the gay author's infecundity (see Binding 1985: 173; Gibson 1989: 356), fails to take into consideration the links between playwright, actress and role made by the Catalan critics. These go some way towards explaining why Xirgu was not permitted to return to Francoist Spain from South America, where she remained between the outbreak of the Civil War in 1936 and her death in 1969 (see Delgado 2003: 56–66).

Fontanals produced a severe scenography conceptualized into six settings of a rural world of hard lines and rigid colours, far removed from the pastoral ideal. The painted backdrop that evoked the hermitage of Act 3, Scene 2 conveyed not a bucolic haven but a prison of sorts hemmed in by the constricting frame of the proscenium. Soufas (1996: 119) sees the concept of the fourth wall that had occupied such a crucial role in shaping the dramaturgy of the late nineteenth and early twentieth centuries as critical in reading Yerma's increasing frustration at containment within the four walls of her home. This is viewed as a metaphor for Lorca's theatrical aspirations in cultivating a theatrical culture that looked beyond the parameters of voyeuristic naturalism (Soufas 1996: 119). Fernández Cifuentes's (1986: 169–70) observations on the terrible power of words in the play appear acutely salient here: language functions, not as a form of communication but to perturb and wound, to incite and inflame. That it should provoke both the characters and the audience is not therefore surprising. This is a play that equates sterility with silence and words with fertility. Juan frequently attempts to silence Yerma but it is his silence that resounds definitely at the end of the play.

Spanish Yermas *under Franco*

While recent productions have trapped the play within Andalusian clichés, both the décor and performer accents in the first production were judged more suggestive of Castile (Haro 1934) and led Dalí to the conclusion that the play was full of 'highly obscure surrealist ideas' (Dalí 1987: 97). Luis Escobar's 1960 production featured a set by Caballero, responsible for the 1934 poster design, dominated by black and white murals with jagged shapes suggestive of jutting rocks. The prominence of red as the action moved to its tragic denouement provided a stain that marked the décor like an ever-more gaping wound. The production, opening at Italy's Spoleto Festival in June 1960, played at Madrid's Eslava Theatre for three months beginning 21 October of that year. While there had been earlier productions of Lorca's work in Franco's Spain, these had been largely positioned within the marginalized university sector or small scale theatre clubs permitted to stage only single performances for selective audiences – as with Teatro Experimental's production of *Yerma* in 1947 and Teatro de Ensayo La Carátula's staging of *The House of Bernarda Alba* in 1950 (see Higuera Estremera 1999: 584; London 1997: 35).

The endorsement of Lorca by Escobar served as an indication of thawing times. The granting of permission by the Lorca estate signalled the beginnings of a willingness to allow Lorca to be staged within the cultural programme of a regime that had negated responsibility for his death. Escobar proved a key arbitrator, trusted by the authorities,[11] 'endorsed' by Dalí who had provided the contentious sets for his staging of *Don Juan Tenorio* (1949), and respected by the profession to the degree that he could assemble a cast that included performers associated with Xirgu and the culture of exile, like Enrique Diosdado and Aurora Bautista, and secure the collaboration of Pittaluga to orchestrate music based on Lorca's templates. The presence of Lorca's sister Concha in the role of the Pagan Woman at the Spoleto Festival served as the most prominent indication that times were changing and Lorca could function as valuable currency in both promoting Spanish theatre on the international theatre circuit and in indicating how far removed the dictatorship supposedly was from the climate of 1936. The police deployed outside the Eslava, however, removed only after Franco's wife attended an early performance (Higuera Estremera 1999: 575), testifies to the precarious climate in which the play was staged and to the authorities' fear of what its performance might engender in the wider body politic.

While Escobar paved the way for further high-profile stagings of Lorca's work in Spain, it was Argentine director Víctor García's *Yerma* for Nuria Espert's company in 1971 that consolidated Lorca's position on the international stage. García and co-designer Fabià Puigserver provided an expansive metaphorical plain for the action in an olive canvas tarpaulin raised and lowered by pulleys and ropes. The tilting pentagonal 18-foot structure could be tightened and slackened as required to provide different environments (see Figure 6). The central membrane could function as an umbrella or plain, with a billowing undulating surface offering a living breathing moving landscape that proffered a visual analogy for the play's references to the female body, crops and fertility.

While García described it as both a lunar landscape and a desert (Monleón 1971: 16), the most poignant correlation was with the stretchable tissue of a womb, serving as a visual metaphor for Yerma's childlessness. Its texture affected the pace and rhythm at which the actors moved, controlling and grounding them as if 'walking on thick sand' (Adams 1977: 198). Unlike Escobar's production, where the largely naturalistic peasant costumes clashed with the abstraction of the décor, García opted for tunic-like garments in shades of charcoal gray (see Figure 6). The performers' movements often resembled those of animals in packs.

Both in the early 1970s and later in 1986 when it was revived to mark the fiftieth anniversary of Lorca's death, the production provoked widespread debate about the legitimacy of the visual and 'ownership' of the text. Its Madrid premiere at the Comedia Theatre on 29 November 1971 and its 1973 Barcelona run saw critics lament a negligent abandonment of language and the stranglehold of a design that seemed wilfully divorced from the text (Álvaro 1972: 131; Martínez Tomás 1973; Romero 1972). At a time when both divorce and abortion were still illegal in Spain, the production's frank sexual register disturbed the more conservative press corps (Marqueríe 1971; Prego 1971). It was

Figure 6 Eschewing mimeticism in favour of the conceptual: *Yerma*, presented by the Nuria Espert Company, directed by Víctor García, 1971. Photo: Montse Faixat

the battle site for those negotiating how far theatre could move away from mimetic referents and what kind of tensions might be played out in the staging of a text with significant historical associations (Laín Entralgo 1972). It is now seen as a fundamental reference point not only for stagings of Lorca but also for the evolution of a mode of stagecraft that redefines authorship in theatrical creation.

Yerma *on film*

The naturalistic acting and typological packaging of Pilar Távora's lavish 1999 film of the play, provides a veritable counterpoint to García's staging in positioning the play in a recognizable Andalusia rooted in period detail from the 1930s and a prevalence of horticultural motifs – the opening sequence captures close-ups of flowers, olive trees, poppies and fields as if to stress the fecundity of the landscape, Aitana Sánchez-Gijón's Yerma is first seen snapping beans, the odd gnarled tree blocks the route of her Little Red Riding Hood-like Yerma as she carries lunch to her husband. The high production values and emphatic flamenco score, commenting relentlessly on Yerma's predicament, ulti-mately undercut its social relevance. References are made in the play to a child of Yerma's not being born 'with a silver spoon in his mouth' (512; 192) and yet this was a sanitized world where the classically handsome Víctor always sported a pristine white shirt, even when tending sheep in the mountains, and Yerma and Juan enjoyed a light, spacious and tastefully furnished cottage. Interestingly the casting of Juan Diego as Juan perceived him as a father-like figure, aligning him with Yerma's absent father who had bartered the marriage (489; 168). The film's clean aesthetic, however – colour-coordinated scarves for the Washerwoman, roaring fires for the fertility shrine – ultimately rendered a problematic nostalgic atemporality and a linguistic text unable to gel within the sepia-tinted naturalism of the cinematic language.

Imre Gyöngyössy and Barna Kabay's Hungarian-language *Yerma* (1985) had similarly negotiated a romanticized pastoral idiom that alluded to Andalusia in the whitewashed mountain village, shawls and smatterings of Spanish. Its focus on mapping the community's rituals and routines – from the orgy-like bathing of the sheep in the opening sequence to the fertility shrine procession – and the rendition of a pruned, prosaic text provided less of a collision between language and *mise en scène*. Even Juan's death, more accident than wilful murder, served to envision the play within restrained parameters. David Stivel's Argentine TV rendition of the play, realized from Xirgu's 1963 production with María Casares in the title role, negotiated Juan's death as frustrated homicide enacted before an audience of local neighbours. Casares's Yerma was an older woman, coming late to marriage and realizing that there was little time left to conceive. The stylized rural setting referenced the Argentine pampa, Casares's native Galicia, and the mannered Fontanals' sets of the premiere production.

International Yermas

Arguably productions that have approached the play through choreographed action and conceptual décor have proved more critically successful than those that have ploughed the more localized route. Helena Kaut-Howson's 2006 staging for London's Arcola Theatre with Kathryn Hunter in the title role framed the play within a particular tradition of movement theatre embodied by Complicité – as with the Washerwomen pummelling wet clothes against the stone floor generating sprays of water and the pagan pilgrimage conceived as a masked ballet-cum-portentous dance of death. Presented on an ominously white traverse set with 'a central vulva-shaped black pool surrounded by rocks' (Marlowe 2006: 928), the Moorish-infused music suggested a sense of place that jarred with the undercurrents of 'a primitive African village complete with a pair of tribesmen on drums' (Walker 2006: 929), and the mélange of accents of the international cast.

Di Trevis's 1987 production at London's National Theatre ostensibly avoided exoticizing details in the spare stone floor with the audience positioned across four sides and washing dripping down from the Cottesloe galleries to further aid the sense of claustrophobia. The restraint of Juliet Stephenson's Hedda

Gabler-like Yerma provided an emphatic contrast to Espert's conception of the role, seen in Edinburgh the previous summer. The pagan fertility rite, decoratively staged with 'some tasteful gipsy dancing accompanied by a decorous trio on guitar and violin' complete with red roses and nods to Saura's *Blood Wedding*, demonstrated the allure of the folkloric as a means of realizing the choral moments (Billington 1987). Ultimately the production failed to resolve 'how to give claustrophobic, private suffering a more human and less mannered resonance' (Peter 1987).

The play has proved a reliable stalwart of the fringe circuit both in the UK and the USA since 1986. Whereas it may be possible to argue that this is because 'it's relatively cheap to stage. Rural Spain is easily evoked with flamenco clapping and the womenfolk wearing bunched hair-styles and shawls tied around their hips' (Hassell 1993: 1116), the transliteration of his folk tragedies to a workable Anglo register offers significant challenges to would be *auteurs*. From Blueprint Theatre Group's staging at New York's The Firehouse (1989) to Tamasha's transposition to Britain's Punjab community, *A Yearning* (1995), the enacted struggle to sustain over an evening what one critic has referred to as 'a single, compulsively reiterated state of mind' (Kerr 1966) has generated audacious experiments in theatrical language.

Heitor Villa-Lobos' opera adaptation, originally commissioned as an English-language piece for all-black singers and premiered posthumously with a Spanish libretto in 1971, 'countered the built-in static quality' of the play 'with music of fascinating complexity and changeability. . . . pages of angular power bump up against lush, semi-folklore sections, and clear-cut, almost Puccini-like vocal lines frequently soar above a harsh, thick-textured instrumental fabric' (Sherman 1971). In dance too, from J. Marks's version for the San Francisco Contemporary Dance Company in 1965 to the flamenco renditions of Carmen Cortés (1996) and Cristina Hoyos (2003), choreography has served as a means of accelerating the pace of the drama through a musical graduation of action, thus pointing to the ways that the play has been written anew through the musical, vocal and physical vocabularies of performance.[12]

Doña Rosita the Spinster (c. 1934–5)

Like *Mariana Pineda*, *Doña Rosita the Spinster* or *The Language of Flowers* is set in Granada and reflects Lorca's schizophrenic relationship to the city. Penned between *Yerma* and *The House of Bernarda Alba*, it enjoyed a lengthy gestation period. In a 1936 interview Lorca refers to its initial conception in 1924 when the poet José Moreno Villa spoke to him of the *rosa mutabile*, a breed of rose whose span life encompasses a day, opening as red, darkening to carmine further before withering to white as it dies (OCIII 631). Significantly one of Lorca's drawings from that same year (titled 'Granadine Girl in a Garden') shows a melancholy woman dressed in yellow clutching what appear to be a bunch of red roses to her chest (reproduced in Hernández 1998: 54). Gibson (1989: 141) alleges its cast list was mapped out as early as 1922.

Set at the time of his parents' youth, Lorca defined *Doña Rosita* as a 'soft-toned' play of middle-class manners, 'full of sweet ironies and touches of gentle caricature . . . permeated by the graces and delicacies of past times and different epochs' (OCIII 541). His mother was born in the same year as Rosita, allowing the latter to be seen as a symbolic figure evocative of women in provincial Spain. Rosita, identified with the *rosa mutabile* cultivated by her horticultural uncle, is presented in similar terms as a object to be admired in the prime of her life and then left to wither in the confines of the house. Her dresses across the play's three acts echo the colours of the *rosa mutabile*. Engaged to her cousin at the play's opening, his departure for Argentina leaves her at home with her uncle, aunt and the family's housekeeper awaiting infrequent letters and his endlessly deferred return. After fifteen years he offers her marriage by proxy, which she willingly accepts. In the play's final act we learn that he has already been married for eight years. Now penniless, Rosita is forced to depart her dead uncle's house with her aged aunt for a new home and perpetual spinsterhood.

Lorca repeatedly referred to the play as a denunciation of the social conventions and small-minded bigotry that imprisons women within limited behavioural codes (OCIII 552, 612, 619) and the play positions spinsterhood as an unfortunate punishment rather than a determined course of action or positive choice. The play's three acts are set in 1885, 1900 and 1911, an immediate past 'too recent to be historic and too distant to be present' (García Lorca 1986: 223). While Lorca's theatre habitually eschews such temporal specificity, the distinct time spans have encouraged critics to draw very precise analogies with the position of family members and acquaintances in Granada.[13] As such the play has been read as a statement on the milieu that shaped Lorca's formative years and an elegy for a city once the jewel of Islamic civilization and now a turgid provincial locale (Anderson 1984: 83; García Lorca 1986: 221–31; Lima 1963: 245).

The plot echoes that of Carlos Arniches's *Miss Trevélez* (1916) which similarly presents a single woman holding out for the promise of marriage in a society that sees spinsters as a source of embarrassment and a butt of communal jokes. Both works interplay both tragic and comic elements and in this respect parallels have also been drawn with Chekhov's *Three Sisters* (1901) and *A Cherry Orchard* (1904). Lorca may have seen Eva Le Gallienne's productions of *The Cherry Orchard* and/or *The Seagull* while he was in New York or the Moscow Art Theatre's staging of *The Cherry Orchard* that visited Madrid in March 1932 (Anderson 1993; Stainton 1999: 396). The play's parodic subtitle 'A Poem of Granada in 1900, Divided into Various Gardens with Scenes of Song and Dance' may allude to a sanitized theatre culture keen to avoid offending audience sensibilities. Grau Sala's poster for the play's 1935 premiere can be seen as a complement for the 'gentle parody of the titles: the lettering is in a flowery cursive hand, and Rosita is surrounded by a swirl of white doves, stars and graceful flowers and vines. It resembles an antique greeting card' (Anderson 1984: 74). Jorge Lavelli, who staged the play in 1980, views Rosita, her aunt and housekeeper as theatrical types lifted from the more generic works of contemporaries like Arniches and Echegaray (Álvarez 1980). There are also echoes of *Romeo and Juliet*'s pragmatic, hearty Nurse in the Housekeeper and the reclusive uncle functions within a long-standing dramatic tradition of ineffectual men engaged in domestic activities that serve to emaciate and disempower them within the wider structures of society. Ultimately the uncle's inaction leads to his widow and niece's destitution.[14]

Fernández Cifuentes (1986: 233–4) reads the play as a study of performative words that promise but never deliver. Lorca's comments on 'provincial Spanish *cursilería*' (pretentiousness), on the 'spectacle' of the spinster (OCIII 552, 620), at once hidden away and displayed object of ridicule, indicate a self-conscious register of performed activity. Rosita is first seen in Act 1 calling for her hat (OCII 531; GL 1987: 100), an indispensable prop in making her public appearance outside the home. The three Spinsters who visit Rosita in Act 2 appear in 'huge hats with tasteless feathers, ridiculous dresses, gloves to the elbow with bracelets over them, and fans dangling from large chains' (552; 124). They represent a past tense of formalized behaviour, all three reiterating each other's lines as if reciting from a well-worn melodrama. The two Ayola girls who follow them onstage are the less reverent future but one equally concerned with fabrication, adornment and storytelling. The Aunt refers to the Housekeeper's 'fine-sounding, sugar-coated words' (548; 119) but it is the Nephew's false promises and empty declarations that ultimately devastate Rosita.

This is a play that, as the consideration of the language of flowers in Act 2 demonstrates, signals a grasp of communication that only allows discussion through abstraction rather than direct expression. The play is not just the tragedy of the Spanish spinster but also its camouflage and disguise (Fernández Cifuentes 1986: 218). The Mother of the three Spinsters laments the material sacrifices involved in assuring that painted parasols, trimmings and hats are on hand to decorously adorn her daughters' outfits (554; 125–6). Appearances must be maintained whatever the physical or emotional cost.

The deployment of the letter in Act 2, a device also deployed by Lorca in *Mariana Pineda* (see p. 55), further locates the work within the realms of the theatrical. The proposed marriage by proxy again presents an incongruity between the performed event – with an 'actor' standing in for the groom – and its aftermath. Who, as the Housekeeper posits, can stand in for the groom on the wedding night? (562; 135). Similarly in Act 3, Rosita's long curls and pale pink dress camouflage the aged flesh beneath the disguise. Her Act 3 declaration that 'Each year that passed was like an intimate piece of clothing torn from my body' (574; 148) presents costume as indispensable to the construction of identity, concurrent with Lorca's reflections that 'Half of the show depends on rhythm, colour, scenography' (OCIII 563).

Rosita wants to leave the house when 'the street is dark' to avoid being seen (573; 147). A lifetime, however, spent 'living outside myself' in the public eye (574; 148) amidst multiple layers of fabrication ensure that only reflections remain. Rosita is as much a cultivated product as the *rosa mutabile* grown by her uncle within the confines of his greenhouse. Her trajectory follows that of the rose in a plot as predictable as that of Chekhov's *The Cherry Orchard*. In *Doña Rosita* the audience's own act of looking is articulated and made conscious. The historical attention paid to costume and attire in the play is significant here. Francisco García Lorca documents the meticulous research undertaken by his brother when crafting the play with books, magazines and almanacs from the turn-of-the-century consulted as a means of capturing the mood of the era (García Lorca 1986: 223).

Rivas Cherif's Doña Rosita *(1935)*

Rivas Cherif directed the production presented by Xirgu's company at Barcelona's Principal Palace Theatre on 12 December 1935. The three constricted locations within the house engendered by Fontanals provided some sense of the diminutive dimensions of the *carmen* in Granada's Albaycín where the action is supposedly set. The shadow of the garden hovered over the first act casting a particular light over the room. The second act saw a plethora of props and objects – ornate curtains, baroque chairs, portraits, side tables – all contained within the receiving-room. The final act was cold, arid and bereft of colour (Cruz Salido 1935). The fashions of each epoch were realized through sharply delineated costumes that evolved into Rosita's final spectral appearance as she leaves the house. Xirgu used vocal depth and shifts in body posture to accent the passing of time, contrasting with the more mannered gestures of the performers playing the trio of Spinsters and the Ayolas (Espina 1935; Haro 1935; Sánchez-Boxa 1935). Costume, décor and performance mannerisms combined in the view of one critic to offer the 'frightful grotesquerie' of this Granadine bourgeioisie (T.B. 1935). Offering a fine line between elegy and satire, this was a production that utilized the full horizontal potential of the stage (Morales 1935).

The presence of a significant proportion of Madrid critics signalled both the pulling power of Xirgu and the growing importance of Lorca as a playwright (rather than poet) (Vilches de Frutos and Dougherty 1992b: 105–11). The production effectively marked his consecration as a dramatist (Artis 1935; Espina 1935; Morales 1935) with only one dissenting voice lamenting its lack of theatricality and overly picturesque staging (Agustí 1935).

The play was linked to *Mariana Pineda* in its poetic register. Ballads (or *allegros* as one critic referred to them) comment on Rosita's predicament with Rosita and the Nephew's Act 1 love duet crafted in verse. Here, however, the fusion between poetry and prose – through which the majority of the dialogue is rendered – was judged to provide a more effective idiom for the dramatic action (Marín Alcalde 1935; Olmedilla 1935). The work was discussed in ways that stressed its international credentials, as a mapping of the way forward for Spanish theatre, with a final act as resonant as that of *The Cherry Orchard* in its expression of that which remains unsaid (Guansé 1935; Haro 1935; Morales 1935).

Doña Rosita: *late twentieth-century revivals*

The play was not seen in Madrid until 1980 when Franco-Argentine director Jorge Lavelli directed Espert in the title role. Max Bignens provided a semicircular set that functioned as much to evoke a period museum as a bourgeois parlour. This is a receiving-room backing onto a botanical garden with the finest gauze separating the blooming flowers from the stolid heavy wooden wardrobes that hold Rosita's trousseau. A series of doors sees characters come and go with choreographed haste in Acts 1 and 2, almost as if dancing a waltz. By Act 3 the parlour, a symbol of bourgeois respectability and the favoured location of naturalist drama, withers into a wasteland where the doors that once led out into the garden are now bereft of plant life.

Espert's Rosita dances across the stage with juvenile energy in Act 1, waving her parasol and wrapping her shawl flamboyantly around herself. As her fiancé mentions his departure she pushes him away with her hand as if in fear of the consequences of his touch. As one critic remarked on the production's outing to the Edinburgh International Festival in 1983, Espert is 'unafraid of the grand gesture: when her lover abandons her she crumbles to the ground and rolls helplessly down stage as if the vitality has been drained out of her' (Billington 1983). In Act 2 she sweeps across the stage like a stately dame, secure in what the future holds as she proudly shows off her trousseau to visitors. By Act 3 she is jittery and clingy, a hunched, pacing figure, choking on her words and holding on to her aunt and housekeeper with palpable insecurity.

This was a performance that made 'every external action seem a spontaneous action of an inner state' (Brennan 1983). Lavelli rendered time, rather than Andalusia, the play's 'silent character' (García Lorca 1986: 229), progressively stressing Rosita's displacement from the world at large. The genteel poverty of the Spinsters and the new money of the photographer's daughters was brought face to face in Act 2 with the trousered Ayolas weaving in and out of the disorientated Spinsters in a motion suggestive of two centuries meeting under Rosita's disorientated eye.

Criticisms of the production's costume anachronisms and a set design more Castilian dourness than Andalusian miniature (Díez Crespo 1980; García Osuna 1980) may have also been rooted in disquiet at a 'foreign' director confounding critical expectations in his staging of a play not seen in Spain since 1935. The battle for 'ownership' of Lorca, brutally in evidence in the celebrations marking the fiftieth anniversary of his death, had effectively begun.

In 2004 Miguel Narros, responsible for the first Spanish staging of *When Five Years Pass*, cast regular Almodóvar collaborator Verónica Forqué in a Beckettian treatment of the play that saw a girlish, broad-grinned Rosita waiting in vain for her Godot in an environment that suggested something of the desolate wasteland of Beckett's play with a lone pot plant holding the symbolic *rosa mutabile*. Costumes alluded both to Lorca's specified time periods and, increasingly as the play progressed, to a more contemporary era – as with Rosita's final appearance in a beige crocheted dress. Andrea D'Odorico's high-walled set peppered with a minimum of functional furniture provided tempting images of the greenery in the landscape beyond the house, always ever so slightly out of Rosita's reach.

Stagings of *Doña Rosita* have often tended to opt for the scenic dominance of floral imagery to reinforce the symbolist credentials of the work. John Olon's production for the Chelsea Theater Center New York (1980) projected shadows of leaves and illustrations from antique botanical books on white fabric screens. Ernest Johns' 2004 reading for the Jean Cocteau Repertory in the same city proffered a courtyard setting filled with branches of red roses that evaporated by the play's close. Rene Buch's staging for New York's Repertorio Español – a stalwart of the dramatist's work in the city – involved a more abstract set mutating like the rose from white to sepia and then to black. *Doña Rosita* may have been judged 'to all appearances, the most "realistic" of all Lorca's plays' (Edwards 1980: 228), but few directors have selected a 'realist' approach to décor. Jennifer Shook's staging for Chicago's Caffeine Theatre (2005) featured plant pots on every table surface and was similarly staged on a set that was only suggestively historically placed with white curtains framing French doors bordered by blacks to give the appearance of a cut-out picture.

In her 1997 Almeida Theatre revival of an earlier 1989 production for Bristol's Old Vic, Phyllida Lloyd presented the action almost like an operatic score with Gary Yershon's music underpinning the lush language. Anthony Ward's set took the play's subdivision into 'various gardens' as a starting point, positioning the first two acts in a conservatory filled with wrought-iron furniture and heavy with pots and plants (see Figure 7), and the final act in a bare room with a vast skylight. Posed tableau suggested posed, poised social rituals and introduced the characters in ways that stressed their affinity with the plants that surround them. The three Spinsters were conceived like a chorus of crowing birds, watched over by Kathryn Hunter as their flapping crone-like mother slyly pocketing delicacies into her handbag whenever the opportunity arose (see Figure 7).[15] The giggling Ayolas were conceived like a duo of bobbing puppets. Lloyd's staging marked the London premiere of the work. Praised during Lorca's lifetime as the pinnacle of his dramaturgy, *Doña Rosita* now unfortunately languishes as 'a kind of dry run for *The House of Bernarda Alba*' (Hanks 1997: 543).

The House of Bernarda Alba (1936)

The House of Bernarda Alba, Lorca's final play, was completed on 19 June 1936 against a backdrop of increasing political unrest in Madrid and read to friends five days later (Morla Lynch 1957: 483–8). Positioned posthumously as the third part of the rural

Figure 7 *Doña Rosita* as an operatic lament for lost youth: The Mother of the Spinsters (Kathryn Hunter) stage left and the Aunt (Eleanor Bron) stage right frame Rosita (Phoebe Nicholls). *Doña Rosita*, directed by Phyllida Lloyd at the Almeida Theatre, London, 1997. Photo: Ivan Kyncl

trilogy initiated with *Blood Wedding* and *Yerma*,[16] it has sub-sequently proved Lorca's most frequently staged play. This may partly be because of its ostensibly realist idiom that poses few of the interpretative challenges of the lyricism of *Doña Rosita* or *Blood Wedding*. Its raunchy plot juggles narrative suspense and rapid-fire dialogue rather than the more contemplative *arias* of *Yerma*. With most of the dramatic canon crafted for male protagonists, Lorca offers an all-female cast. Here women exist not merely as chattels of exchange or subsidiary figures. As such the play has proved an attractive proposition for school, university and conservatoire stagings.

It is now thought that the play's overt reference to his neighbours in Asquerosa may have played a part in Lorca's assassination (see Ruiz Barrachina's 2006 film, *Lorca: The Sea Stops Still*). Bernarda Alba appears to have been based on Lorca's distant cousin Frasquita Alba Sierra, a mother of seven children, who lived a few doors away from the family. Here, according to Lorca, she ruled tyrannically over her unmarried shadow-like daughters 'always silent and dressed in black' (Morla Lynch 1957: 489). Whether this Frasquita Alba was a figure conjured from Lorca's imagination remains unknown. His mother and brother pleaded during the month leading up to his assassination to modify the protagonist's name but Lorca refused to do so, supposedly passing a copy of the play to his cousin Alejandro not long before his arrest. Whether the irk of the Albas played a role in events leading to his arrest may remain for the moment conjecture but it suggests reasons as to why the play was looked upon with suspicion during the Franco era and not produced until 1945.

The play takes place in three locations in the house of Bernarda Alba. As it opens Bernarda's second husband is being buried and servants are preparing the house to receive the funeral guests. Once they have departed Bernarda announces to her five daughters that they are to remain locked in mourning within the walls of the house for eight years. Only Bernarda's eldest daughter, Angustias, from the former's first marriage, has a prospect of escape for she is to be married to Pepe el Romano, a local lad some years her junior, who also seems to have attracted the eye of her half-sisters. As the sisters prepare Angustias's trousseau under the supervision of the housekeeper Poncia, we learn that the former is the greatest beneficiary of her stepfather's will. Resentment between Angustias, Adela and Martirio grows as it becomes clear that Adela is having an affair with Pepe el Romano under her half-sister's nose. Martirio follows Adela as she meets with Pepe and informs the house of her sister's actions. Bernarda takes a shotgun to Pepe but misses. Martirio maliciously tells Adela that Pepe has been killed and Adela hangs herself in horror.

The House of Bernarda Alba is built on the premise of negation. Bernarda's opening and closing lines are 'Silence' (OCII 587/634; GL 2007: 131/180) and she imposes on her daughters a regime that will not allow amorous contact, conversation, agency, or occupation of the public sphere (Newberry 1976). The play is subtitled 'A Drama of Women in the Villages of Spain' and the home functions, much like the House of Atrius, as a social microcosm representative of a wider body politic. This is the story of a dynasty, only here Clytemnestra has been reconceived as a 60-year-old matriarch for whom social control is inextricably bound up with religious display. Lorca's oft-quoted remark on finishing the play that 'Not a drop of poetry! Reality! Realism!' (Río 1952: 141–2) and his statement following the cast list that 'these three acts are intended as a photographic document' (583; 127) positioned the play as a statement on tyranny at a time when the country was facing the distinct possibility of a military coup and a return to dictatorship.

Tyranny is a prominent motif in the play and the authoritarian Bernarda, aligned to the patriarchal order, has been conceived by directors as a male figure – as with Ismael Merlo's characterization for Ángel Facio's 1976 Madrid production. The house is repeatedly conjured by Bernarda, its different elements summoned as a means of reinforcing its boundaries. The outside world is perceived through shutters and upstairs windows or as sounds in the distance. Tolling bells (584, 586, 608; 128, 130, 153), the cacophony of dogs and baying villagers chasing La Librada's daughter (617–19; 163–5), the song of the reapers as they head out to the fields (609–10; 154–5), plates and cutlery

(620; 165), the stallion kicking in the stable (621; 166), Pepe's coded whistle to Adela (631; 178), the sound of a gunshot (633; 179), the thud that marks Adela's suicide (633; 179) constantly cut into the silence of the play. As with *Yerma* and *Blood Wedding* sound provides an auditory texture, but here it is largely an offstage presence that suggests the world beyond the house.

Visually too the play's palette of black and white may serve to evoke the colour scheme of a black and white photograph. White is the colour of Bernarda's surname: Alba translates as dawn or brightness. The white walls of Bernarda's house make the sisters' dark profiles stand out: all are like black stains on a landscape primed for visibility. Bernarda demands a whitewashing of all that is undesirable; her house an immaculate image of antiseptic sterility. The play opens with Poncia and the Servant cleaning the house. Bernarda orders the patio to be whitewashed again after the funeral to erase all traces of the neighbours' presence (594; 138). White is an organizing motif, associated both with the rebellious stallion of Act 3 and Adela's nightdress. White is also the colour of the foam of the sea that Bernarda's mother, María Josefa, yearns for (600–1, 629; 145–6, 175); it represents the sisters' present and their future as evident in the white hair of their grandmother.[17] The play may have been positioned as social realism (Anderson 1984: 119–21; Morris 1990: 24–7), but its mechanics are as ostentatious as those of Williams' *A Streetcar Named Desire* (1947).

Binding (1985: 187) sees a debt to Strindberg's *Miss Julie* and Wedekind's *Spring Awakening* in the painterly manner in which the play saturates 'all colours and incidents in one colour, one mood'; 'the imprisonment, immobility or tragic fixity associated with a character's situation is often expressed visually in terms of physical or visual restrictiveness' (Wright 2000: 51). Adela's rebellion is plotted in visual terms first through the green dress and then through placing herself at the window to attract her sisters' attention. Like her sisters she derives pleasure not so much from agency but from being the subject of the gaze (Wright 2000: 51). She is willing to go from imprisonment in her mother's house to imprisonment in her lover's and is, as I will go on to indicate, prominently implicated in the culture of surveillance that exists in the home.

Adela and her sisters exist in a society that views women's place as within the home (591; 135). Women are perceived as the lesser sex. 'To be born a woman is the greatest punishment', moans Amelia as Poncia regales the sisters with tales of fields animated by lusty visiting harvesters (609; 154). Women who transgress sexually, like La Librada's daughter and Paca la Roseta, or disobey the law of the father, like Prudencia's daughter, are seen as wayward outsiders, spurned by respectable society.

Martirio is aware of how men cover up for each other and marry for blatant financial gain (595; 140). Magdalena longs for the open air of the public sphere (591; 135). The house is rarely described as a home, rather a convent or fortress where the daughters are sealed as if in a coffin. Bernarda metes out a culture of physical and mental abuse, advocating chains for her daughters (614; 159). While scathing of the society around her, she also endorses and upholds it. As Smith (1989: 117–25) has argued in his persuasive analysis of the play, all the characters are implicated in maintaining the culture of surveillance that operates in the house. Just as the neighbours scrupulously observe Bernarda, so the sisters furtively watch over each other. They collaborate in locking away the supposed 'madwoman in the attic', María Josefa, and are all involved in preventing Adela's elopement with Pepe el Romano.[18]

Family functions as a disciplinary institution in the play. According to Michel Foucault (1985: 195–228) incitement to regulation rather than the exertion of force is the pivot of a disciplinary society. As in Genet's *The Balcony* (1956) continuous observation regulates the individual. Bernarda 'confronts her daughters with images of their own poverty and undesirability. . . . The sisters do not beat or confined themselves; but they can and do make themselves silent' and 'remind themselves of their physical and financial inadequacies' (Smith 1989: 121). All derive some perverse sense of comfort in the known routine of tyranny. They may talk about being free and yet continuously prevent each other from escaping the house. In Act 1 Angustias is reported peeping through the cracks in the back door to watch the men leaving the house (592; 136). Adela informs Bernarda of Angustias's activity as later Martirio announces Adela's rendezvous with Pepe (632; 178). If any sister threatens to transgress, the surveillance intensifies. All pretend to be pleased that Angustias is to marry Pepe, but all desire him. Only Magdalena is willing to confront Martirio about this but Martirio denies it just as she initially tries to shrug off the theft of Pepe's photo from Angustias's room as a joke (597, 613; 141–2, 159). Magdalena, the least hypocritical of the sisters, is aware that we see only what we want to see. 'Even our eyes aren't our own' she states to her sisters in Act 2 indicating the ways in which vision betrays and appearances deceive (609; 154). Poncia tells Bernarda to open her eyes to Martirio's motives for stealing the photo (614–15; 160–1) but Bernarda's vigilance prioritizes a 'respectable' appearance that no-one can penetrate (623; 169). Poncia describes her head and hands as 'full of eyes' (606; 151) as she polices Adela's behaviour. The sisters follow Pepe's moves with almost military precision.

Smith (1989: 119–25) has delineated the ways in which the house's structure follows the model of other disciplinary institutions like the asylum and the prison where 'surveillance is based on a system of permanent registration' (Foucault 1985: 196). It holds the supposedly insane María Josefa within its walls and its rooms are a labyrinthine structure of interconnecting 'theatres' or 'cells' where, following Foucault's prototype, 'the subject is caught in the "trap of visibility"' (Smith 1989: 122). The house induces in the daughter-inmates 'a state of conscious and permanent visibility that assures the automatic functioning of power' (Foucault 1985: 201). As with Genet's *Death Watch* (1949) and *Un Chant d'amour* (1950) the play demonstrates how we define ourselves through the act of looking, marking out our sameness and our difference. Looking is always coded and signified in relation to power. Adela's body performs for the invisible 'other' of Pepe el Romano, a figure constructed through the language of the sisters but never seen. He is as much a product of the imagination as the nymphs on the pictures that hang on the walls in Act 1 (584; 128).

The House of Bernarda Alba articulates its ideas through an interplay of theatrical surfaces that interrogate the relationship of the real to the imagined. The sisters' names indicate emotional states – Martirio/martyrdom; Angustias/anguish – pointing to roles that they are expected to play. Alliteration proliferates – note the sonic association of Adela and the transgressive Adelaida; the dominance of the *a* sound across the title and in the sisters' names. Adela and her mother may be positioned as antagonists in the play but both are referenced by Poncia through animal imagery; both argue for female subjugation to the male. Adela smashes Bernarda's stick in two because she will recognize no other authority than Pepe (632; 178). She welcomes the punishment of the crown of thorns that accompanies the fallen woman because for her, as with so many of Lorca's female protagonists, love is bound up with masochism and punishment (see Smith 1989: 122–5). Notions of plenitude and fulfilment are inextricably linked to endorsement from the desired male.

The form of the play proffers a distinct break from the 'impossible' theatre that Lorca was advocating at the time. The photographic document that Lorca specifies as the preferred aesthetic for the play serves as a model precisely because, like Bernarda, it imposes 'linguistic censorship' (Hart 1989: 64). *The House of Bernarda Alba* constructs a world where language is evasive and little is conveyed directly, characters talk of what they've seen but give few details. Insinuation prevails and much remains unsaid.

This is part of the pleasure of interpreting the play, it allows us to 'read' between the gaps and construct truths, partial or otherwise, from what is unspoken. Speculation ensues as to why Bernarda's second husband leaves more in his will to his already wealthy stepdaughter rather than his impoverished daughters. We know that Antonio María Benavides was involved with the family servant (587; 131). Was Angustias involved in a sexual relationship with him? She defiantly insists that he was not her father when her mother accuses her of defaming his memory by powdering her face on the day of his funeral (599; 144). Much information is displaced in the play as metaphor; as with the stallion's association with Pepe and the narrated stories about Adelaida, La Librada's daughter and Paca la Roseta that all comment in some way or other on the sisters' predicament.

The House of Bernarda Alba *in production:*
from Xirgu (1945) to Plaza (1984)

Productions often read the play through metaphorical terms, setting it within the confines of a prison, convent, colonialist villa, Italian country home or Andalusian whitewashed *finca*. Ontañón, designer of the 1945 premiere directed by Xirgu at Buenos Aires's Avenida Theatre, provided three different locations for the action, following the guidelines laid out in the stage directions. The first was a white reception room featuring curtains adorned with red tassels; the second an arched passageway with heavy wooden doors running off it and the final an interior moonlit patio. Each space appeared to lead the action further into the inner recesses of a house rigidly controlled by Xirgu's inflexible Bernarda. This was a highly politicized inflection with Bernarda viewed as both a vocal and gestural embodiment of authoritarianism (Monleón 1986: 375–6). The interplay between silence and malicious accusations that Xirgu's staging delineated revealed a microcosm of the larger conflicts played out on Spanish's political stages at the time Lorca wrote the piece. Opening on 8 March as the Second World War was laying to rest the spectres of fascism elsewhere in Europe, Bernarda's opening and closing words articulated the fate of a Spanish populace still suffering fascist rule and a dramatist whose works were silenced within its cultural landscape.

   The first commercial production seen in Spain, directed by film director Juan Antonio Bardem, opened at Madrid's Goya Theatre on 10 January 1964. Abstract painter Antonio Saura, brother of the filmmaker Carlos Saura, supplied a glistening, antiseptic décor devoid of folkloric hangings or adornments. While there were variations in three locations, the final act remained within the confines of a room rather than the outdoor *corral*, reinforcing the sense of unchanging insularity. The dark grey floor, the slightly oppressive perspectives of the high doors, the single ornament prevailing in each act afforded a bleak reflective interior (Cornago Bernal 2001: 312). There were no headscarves here, no mantillas; the high-necked dresses had almost a nineteenth-century feel. In contrast to José Tamayo's affective *Blood Wedding* seen at Madrid's Bellas Artes Theatre in 1962 offering a plethora of localized references, Bardem envisaged a Lorca distant from the Andalusian locale that perturbed Madrid's more conservative press elements (Álvaro 1965: 3–8).

José Carlos Plaza's 1984 staging followed the lead established by Bardem's reading. Here again the sisters were individualized with Amelia presented as the most naive, Magdalena as mournfully resigned, and Angustias as withered by age. Berta Riaza's wizened Bernarda was steelier than Bardem's less abrasive Cándida Losada. Plaza presented a Foucauldian reading that saw the sisters not as passive victims but as compliant perpetrators of the surveillance culture in a space that facilitated vigilance (Plaza 1984: 197–8). The play was placed firmly in the 1930s, alongside the rise of fascism in Spain, on a single large parlour set with labyrinthine corridors at the back of the stage leading off into the different rooms of the house.

Although the servant spoke with an Andalusian accent and the popular flamenco of *sevillanas* peppered the action, this was more ostensibly Castile than Andalusia, following the lead of a range of critics from Guardia (Honig 1945: 176) to Sánchez (1950: 67–8) who have located more of the dour ochre of Machado's Castile in the play than the ostentatious Andalusia of *Gypsy Ballads*. The focus was on presenting a comfortable physical environment with period detail evident in costume, hair and the dark weighty wood design of the household furniture. This was not a poverty-striken milieu but a bourgeois home where the sisters' material comforts suffocated any ambitions to flee (Plaza 1984: 198). The off-black costumes suggested a family caught unawares by the patriarch's death, forced to dye their wardrobe to meet societal mourning conventions (Moreno 1984: 241).

The House of Bernarda Alba *on the London stage*

Nuria Espert's 1986 English-language production occupied similar naturalistic terrain, similarly opting for a single scenic environment for the action – a decision followed by Calixto Bieito, Katie Mitchell and Polly Teale in their subsequent stagings of the play. Ezio Frigerio's courtyard fortress featured weather-worn

white walls well past their best and miniature barred windows
that could offer only a partial view of the outside world. Part-
nunnery, part-prison, part-asylum the daughters, clad in Franca
Squarciapino's 1930s redolent costumes enacted their daily rituals
with weary resignation. Transferring from the Lyric Hammer-
smith to London's West End, this was a production devoid of
Andalusian exoticisms, where self-effacing direction avoiding
'grinding stylistic gear-changes' (Hoyle 1987) and an understated
translation was judged by dramatist Arnold Wesker (1986: 3) to
have located a successful stage register for Lorca's work in Britain.
The effacement of the Spanish context was, nevertheless, considered problematic by certain critics who thought the 'nice'
accents wedged the play too firmly within 'an English theatrical
drawing-room' (Preston 1986; Shorter 1987). The received
pronunciation of the cast was also felt to erase the class differences
between Joan Plowright's Poncia and Glenda Jackson's Bernarda
(Edwards 2000: 722–3).

Other London productions have opted for overtly political
readings. Polly Teale's staging for Shared Experience in 1999
favoured an imposing portal of bolted prison-like doors with
grilles and slats that filtered in light from the outside world. Here
characters read newspapers announcing 'Franco Advances' and
'Civil War Possible' and Franco's voice intruded into the house
through a crackly wireless. The merged time frames may have
sought to provide a decisive political context for the action but
were ultimately unable to inscribe a historical moment that was
realized neither in the colloquial English translation nor in the
generalized costume aesthetic. Katie Mitchell opted for a more
openly religious setting for her 1992 reading at London's Gate
Theatre. Here the family's salute to *il duce* as the mob passed by
in search of La Librada's daughter as well as the visual recreation
of Leonardo da Vinci's 'The Last Supper' at the opening of Act 3
with Adela positioned poised for sacrifice in a crown of thorns
suggested fascist Italy.

The earliest English-language production in the UK, directed
by Robin Phillips at London's Greenwich Theatre in 1973, opted
for a cool, clinical 'convent furnished by Habitat' that failed to
create any sense of claustrophobia (Wardle 1973). Mia Farrow's

Adela was judged 'too ethereal and Bohemian' – more late 1960s hippy than angry adolescent – and June Jago's Bernarda was viewed as 'a suburban English matron, or a Trust House Lady who has been interrupted at tea by tourists who have mistakenly entered the private quarters' (Brustein 1973).

The criticisms of a 'home counties' idiom, also raised in respect to Espert's 1986 staging, were perhaps most noticeable in Howard Davies's 2005 National Theatre production, which was conceived almost as a drawing-room farce set in an English public school with Penelope Wilton as a 'headmistress rebuking a dorm of overboisterous gels' (Clapp 2005: 339–40). The overhead planes and Republican songs in the distance may have alluded to 1930s Spain but David Hare's translation was resolutely contemporary. Vicki Mortimer's set evoked the decayed glamour of a spacious domed Moorish courtyard villa. The languid world of the sisters conveyed a stunted environment of infantilized sniping schoolgirls who had failed to grow up, smoking and dancing to the wireless when their mother was out of the room. Black was simply for public show, around the house all were more informally clad. This was an ex-pat colonialist world of siblings who feared the unknown of the outside world much more than their controlling mother.

American relocations

In the USA too the tendency has been to play Bernarda as an unflinching autocrat. In 1951 Greek actress Katina Paxinou offered a high-octave 'bitter and arid' virago, presiding over her household with 'monstrous authority' (Atkinson 1951). Fifty-one years later at New York's INTAR, Ofelia González continued the long line of Latino performers (including Chita Rivera, Adria Santana and Virginia Rambal) who had conceived the character as a wilful metatheatrical *directrice* issuing orders to a resentful cast.

Arguably, the most radical English-language reading of the play was provided by Emily Mann for the McCarter Theater, Princeton, NJ, in 1997. Thomas Lynch's set of patchy grey granite walls avoided black and white absolutes. There was no aim to provide physical referents for Spain, but a rural location that suggested small-town America. Lucille Patton's María Josefa was a glamorous wiry, grey-haired grandmother, adorned Gloria Swanson-like, in layers of jewelry. Isa Thomas's Poncia was a first generation Irish immigrant, an older shadow to Helen Carey's still attractive Bernarda. The production did not shy from cruelty. The Servant wept in anguish as she recalled Antonio María Benavides's inappropriate advances. Bernarda's first entrance, snapping her lines like rapid bullet-shots, silenced the kneeling Servant by stepping unceremoniously on her hand. Importantly, however, there was also compassion: Bernarda weeping over her senile mother and resting her hand consolingly on Angustias as the latter shared concerns about her indifferent fiancé. This was a mother despairing of her eldest daughter's ungainly ways and her youngest daughter's surly petulance. The shadows on the wall in Act 3 conveyed the sense of prying eyes and constant vigilance. The play's final sequence was a cacophony of raised voices and chaotic pockets of activity. Bernarda's final cries of anguish as she was held from crumpling to the floor by Poncia pointed to agony in the realization that Pepe's 'disappearance' had generated Adela's suicide.

From Calixto Bieito's abstractions to danztheater

If Mann demonstrated to English-speaking directors how to conceive the play within realist paradigms that recognized the play's lyrical outbursts, in 1998 Catalan director Calixto Bieito pointed the Spanish-speaking world to more abstract ways in which the physical urgency of the play might be realized. With scenographer Alfons Flores, Bieito conceived an austere indeterminate space dominated by a white vertical panel against which the black clad performers moved like eerie shadows. In the final act the white wall collapsed to leave a bare space enveloped in black. The sense of enclosure in an anonymized locale with few historical pointers suggested parallels with Sartre's *Huis Clos*, delineated by Fernández Cifuentes (1986: 204) in his treatment of the play. Chairs were lowered from the flies for the funeral (see Figure 8); the sisters sat formally in rows undertaking needlework;

Figure 8 Abandoning the iconography of Andalusia for abstraction: *The House of Bernarda Alba*, directed by Calixto Bieito at Madrid's CDN, 1998. Photo: Chicho/CDT

a naked trapeze artist encased in a white shadowy moon hovered above the action commenting physically on the sexual angst contained within. This appeared both as a homage to Buñuel's *Viridiana* (1961) and as a means of stressing conceptual links with the dramaturgy of *Blood Wedding* and *The Public*.

The process of enculturation visibly enacted on and through the body in Bieito's reading intimates why the play has been so frequently reconceived within dance paradigms. Physical expression has allowed for the delineation of both political and cultural values, shifting the focus from the various intrigues in the house to Adela and Pepe's illicit liaison and renaming it appropriately in the process.

The absent object of desire in the play, Pepe el Romano, is often conjured as a physical entity and Adela's sacrificed body remains on display as the final image of the climatic finale. Kenneth MacMillan's *Las hermanas* (1963), set within a church with a pew of rocking chairs, dispensed with both Poncia and María Josefa in placing the relationship with Pepe and Adela centre stage. Eleo Pomare's *Las desenamoradas* (1967) had the sisters as an almost military chorus that Adela repeatedly broke away from. Bernarda's stick, an embodiment of her authority, was conceived as a martial arts pole negotiated by Pepe and Adela in their encounters. Alvin Alley's *Feast of Ashes* (1976) fused elements of *Blood Wedding* and Bizet's *Carmen* into a retelling of the story that cast Pepe as the bullfighter Escamillo, killed by a personification of Death that colludes with Bernarda in his murder. The proliferation of fans, polka-dot ruffles, high-waisted *señoritos* and flamenco-infused dance numbers presented the play as a narrative hinge for the realization of the exotic depiction of Spain created by the Western imagination.

Flamenco dancer Antonio Canales (working with Lluís Pasqual) followed the example of Saura's *Blood Wedding* in stripping the play of decorative clichés, reshaping it as *Bengues* (1998) (from the gypsy word for Devils). Unlike Rafael Aguilar's version for Antonio Gades in the 1970s and Mats Ek's 1978 reading, where the lone figure of Bernarda functioned as an abhorrent 'male' outsider distanced from the female society in which she functions, here all the cast, excepting María la Coneja's María Josefa, were male. Gender was viewed as visibly imitative with selected signs of femininity (the ankle boots and earrings) worn by Canales's Bernarda serving to locate the feminine on the male performing body. This was the female inscribed through its relation to the male with the body as both instrument and site of socio-cultural critique.

In Mats Ek's *Bernardas hus* (1978) violent thrusting architectural sweeps of the body were used to suggest psychological states. The sisters slumped across the furniture, squatted at the table screaming, tore at their clothes and fought over the chairs. A statue of Bernarda's husband was knocked off its pedestal by the Servant in the opening scenario but the entry of Luc Bouy's buttoned up Bernarda and later George Elkin's suitor suggested a continuing male control over every aspect of the sisters' lives in the blue box set that contained them.

The House of Bernarda Alba *as music theatre*

Composers too have appropriated the play's nineteenth-century dramaturgy to underpin their own explorations of the limits of vocality and the rituals of musical performance. Aribert Reimann's German-language opera *Bernarda Albas haus* (2000) pushed the borders of the operatic in its treatment of a fascist past inflected through Lorca's text. As with Flores's décor for Bieito's staging, the conceptual scenography of Frank Philipp Schlossmann situated the action within a nondescript white set. The sparse seats of Bieito's reading were here replaced by a web of chairs scattered across the floor, falling like giant raindrops from the ceiling and suspended from the wings. As with Pina Bausch's *Café Müller*, these were obstacles containing and shaping movement, a physical representation of social restraint. The musical sound world created by Reimann evolved around dark percussive orchestration offset by the edgy hysteria of the vocal line. The effect was almost expressionistic with declaimed text set against the leitmotifs associated with each role.[19]

Michael John LaChiusa's musical rendition, premiered at New York's Lincoln Center in 2005, also featured recurring melodic lines. Here a restricted chromatic palette never allowed for melodic release thus providing a musical analogy for the pent-up tension in the play. Certainly the critics saw the piece more as music theatre than musical theatre: 'The punctuating yelps; the wavering sustained notes in minor keys; the labyrinthine interior musical paths; the eruptions into antimelodic harshness – these are all more the stuff of mid-twentieth-century chamber operas than conventional show tunes' (Brantley 2006). The flamenco allusions and gospel-infused numbers, however, pointed to a broader musical genealogy. The decision to sharply differentiate all the siblings in ways that never allowed them to blend into the landscape and the rendering explicit of that which is only implicit in the play – the dead father's physical relationship with Angustias, Magdalena's narcolepsia, the physical presence of Pepe and his equation with the stallion – indicated a mode of theatrical communication where information could be conveyed in very direct modes both through song and through the thematic patterns of Graciela Daniele's choreography.

Film adaptations and dramatic reworkings

Mario Camus's 1987 film operated a similar strategy of 'making visible' that which is suggested or alluded to. The sisters are thus individualized during the funeral service for the dead father that opens the film; Pepe appears as a *Zorro*-like matinee idol horse-man passing by a window; the men at the funeral are glimpsed as partial mirages in the yard; Martirio is seen hiding the portrait of Pepe; Pepe and Adela embrace through the bars of the window in the moonlight; La Librada's daughter is aggressively pursued through the streets; Pepe is fleetingly seen as he flees the stable; Adela's dead listless body hangs before our eyes from the room that holds Angustias's wedding furniture. The 'opening out' of the work beyond the confines of the house allows for Bernarda's behaviour to be read as reproducing that of a wider body of male institutions (like the church) and for an identification with the female gaze (Smith 1996: 21–7). Nevertheless the production's lush aesthetic, soft-focus cinematography, tasteful interiors, winding streets of whitewashed houses, flawless make-up and hair, and elegant corporeal compositions ultimately sanitize the play's unruly facets. The film, realized with the approval of the Lorca estate, allegedly paid a record-breaking 12 million pesetas (approximately $120,000) for the rights (Fernández 1986), allowed no discordant imperfections to mark its shiny surface of reverent realism.

A film version of the play had been proposed to Luis Buñuel as early as 1944 and, while possibilities were mooted of Sophia Loren's involvement in a Carlo Ponti production (Aub 1985: 155, 276; Buñuel 1985: 190), rights for the play ultimately lay beyond Buñuel's financial means. The figure of Bernarda, however, is inflected through the monstrous mother of *Los olvidados* (1950). The unbending matriarch maintaining discipline within the home was a powerful symbol of authoritarianism for a significant number of film directors working during the Franco regime (see Hopewell 1986: 78–104). Even in the post-democratic era, Lourdes Ortiz's *The Joint of Bernardeta A.* (1995), resetting the play in a brothel that's fallen on hard times, indicates the ways in which Bernarda's ghost similarly haunts the country's theatrical landscape.

Other refractions have involved the Andalusian company Teatroz's *Casting* (1995–8). This two-part comment on the play juggled a fabricated audition for *The House of Bernarda Alba* and an upbeat pastiche musical of the play (see McDermid 2007: 180). The emphasis was on metatheatricality and narrative excess, on indicating the ways in which the play negotiates the boundaries between naturalism and melodrama. Beyond Spain, North American dramatic workings include Óscar Colón's prequel *Becoming Bernarda* (2002) and Tanya Kane-Perry's *Bernarda's Coffin* (1996), an experiment at the borders of dance-theater and the visual arts. Eduardo Machado's *Crocodile Eyes* (1999) refracts the play through Pepe's eyes. Migdalia Cruz's *Another Part of the House* (1997) offers a deconstruction of the play focusing on the madwoman in the attic, María Josefa, here a complicit ally in Adela's relationship with Pepe. Relocated to 1895 Cuba, still then under Spanish colonialist rule, Cruz interweaves the political into the fabric of the tale suggesting links between the women's predicament and that of the island explicitly through Magdalena's infatuation with the revolutionary poet José Martí. Revelations tumble in quick succession: María Josefa's affair with her daughter's first husband, a lesbian relationship between two of the sisters. Pepe haunts the stage as an inescapable source of temptation.

What these reworkings demonstrate is that the legacy of *The House of Bernarda Alba* goes beyond translations and productions. For those who have dismissed the play as 'Ibsen in fancy dress' (Taylor 1999: 626), its operatic, dance and theatrical afterlives point to the hold it exerts on the dramatic imagination and the manner in which its treatment of sexuality, nationality and gender can be harnessed to 'speak' to the multiple subjectivities of our fractured, contemporary world.

3 The 'unknown' Lorcas

While Lorca's reputation as a dramatist was forged first in Spain and Argentina in the 1930s and then in the aftermath of his death across Europe and the Americas, this was based on the limited number of his works then in circulation. The dramaturgy that Lorca was to refer to as his 'real objective' (OCIII 631) remarkably filtered into the public domain only from the 1970s, beginning with *When Five Years Pass*, scheduled for production in late 1936 but not produced in Spain until 1978, forty years after its first print run. *The Public*, published in its extant incomplete form, did not appear until 1976, opening at Milan's Piccolo Theatre in Lluís Pasqual's premiere production ten years later. The single act of *Play Without a Title*, now often known as *The Dream of Life*, was first published in 1976 and premiered, again by Pasqual, for Spain's Centro Dramático Nacional, in 1989. Both a process of reappropriation and scholarship, the staging of these unfamiliar 'impossible' works served to re-envisage Lorca, introducing audiences to hitherto unknown areas of his repertoire.

Other shorter plays and sketches from his adolescence and early twenties came into print in 1994 and this together with the fragments, notes and drafts of later projects, like *Dialogue with Luis Buñuel* (1925) and the film script to *Trip to the Moon* (1929–30) have allowed for a reassessment of Lorca's *oeuvre* that questions the 'colourful, castanet-clicking gypsy with a tragic, social conscience' of popular mythology (London 1996: 7).

This chapter examines some of the 'unknown' works that have shifted the ways in which Lorca's work is mapped. These are considered alongside Lorca's own writings and declarations on the function and role of theatre that proliferated in the 1930s with his increased involvement in the mechanics and 'business' of the industry. Our knowledge of the chronology of the works is partly based on the dates of existing manuscripts, partly on conjecture and partly on the oral and written testaments of those who heard them in more complete versions than those that have survived in manuscript form.

These 'impossible' plays are positioned alongside *Poet in New York* (1940) as embodiments of the surrealist ethos in Spain, discernable also in Rafael Alberti's *Concerning the Angels* (1929) and Buñuel and Dalí's *Un Chien andalou* (1929). *Poet in New York* sees Lorca as 'poet-seer' (Havard 2001: 112), the suffering, visionary prophet chronicling a Babylonian excess of savagery, impassable dehumanizing skyscrapers, human indifference, material gluttony, and spiritual vacuity. The '"I" of his New York poems is just as much an invention as the carefree "I" of the letters Lorca sent to his family from America' (Stainton 1999: 237) and the mantic voice of the former 'I' has been viewed as the prevailing idiom of the 'impossible' plays. Written in the aftermath of his time in New York, they have been judged abrasive commentaries on the petty concerns and tired formulae of prevalent forms of dramaturgy (Anderson 1984: 133–61; Harretche 2000). *When Five Years Pass*, *The Public* and *Play Without a Title*'s playfully interrogate linguistic certainty and dramatic norms. But theatrical innovation is arguably present in much earlier pieces that acknowledge a vibrant cross-cultural fertilization between theatre and the visual arts.

Dialogues and sketches

In a 1935 interview Lorca referred to *Yerma* as the fourth work of a dramatist 'learning to negotiate his craft' (OCIII 615), effectively negating the importance of much of the adolescent work that first appeared in print in 1996. Dramatic vignettes, poems and dialogues crafted as early as 1917 function as valuable markers of an apprenticeship served out in the symbolist sphere. As such, the earliest piece, *A Perfect Little Play* (1917), shares the static abstraction of *The Butterfly's Evil Spell*. Here the forest location, filled with an array of fragrant trees heavy with fruits and wide coverings of flowers, is a rounded, uterine world. The play moves between dusk and dawn, a twilight hour where fantastic beings come out to play. The physical world is little more than a projection of characters assimilated from legend who function as psychic states. A horned man with glass hands emerges from a shell to talk with a blue-eyed creature 'of indefinable form' (OCIV 878); neither is individualized. Both are prototypes of sorts for the *duende* sprite-goblins in *Don Perlimplín* and the figures in Vine Leaves and Bells in *The Public* (Soria Olmedo 1996: 15). Bees, Lights and Flowers scream as the figures mutate and disappear. Mysterious voices speak of completed prophesies and debate the need to live for and in the present. Death is conceived as an omniscient figure in search of vulnerable prey, clad in blue and 'crowned with bloody lotuses and violet *sempervivum* flowers' (OCIV 881). The Ashes (representing the voices of the dead), nevertheless, refuse to recognize Death as absolute or definitive. The surviving fragment of the second scene opens on an island of souls protected by treacherous iron rocks and a coral castle evocative of the equally unassailable edifice of Maeterlinck's *Pelléas and Mélisande* (1892). The referent appears to be the river Styx, passage between the world of the living and that of the dead, where the chorus of predatory satyrs searches out its next meal. The chorus of Poets enclosed within the castle search for an impossible ideal, tortured beings separated from the world of 'happy men' (OCIV 883).

The symbolic premise of the agonized poet negotiating the thorny trajectory of existence also governs *Theatre of Souls* (1917). Here again the poet-seer is positioned precariously between rational and irrational forces, conscious and unconscious worlds. The play similarly juggles abstract figures – Dreams, Love, Goodness, Evil, A Star, Christ's Shadow, Lust, Death – with states of mind projected in visual terms.

The pull of the subjective proves a determining ethos, translated, as in *A Perfect Little Play*, into stage terms. The symbolist inflections of the piece link it to the later *Shadows* (1920). The abstractions that pass as characters are introduced by an Actor who classifies them as the embodiment of humanity's 'suffering' and 'pain' (OCIV 885). It is both a journey into the psyche of the self, marked by essentialist leanings and impressionistic archetypes, and an attempt to impose the structure of dreams and the subconscious onto theatrical composition. The Actor's intervention announces a metatheatrical agenda, a 'marvellous theatre of our interior world' (OCIV 885) that positions itself against the conventional plot construction of cause and effect rationale and psychologically credible characters favoured by Echegaray and Benavente.

In addition, *Theatre of Souls* is also an *auto sacramental*, the one-act allegorical drama that had emerged from medieval morality and mystery plays. Its religious slant links it both to two further fabulist *autos, God, Evil, and Man* and *The Primitive Sentimental 'auto'*, drafted in the same year, as well as to a prose treatment of Christ at 19, *Christ: A Religious Tragedy* (c. 1919–20). Gibson (1989: 67) views 'a strong tendency on the part of the young poet to identify with Christ' and links the narrative of Jesus unable to respond to Esther's carnal desires to Lorca's homosexuality. Sexual angst and physical desire are recurrent concerns in his early writings. However, the mystical and mythical vein of many of the sketches, the grounding of the (in)action in a primitive landscape where ceremonial purification or resurrection of some sort is aspired to, the adaptation of structures and belief systems from Christianity and the endeavour to recreate dream states link the dramatic experiments to wider transnational incentives to transform the stage into an arena for exploring metaphysical questions around the role of performance and identity.

Portraits of these works as the projections of the poet's 'tormented soul' (Gibson 1989: 67) fail to account for the plays' playful currents. *Shadows*, for example, presents a group of shadows (possibly souls) in an ancient garden debating their current predicament and in what form they might be reincarnated back on earth. The arguments veer between the sublime (as with Socrates' shadow whose ego is boosted by the Sixth Shadow) and the ridiculous (as with the Second Shadow, who was a lettuce in a previous life). As in *Of Love. Animal Theatre* (1919) there is an incongruity between the subjects debated (poetic prophesy, innocence and agency) and the means through which they are handled – in the latter play through the dialogue between a dove and a pig.[1]

A further grouping of scenarios from the mid-1920s are similarly grounded in a non-representational world, although this has been linked more specifically to that of Dalí and Buñuel, with whom Lorca enjoyed a close association during his time at Madrid's Residencia de Estudiantes (see pp. 21–6). Lorca's short play *Dialogue with Luis Buñuel* (1925) is one of a series of 'conversations' realized with figures both real and imagined, human and animal, historical and contemporary, religious and secular. Here the dialogue between the two friends, mediated by a third colleague at the Residencia, Augusto Centeno, points to differences and disagreements between a Lorca who prefers 'travelling round my garden' and a Buñuel obsessively impatient for travel (OCII 637; GL 1996b: 70). Most are fragmented, incomplete moments of dialogue (as with the Siren's encounter with the sexually predatory goat-god Pan who irreverently urinates on stage before falling asleep) in the undated *Dialogue of the God Pan*. Some can be conceived almost as silent films, as with *Silent Dialogue of the Carthusians* (1925) and *Buster Keaton Takes a Walk* (1925).

This latter sketch, first published in 1928, superimposes characters from ostensibly different realms. Silent movie actor Buster Keaton is no longer the intrepid, ingenious athletic hero of such works as *Sherlock Junior* (1924) or *The Navigator* (1924), but a child-murderer peddling his bicycle across a pseudo-rural landscape populated by a parrot, an owl, butterflies, a girl with the head of a nightingale, four seraphim's, a black man who eats his hat and an American woman 'with celluloid eyes' (OCII 182; GL 2000: 3). The urban metropolis of Philadelphia hovers over the landscape appearing ever more present as the protagonist cycles on. His assailants are the objects of urbanity – a Singer sewing machine, a gramophone, a bicycle that slips away from him. In Lindsay Kemp's 1986 staging for the CDN, the sense of Keaton's dislocation was conveyed by his cycling above the stage suspended in time and space as a dislocated trapeze artist. The characters he came into contact with were presented as personifications of his imagination, fleeting visions rollerskating and dancing by. Robert Delamere's 1990 staging at London's Battersea Arts Centre conjured a silent cinema world, not merely as Kemp had done through Keaton's whitened face, boater and trademark suit, but also through 'flickering cogs, whirring projectors and precise yet unobtrusive violins' (Gray 1990).

In *The Maiden, the Sailor and the Student* (1925), Lorca's friends, the poets and publishers Emilio Prados and Manuel Altolaguirre, make timely entrances at the close of the play to remove a suicidal Maiden from the railings where she has positioned herself. The Maiden is the faceless entity that the Sailor and the Student – masculine prowess versus male intelligence – vie to control. Each brings on an instrument to seduce her – the former a tired accordion, the latter his lethargy. Again here 'images are presented seemingly undigested' (Svich 2000: xv). The encounters take place in an environment defined only in relation to an unplaced balcony. Occupying an uneasy space between film and performance script, the play is almost the crystallization of a moment of decision, challenging the reassuring tendencies of the realist play with a fluid, undetermined conception of time.

Chimera (1926) too shows the human figure merging with the stage landscape in an undefined space, only here time shapes the restless protagonist's moves. The dismembered voices of his children haunt the action like spectres, *revenants* whose anguished cries reverberate across the stage unheeded by the now distant father. This is a liminal world, shaped both by the language of cinema – jump cuts, close-ups, fades and dissolves – and by art works that Lorca was to evoke in specific stage moments. Lorca's favourite artwork in the Prado was Mantegna's *The Death of the Virgin* (c. 1491), positioning the dying Mary between the world of the living and that of the dead and painted 'with the light of an eclipse' (Dalí 1950: 94). In his 1928 lecture on modern art, Lorca celebrated cubism's communication between 'colour and volume . . . valued for themselves' as a release of art from the 'service of portraits and religious paintings. . . . towards the absurd' (OCIII 89–90, 97; Oppenheimer 1986: 128, 135). In pieces like *Buster Keaton Takes a Walk* and *Chimera*, perspective is similarly reconfigured, connoting a stage world where established logics do not operate. The vanishing point perspective of the proscenium stage emerged from landscape painting. Here Lorca, like Gertrude Stein, provides more panoramic positions that foreground the process of illusion. Mimesis and experiential unity are no longer criteria for composition.

The elusive abstraction of the plays, their brevity, their idiosyncratic combination of elements, the lack of denouement or narrative progression, the overt self-reflexivity and suspension within a continuous present has resulted in their having only a sporadic stage life. *Buster Keaton Takes a Walk* and *The Maiden, the Sailor and the Student* were premiered in Spain only in 1986 as part of a season of Lorca's short works entitled '5 Lorca 5'. In 1935 Lorca reflected that it took him four or five years to negotiate the genesis of a work that he then wrote within fifteen days (OCIII 565). The works presented as part of the '5 Lorca 5' season often read like ideas for larger works – *Dialogue of Amargo, the Bitter One* (1925) is a cautionary tale of a nocturnal encounter between a mysterious rider and a Granadine traveller that negotiates the symbolist terrain of *Blood Wedding*'s Act 3, Scene 1. Like the *Scene of the Lieutenant Colonel of the Civil Guard* (1925) it initially appeared as part of the *Poem of the Deep Song* in 1931. Crucially it points to a dramatist whose work falls elusively between the paradigms of poetry and drama and whose unknown sketches are often positioned alongside scenarios conceived around more familiar poetic tropes.[2]

Cinema and *Trip to the Moon* (1929–30)

A number of Lorca's 'impossible' works negotiate the vocabulary of cinema. Jump-cuts allow characters to be introduced without any prior exposition. Close-ups give the impression of focusing on the intensity of an instant or on an inner sense that can be suspended from the narrative moment that generated it. The photographic enlargement is both a formal conceit – as with an unrealized treatment referred to later in this chapter (see p. 170) – and a mode of conceiving character, as in *When Five Years Pass*. Here character fits with Roland Barthes's (1982: 89–94) dictum of the photograph as a dead image, 'posed' and frozen in time. The characters have little interior life, they are like 'a pack of cards', arrested types that float across the stage and point 'metaphorically to the halting and flow of the narrative' (Wright 2000: 83). For Barthes (1982: 32) photography was 'a kind of primitive theater', representing not authentification of 'the real' but a surface image. The 'impossible' plays show us how that surface can be manipulated and reconfigured.

Lorca's specification in the opening Act 2 stage directions of *The Shoemaker's Wonderful Wife* that the entry of the two suitors, the Young Man and Don Blackbird, is like 'a sequence in a film', also harnesses techniques of shot/reverse in capturing how 'the looks and expressions create the mood of the scene' (OCII 216; GL 1990: 21). Lorca once referred to Walt Disney's Mickey Mouse as a symbol of America (Burgín 1973: 111) and animation haunts the vocabulary of these plays. Here animals talk, as with the Dead Cat in *When Five Years Pass* and the horses of *The Public*, and objects acquire agency as with the weeping mannequin in the former play and the bicycle of *Buster Keaton Takes a Walk*. Lorca visited the cinema with fellow students from the Residencia and liked American comedy, especially Keaton, Harold Lloyd and Ben Turpin. He frequented Madrid's Cine Club, founded in 1928, which screened a breadth of material from Murnau's *Tartuffe* (1926) to Man Ray and Robert Desnos's *L'Etoile de mer* (1928) (Gibson 1989: 233–5). In New York the following year, he wrote of his fascination with the talkies (OCIII 1146). Varied textures of vocality and sound inform (and disrupt) his storytelling processes in the post-1930 plays.

Buñuel had requested a screenplay from Lorca for his cinematic debut in 1926 (Buñuel 1926) but his only known filmscript, the 72-sequence visual poem *Trip to the Moon*, was written in New York for the Mexican avant-garde artist Emilio Amero. According to Amero, the genesis for *Trip to the Moon* came from a shared conversation over *Un Chien andalou* (Sánchez Vidal 1996: 221–2, 356). There is a strong degree of critical consensus that the film targeted Lorca's homosexuality both through Pierre Batcheff's impotent man and the androgynous woman pushing her cane at the severed hand (see McDermott 1996: 122, 131). *Trip to the*

Moon negotiates areas of sexual difference in ways that challenge the heterosexual thrust of *Un Chien andalou*. Male–female encounters are balanced by male–male liaisons (as with the man in the white coat and the boy of sequences 23–5, and the three men of sequence 46 who run in panic from the moon that mutates into a sexual organ).[3] Male–female meetings are marked by aggression: the boy that bites the girl in the neck like a vampire and then 'violently pulls her hair' in sequence 59; violent kisses followed by thumbs stabbing eye sockets in sequence 61. While the title suggests a reference to Méliès's *Le Voyage dans la lune* (1902), it may have been Méliès's *Illusions funambulesques* (1903) and *L'enchanteur Alcofrisbas* (1903), oscillating 'between the magical aura of the photograph as wizardry, and the exposure of the slight of hand techniques involved in the production of the illusion' (Wright 2000: 19) that prove more palpable structural referents. Patricia McDermott (1996: 121–2) follows C.B. Morris (1972: 51) in reading the script as a visual synthesis of verbal images in *Poet in New York*.

While the script demonstrates a familiarity with the cinematic principles of montage editing, point-of-view camerawork, and triple exposures gleaned from sources as far removed as Eisenstein and Keaton, it is also defiantly self-referential. The references to dismembered body parts in the opening section (sequences 2–10) mirror the compositional make-up of his own drawings from this period including 'Self-Portrait of the Poet in New York' (c. 1929–30) and 'Eye and Foot on a Plane Surface' (c. 1929–30) as well as the later 'Severed Hands' (c. 1935–6). Both drawings and screenplay highlight the concerns of Freud's 1919 essay on 'The Uncanny' which significantly refers to severed limbs in its evocation of those things that arouse 'dread and horror . . . that class of the frightening which leads back to what is known of old and long familiar' but alienated through repression (Freud 2001: 930). As metaphorical embodiments of unknown fears and desires, they point to a conceptual realm projected onto the screen. His own drawing, 'Death of Saint Radegund', completed in New York in 1929, is cited in Sequence 38. In the drawing the sixth-century saint is seen vomiting into a bowl. As with his c. 1927–8 'Saint Sebastian', wounds protrude from the chest. Here, however, there is also rectal/vaginal bleeding that provides compositional symmetry with the vomiting and the saint is positioned in a far more submissive position than the vertical Saint Sebastian.[4] This is as much a symbol of that which is disavowed or repressed by society as the severed hands.

The Harlequin of Lorca's 1927–8 sequences of drawings, later featured in *When Five Years Pass* and *The Puppet Play of Don Cristóbal*, is, in *Trip to the Moon*, just a costume imposed onto a boy (sequences 25–6), dragged across the ground by the anatomical nude (sequence 43) and used to deceptive ends as a disguise for the aforementioned nude in his role as the loverboy in the lift (sequence 62).[5] The moon, another persistent symbol in his writing, is positioned as feminine (sequences 17–18), associated with death and a threatening visibility that wounds, threatens and implodes – as with the vomiting that follows her appearance in sequence 18. Vomiting is a persistent action in the screenplay, a leitmotif and form of punctuation, a comment on the action and the return of the repressed. Orifices feature conspicuously – mouths, nostrils, sexual organs. Carnality is a recurring motif – embraces, kisses, close dances in slow motion, playing hands. The circle of birth and death repeatedly enacted in the screenplay is framed within feats of abuse, as with the 'parody of the traditional Madonna and Child icon' in sequence 11 (McDermott 1996: 124) or the anatomical nude with hands outstretched in sequence 47, a crucified post that is later replicated by the Red Nude in *The Public*. Duplication, replication and reiteration runs as a pervasive organizing pattern – as with the numbers mutating into ants in the opening sequence and the revisiting of Helen (sequences 34, 65) in her varied manifestations ('Elena, Helena, elhena, eLHeNA' [OCII 272; GL 2002: 752]).

Helen of Troy, the face who launched a thousand ships, is reconceived as the blank canvas on which the male imagination projects its fear of the 'other'. Fear of death translates into fear of Woman and Helen represents a feminine 'other' capable of destroying the most entrenched kingdoms: a site where male desires are both projected and enacted. Significantly, the screenplay opens with a reference to a white bed – later returned to in Sequence 68 – a place of temptation and fornication. *Trip to the Moon* is a parable of the seven ages of man, forever imprisoned by a cloying, castrating female sexuality that knows no bounds.

Amero began filming the work in 1936 but it was never completed. A short was realized in 1993 by Ángel Gil Orrios that merged images from the screenplay with verses from *Poet in New York*, but it was only in 1998 that Catalan artist Frederic Amat rendered a twenty-minute reading of the screenplay. To a score by composer Pascal Comelade, Amat provided a visual language that conspiciously drew on the designs he had conceived with Fabià Puigserver for Pasqual's 1986 staging of *The Public*. The figurative was a fleeting presence in the film; signs abstracted into mutating geometric forms; the familiar was conceived as suggestion. Cesc Gelabert's choreography and Amat's recourse to virtual technologies situated the piece within the contemporary present but it was a present that Amat acknowledged as haunted by the ghosts whose languages echo both through Lorca's screenplay and Amat's interpretation of it. Visual nods to Duchamp, Ernst, Man Ray, Mantegna and Magritte were positioned alongside citations to Buñuel and Dalí as well as to *Poet in New York* and the New York drawings. In providing a visual language for the film, Amat refracted his own process of engagement, both intellectual and artistic, with the screenplay. Amat's *Trip to the Moon* is the encounter of his baroque blending of primary colours with a screenplay that announces itself as the product of an earlier era. 'Making visible' the body of the screenplay, Amat opted not for the imitative tradition of the photographic but for a laborious process of inscription that recognized the art/ifice involved in shaping the screenplay as the flicking images of celluloid.

On theatre, metatheatricality and directing

> Theatre is, above all, a good director.
>
> (OCIII 426)

Lorca identified with theatre in ways that were incomprehensible to more senior literary figures of his era, like Juan Ramón Jiménez, who viewed theatre as a lesser art and actively dissuaded him from playwriting (Sánchez Vidal 1996: 57): even a male poet in 1920s Spain was tainted by his proximity to an industry ontologically dependent on deception, delusion and dissemblance.

The pragmatics of performance impacted significantly on Lorca's dramaturgy. The figure of Don Cristóbal, Andalusia's guignol Punch, framed the triptych of plays directed by Lorca for the Epiphany entertainment organized for his sister in 1923. Mora Guarnido (1958: 164–5) asserts that the event served as a model for ideas realized more convincingly in *Don Perlimplín*. The mottled treatments of Don Cristóbal realized by Lorca in *The Billy-Club Puppets* and *The Puppet Play of Don Cristóbal* demonstrate the difficulty of identifying any of the extant versions of the dramatic works as definitive. Lorca's trajectory as a director is fundamental to an understanding of the variant drafts of his dramatic works.

Lorca was to direct productions of *The Shoemaker's Wonderful Wife*, *Don Perlimplín* (1933), Franz Molnar's *Liliom* (1934) and Lope de Vega's *Peribañez* (1935) for the amateur Club Teatral Anfistora run by Pura Ucelay, advocating theatre clubs in the mould of the Anfistora be created across the country with a remit to stage works that commercial enterprises would not touch (OCIII 409). He was a regular presence in rehearsals of his plays – bemoaning the rigidity of the actors while preparing *Blood Wedding* in 1933, shaping musical pacing in *Doña Rosita* (1935). He advocated a consistency of characterization and accents across all roles, fine-tuning the text in an approach that treated the texts like an operatic score (Guerenabarrena 1989). Directing involved the creation of a stage language for the works (OCIII 246). The analogy he provided was musical: Chopin sounds different when played by Rubinstein or Brailovski (OCIII 587).

During the 1930s, both as director of La Barraca and after his return from Argentina when his position as poet and dramatist was firmly consolidated, he missed few opportunities to stress the importance of theatre to Spain's cultural identity. As he stated in 1935:

> The theater is an extremely useful instrument for the edification of a country, and the barometer that measures its

greatness or decline. A sensitive theater, well oriented in all its branches, from tragedy to vaudeville, can alter a people's sensitivity in just a few years, while a decadent theater . . . can cheapen and lull to sleep an entire nation.

(OCIII 255; GL 1991: 124)

It is beyond the remit of this book to trace the evolution of Lorca's theatrical thinking but suffice to state that theatrical analogies, commentaries and debates feature conspicuously in his writings. There is no cumulative ideological position, rather ruminations and observations that give the writings the sense of an unfinished work in progress. The frustration with Spain's theatrical culture articulated in his interviews, lectures and correspondence, may, in part, have been generated by the difficulties he experienced getting *Mariana Pineda* staged. 'Theatre is in my blood' he professed in 1926 as he vented his wrath against director Gregorio Martínez Sierra, who had withdrawn an earlier promise to stage the play (OCIII 882). A month later he ranted against a theatrical culture in the hands of actors and writers who were nothing but 'riff-raff' (OCIII 893). Avaricious impresarios who used their economic clout to police what was staged proved further targets of his tirades (OCIII 893). In the absence of dramatic outputs validated by productions and critical approval, Lorca stressed his own romanticist credentials as an 'artist' ignored by a wider establishment that confuses art and commerce (OCIII 769).

By August 1933, he could no longer claim to be slighted but he nevertheless denounced the Spanish theatre as a theatre 'made by and for pigs', situating his work within a European, instead of a national, context (OCIII 424). Lorca positioned himself repeatedly as a teacher at the service of the nation, both in a mandate to 'educate the masses' and to exert control over the unruly tastes of Madrid's undiscerning audiences (OCIII 598, 256; GL 1991: 125). Aspirations towards a rarefied theatre, rarely staged and generated by discontent, go cheek by jowl with the drive towards a popular theatre (OCIII 374, 424, 566). As early as 1926 he had distanced himself from the theatrical culture of Spain, which he denounced as 'loathsome' (OCIII 928), and yet it was a culture he courted and aspired to form part of, as evidenced by his pursuit of the powerful actress-managers of the day.

The placing of his own dramaturgy outside such commercial parameters, insusceptible to 'sirens, congratulations and false voices' (OCIII 254; GL 1991: 124) fails to acknowledge his own evolution as a product of that very culture or his delight at finally receiving significant capital recompense for his plays (OCIII 1242–53). The writings articulate a series of contradictory positions: Lorca at once viewing himself as a playwright of the people while polarizing audiences into two binaries: the idealized rural communities of La Barraca versus the frivolous, conservative audiences of the commercial bourgeois theatre who arrived late, left early and didn't want any kind of moral conjectures to form part of their evening's entertainment (OCIII 539, 545). 'Theater', Lorca argued in 1935, 'ought to impose itself on its audience, not the audience on the theater': he advocated the 'imposition' of authors on reluctant audiences 'by lofty authoritative criteria superior to their own' (OCIII 256; GL 1991: 125).

The assumptions that underpin these statements are evidently problematic. 'Art' is protected by a sacred aura and imbued with a civilizing function that is threatened by economic imperatives. In his 1934 homage to Lola Membrives, the actress-manager whose productions rendered Lorca financially independent for the first time in his life, Lorca bemoans the contamination of art by the business model (OCIII 243). Alberti's (1988: 228) observations that many who had ridiculed Lorca's early theatre flocked to secure rights to his work once they had realized there was an audience for it, may have conditioned the latter's own disparaging comments, Xirgu and the actors of La Barraca excepted, on performers in Spain (OCIII 397).

There is, nevertheless, an evangelism in Lorca's statements on theatre, professing his own superior position as messiah for a new order largely bereft of significant new dramatists (OCIII 362–3). During his time with La Barraca Lorca pushed for a theatre of 'social action' (OCIII 255; GL 1991: 124) that brought together 'the complete drama of real life' (OCIII 563). Poetry (rather than verse) was both an end product and the means to a dramaturgy that moved beyond the equation of 'real life' with the ideology of mimeticism (OCIII 568). In one of his oft-quoted interviews from 1936, Lorca fashions a concept of theatre that 'rises up from the page and is made human. And when this happens it talks and shouts, cries and despairs' (OCIII 630). The emphasis is on a theatre that intervenes at grass roots level rather than being directed solely at the dress circle and the stalls and that recognizes the precariousness of its own position. His theoretical writings locate the idea of crisis as inherent to theatre's very being (OCIII 255; GL 1991: 124). Self-questioning becomes the means through which to formulate preoccupations around the role of theatre in an age of social unrest. 'His success as a dramatist rests on that ability to interpret the sensibility of his age, and his legacy is to have suggested ways of breaking through the crisis' (Boyle 2006: 163). Thus he has proved such a potent referent for directors and dramatists grappling with the conceptual, philosophical and material remains of an artform rooted in the ephemeral.

Engagement with the politics and function of theatre is evident also in the metatheatricality of the plays. A number feature prologues where an author figure – usually referred to as Author, Director or Poet – bridges the world of the stage with that of the auditorium, offering a framing device and commentary on what is to come. They deal with the commercial imperatives of theatre, as in *The Shoemaker's Wonderful Wife*; the bland dramatic fare provided by dramatists providing easy escapism, as in *The Billy-Club Puppets*; dramatists at the mercy of audiences baying for entertainment, as in the incomplete *Dragon* (1929–30). Audiences are urged to be open-minded about what they are about to see, as in *The Billy-Club Puppets*. In *The Butterfly's Evil Spell* there is even a qualification of the play as 'of no great consequence' (OCIV 168; GL 1983: 195).

By the time Lorca came to write *Play Without a Title*, fifteen years later, he was far less apologetic, preaching 'a sermon' in no uncertain terms to the audience to wake up and engage with the material before them, even though it may show 'the things you do not wish to see' (OCII 769; GL 1994: 107). In *The Puppet Play of Don Cristóbal* the Director talks to Cristóbal, thus diffusing the distinction between the psychological world of individual experience the former represents and the surrogate, surface world of the puppet. In *Play Without a Title* the Author is a conduit, a guide that leads a reluctant audience to a realization that agency is desirable in both theatre and life (771; 109). As in *Dragon*, there is open critique of a theatre bound to outdated conventions where materialist concerns don't intrude. Increasingly in these late works, the prologues understand theatrical texts as inextricably bound up with the conditions of their production: Lorca's performance of the author-role in a number of these pieces further legitimizes the dilemmas articulated therein.

Paratheatrical gameplay informs a number of these plays. The worlds of circus and ballet intervene in *When Five Years Pass*. The Author appears dressed as a magician in a cape decorated with stars in *The Shoemaker's Wonderful Wife* and a Magician reappears in *The Public* as the Director's final and most deadly antagonist. The magician is a repository of theatrical tricks, a conjurer able to invoke spectacles from the slightest of words and imaginative rigour. In many ways the magician can be positioned as the supreme example of 'the theatre of the open air' promoted by the Director in *The Public*, a 'spectacle of light and show' (Wright 2000: 35) that is juxtaposed with the imaginary 'theatre beneath the sand' advocated by the First Man (see pp. 157–8).

There is pause for critical reflection built into the plays' structure: the Magician in *The Public*, the sprite-goblins in *Don Perlimplín*, the Idiot Shepherd in *The Public* and the Harlequin and Clown in *When Five Years Pass*, serve as mechanisms for breaking down the fourth wall. Scenes distanced in terms of time and location present disparate characters from different socio-political or historical realms. Lorca's own statements on theatre may have occasionally proved naive in their castigation of the commercial imperatives of theatre but these 'impossible' plays recognize that human action is determined by social environment and material forces. Even *The Puppet Play of Don Cristóbal* acknowledges this when the Poet closes his opening monologue by stating that he's off 'to iron the company's costumes' (OCII 399; GL 1990: 67). More so in *Play Without a Title*, the practicalities of 'making' theatre are consistently on display.

Like Brecht, Lorca's work as a director brought him into contact with some of the theatrical practitioners moving towards a more musical form of dramaturgy: a stage practice tied to European modernism and its rupturing of linear narrative structures. There are references to Reinhardt and Tairov in 1933 interviews (OCIII 408, 482). Lenormand and Kaiser are seen as further points of contact in discussing *Yerma* (OCIII 616). Piscator's 'courage' and scenic organization are commended in a 1935 interview (OCIII 599). Pirandello, as author, director and crucially innovator, is a comparative model (OCIII 577, 1259–60). Lorca's directorial trajectory cannot be excluded from a discussion of his playtexts. He was involved both in the commercial sector as assistant director and director of his own works for the stage and in amateur and student theatre as artistic director of La Barraca and a regular collaborative associate with the Anfistora. His correspondence and interviews guide us through the puppet theatre companies he had planned to found in the early 1920s, the amateur dramatics at the Residencia de Estudiantes in the mid-1920s, the compilations of folk songs he directed for Membrives's company in Buenos Aires in December 1933, and the rough premiere of *The Puppet Play of Don Cristóbal* at the foyer of Buenos Aires's Avenida Theatre in 1934 (OCIII 729, 690, 482–3, 518–19).

The testimonies of actors and designers who worked with him also point to a marked awareness of the representational discourses that shape theatrical practices. His plays contain instructions to actors on gesture, posture, register and tone. Lorca analogized the verbal to the visual in ways that recognize how theatrical vocabularies intervene in shaping a play. 'Half the production', he stated in 1935, 'depends on rhythm, colour and scenography' (OCIII 563). He affiliated himself with the craft of directing at a time where the role of 'director' was frequently assumed by the actor/actress-manager and saw his theatrical training as ongoing (OCIII 396), as evidenced by his continued presence at Rivas Cherif's side in rehearsals with Xirgu's company. Set designer Manuel Fontanals's contribution in shaping the visual contours of the stagings was acknowledged by Lorca in a 1935 interview that understands scenography as moving beyond the decorative to embrace the technical, the architectural and the dynamics of geography and space (OCIII 553).

For scenographer José Caballero, Lorca viewed a production like the mechanisms of a watch, each needing to run in perfect time and appropriately positioned in relation to the larger organizational body. A production was like a poem interpreted by multiple voices where the quality of each voice's particular inflections is never subsumed by the larger demands of the choral body (Caballero 1984). For Lorca directing involved not merely the rehearsal process but the preparatory selection of material, casting, research, cutting, and musical composition that framed the work with the actors and design team (OCIII 571–2).[6] In intersecting the 'holy' qualities of theatre – he once referred to the mass as the most perfect theatrical act (OCIII 244) – with the 'rough', both in the theoretical writings and the practice (the plays and directing), Lorca sculpts a theatrical idiom that juggles the material and the immaterial without ever effacing the concrete forces that shaped his own theatrical disaffection.

Antiforms and the 'impossible' theatre

While critics have constructed a canon that sees the pinnacle of his theatre as the rural trilogy made up of *Blood Wedding*, *Yerma* and *The House of Bernarda Alba*, his writings refuse to see the avant-garde, surrealist or, as he was to term them, 'impossible' plays, as mere conduits to the better known works. The latter were located by Lorca as the means to gaining the respect that would allow him to stage the 'impossible' plays (OCIII 631). Notes in his papers about prospective projects suggest that this may not be as clear-cut as he would have liked to believe, but the 'impossible' works do provide alternative modes of dramatic composition that eschew the cumulative effect of the three-act tragedy.

When Five Years Pass, *The Public* and *Play Without a Title* all signal an acknowledgement of the breathing, kinetic relationship between the moving living body and its performance environment. The focus on spectatorship situates these works within an evolving fascination with new vocabularies of perception probed by surrealism and other modernist movements in the aftermath of the First World War. The concerns and techniques of the plays are picked up in the site specific and environmental theatre of the 1960s and 1970s which probed and rethought the boundaries around theatre, dance and the visual arts, reconfiguring dramatic focus around the place of performance while asking decisive questions around the exposure and politics of the gaze. The masquerading bodies conjured by Lorca serve as metaphors for a range of elusive desires and compromised allegiances. Overt theatricality becomes the prism through which both characters and audience are given a threshold of revelation. Rather than tell stories, all three prioritize the theatrical experience itself with its inherent reliance on audience reciprocity and reflection. It is perhaps not surprising that *The Public* and *Play Without a Title* gravitate around situations in a theatre with the spectator as voyeur often positioned against the actor as agent.

When Five Years Pass, *The Public* and *Play Without a Title* are certainly political plays but they reject the model of judicial theatre that Sartre was later to employ. Rather it is a theatre that anticipates Genet who similarly posits that political change comes not from characters singing about liberty and revolution in abstract terms but by provoking suffering and 'evil'; what can be seen as 'radical negativity' (Genet 2002: 262). In response to the critical controversy provoked by *Yerma* in 1934, Lorca articulated a desire to scandalize with his theatre: 'I want to provoke a short, sharp shock, to see if all the nastiness of the contemporary theatre can be vomited all at once' (OCIII 612). In the same interview he declares that the two problems that most interest him in his writing are the social and the sexual, stressing that the sexual 'is more attractive to me' (OCIII 612). Lorca moves beyond a theatre of utility. 'Meaning' is no longer its driving force, feeling and/or emotion become more dominant targets (OCIII 546). This is a theatre that requires that the characters who appear on stage 'be dressed as poetry' but that 'their bones, their blood' be visible at all times (OCIII 630).

The desire to stage 'horrible themes' (OCIII 612) thus becomes a way of igniting the audience without ever resorting to didacticism. There are palpable points of contact between Lorca's impossible plays and philosopher Theodor Adorno's (1978: 222) reflections on the task of art as being 'to bring chaos into order'.

For Adorno (1973: 135–207) artistic commitment involved the use of negative aesthetics that dismantle situations, antiforms and structures that recognize that all cannot be reduced to reasoned ideas. Lorca's own sense of unease at the capitalist imperative of theatrical transactions finds an echo in Adorno's views that 'the culture industry not so much adapts to the reactions of its customers as it counterfeits them' (Adorno 1978: 200). Barter or commercial exchange encourages 'non-identical individuals and performances' to 'become commensurable and identical' (Adorno 1973: 146). Written at a time when Walter Benjamin was also questioning the aura of art in an age of mechanically produced art and mass reproduction, these plays each feature protagonists whose realities and perceptions are questioned, dismantled and reconfigured. The focus is not on easy empathy but rather on multiple subjectivities that supersede all encompassing generalizations and challenge dominant ways of seeing in the representational arts.

All three plays merge characters from the world of living and the dead, fiction and the supposedly real to a more emphatic degree than *Blood Wedding* or *Don Perlimplín*. *Play Without a Title* talks about the interaction of 'Angels, shadows, voices, lyres of snow and dreams': phenomema as real as 'the coins you carry in your pocket' (OCIII 769; GL 1994: 107). The idea of dramatizing the subconscious in these plays has led certain critics to use expressionism, rather than surrealism, as a mode of reading their theatrical language (Anderson 1992; Guardia 1952: 190; Jerez Farrán 2004). Lorca's writings betray an awareness of expressionist trends and dramatists (OCIII 256, 616). The blocks of characters (the Card Players of *When Five Years Pass*, the White Horses and Students of *The Public*, the audience of *Play Without a Title*) all point to an abstracted, generic conception of role (Anderson 1992: 217). Names are replaced by generic classifications (Old Man, Young Man, Girlfriend and so on) that further serve to abstract the action. The formal wear of the Three Men in *The Public* and the Young Man and the Card Players in *When Five Years Pass* has been traced back to Kaiser's *Gas* (Anderson 1992: 218). The rhetorical performance style of expressionism with its angular moves and projection of mood onto the contours of the *mise en scène* is captured in the expressionist films that were projected in Madrid in the 1920s. *The Cabinet of Doctor Caligari* (1919) and the later *Metrópolis* (1926) present a dehumanized vision of the technological city that shaped *Poet in New York* and haunt the wider landscape of *The Public* and *Play Without a Title*.

Other critics have seen more of a surrealist ethos in these plays. Severed limbs reoccur in both plays and drawings – as with 'Severed Hands' (1935–6) and 'Severed Heads of Federico García Lorca and Pablo Neruda' (1934) and the maimed mannequin of *When Five Years Pass* (OCII 387; GL 1990: 175).[7] Morris traces the lost solitary men who drift through the plays and the shifting of 'familiar, concrete objects' to 'new contexts' where 'familiar actions become sinister and sinister actions become familiar' to surrealism's restlessness and inverted inference (Morris 1972: 50–1). As with *Un Chien andalou*, the interpretative logic that the plays demand often dispenses with the determinant of psychologically detailed characterization. Surrealism, as Lorca recognized in his 1928 lecture on modern art, allows for the expression of the inexpressible (OCIII 94; Oppenheimer 1986: 132).

When Five Years Pass (1931)

Lorca reportedly began work on *When Five Years Pass* in New York, continued to work on the play in Cuba and then completed it in Granada in 1931. That Lorca died five years to the day of completing the play has led to an almost ghoulish fascination with it as a premonition of the playwright's own death. Critics have positioned the Young Man as a thinly veiled version of Lorca and traced the former's journey to autobiographical concerns (Auclair 1968: 232–40; Guillén 1990; Ucelay 2003: 36–109). Lorca's homosexuality certainly provides a mode of reading the play but it is, as Paul Julian Smith astutely observes, fraught with contradictions in its split between 'anecdote and allegory – between an urge to acknowledge the experience of the historical García Lorca and a desire to impose a transcendent meaning on a text . . . that, unlike *The Public*, does not speak aloud that meaning' (Smith 1998: 73).

The play has survived in what is believed to be a complete manuscript – unlike *The Public* or *Play Without a Title* – and is organized around a familiar three-act structure. A Young Man is to wait five years before marrying his Girlfriend but when they meet again she no longer wants this, having fallen for a Football Player. The Young Man then turns to the Secretary who had been in love with him through the first act but she insists they wait a further five years before they can finally be together. In his deliberations the Young Man is given conflicting advice by two Friends and an Old Man. The narrative is halted as otherworldly characters invade the stage at regular intervals: a Dead Cat and Dead Child in Act 1; the shop-window Mannequin that wears the Girlfriend's bridal gown in Act 2; the Harlequin, a Girl whose lover has drowned, the Sequined Clown and the Mask of Act 3, Scene 1. At times the characters converse in ways that remain largely outside the main tale – as with the Dead Child and the Dead Cat. At others they intersect with the Young Man or the Secretary to illustrate predicaments or manoeuvre the action in particular directions – as with the Clown and Harlequin's pushing of the Young Man and the Secretary together in Act 3, Scene 1. The latter's deferral of their union sees the Young Man face the deadly trio of Card Players in the final scene.

Subtitled 'A Legend of Time in Three Acts and Five Scenes', the passing of time has proved the dominant organizing motif for critical readings of the play. Act 1 appears suspended in time, beginning just prior to the clock striking six and ending with the Young Man's servant, John, reiterating that it remains six o'clock. It is as if the Young Man's inaction fails to move time on. Acts 1 and 2 are separated by a five-year period; Acts 2 and 3 by a lunar eclipse. The first scene of Act 3 takes place in a forest of 'Huge tree-trunks' (OCII 370; GL 1990: 161), a metatheatrical space as removed from the library and bedroom of the first two acts as *Blood Wedding*'s forest from the other locations of the play. At the end of the play the clock strikes twelve although the Servant still insists it's six o'clock. The play takes place in the twilight zone between dusk and dawn, beginning in the evening and ending at midnight; a phantasmagoric time of unknowability and poor visibility.

Representational visibility in the play is anything but constant, rather subject to the multiple subjective positions that we bring to the texts we read. In *When Five Years Pass* like *Trip to the Moon*, the pictorial space of performance evolves before our eyes in a brutal interrogation of the reality of reality. Time is thus shown to be less a concrete, measurable absolute than a subjective concern; fluid rather than fixed, subject to interpretation and reformulation. Time is both interiorized and exteriorized and parallels can be drawn with an allegorical tradition of dramaturgy, the *auto sacramental*, that presents conflicts and crises through the filter of a single male imagination grappling with the personifications of its discontents.

In defining *When Five Years Pass* as 'a mystery play' (OCIII 444), Lorca points to its relationship with the *auto*'s enactment of moral debates in the public sphere. If we read the early *autos* as partly 'a response to Northern attacks on the doctrines of transubstantiation' (Sullivan 1983: 23) – the bread and wine of the Eucharist becoming the body and blood of Christ – then the play's treatment of metamorphosis can be better contextualized. Objects and entities are reformed and reformulated into other beings in ways that may initially appear irrational but can be linked to wider conceits around display and concealment that inform the play. The characters have no back-life. There is little exposition and no endorsed sense of the motivation that propels the action. The opening act and final scene take place in a 'room full of books' (332; 125), the library location pointing to an intertextual space defined by literary paradigms – Lenormand's *Time is a Dream* (1919) and Lorca's earlier *Theatre of Souls* have been cited as particular reference points, with more general comparisons made with the writings of Jorge Manrique, Jean Cocteau and Luigi Pirandello (Guardia 1952: 288; Stainton 1999: 279). The bookish Young Man in whose head the play could be seen to take place remains trapped in a repeatedly evoked past or an implausible future. It is in many ways a prototype for the similarly suspended landscape of Beckett's *Waiting for Godot* (1953) where fulfilment is forever deferred. Significantly, waiting is the most important verb in the play (Fernández Cifuentes 1986: 267).

Sarah Wright (2000) follows the example of Anderson (1984: 135) and Edwards (1980: 99) in viewing the play as a journey into the interior psyche of the protagonist with the onstage characters as guises for the facets of his tortured self, manifestations of decisions made or what might have been, and elements of the world beyond. References made to the Young Man's discomfort at the sounds of the street permeating the room further delineate this sense of a retreat into the self (OCII 333, 337; GL 1990: 126, 131). Wright (2000: 66) positions the Old Man as analogous to Dante's Virgil, leading the Young Man through the journey into the mind. The Old Man ruminates on the importance of an inner life that transcends 'anything outside us, that's exposed to the air and to death' (336; 129), echoing the position of the sages of Calderón's *autos* who extol the merits of an afterlife that remains untainted by the material concerns of the present.

The Old Man is nurtured by past memories (the word 'remember' features repeatedly in the opening sequence: 332–6; 125–8), and trapped by an inaction suspended precariously between tenses: 'one should remember with an eye to the future' (333; 126); 'I'm going to forget my hat' (339; 132). As with the Young Man he shares a view that tomorrow is forever in the future and deferment is, as with *Waiting for Godot*'s Estragon and Vladimir, a way of life. The Old Man can be seen as a projection of what lies ahead for the Young Man although the critics have also viewed him as the Young Man looking back on his derelict life, the split selves of the Young Man sharing different perspectives on their past, and the coexisting 'I's of the Young Man meeting in the sphere of dreams (Harretche 2000: 136–58; Soufas 1996: 69–77). The play accommodates all these possible readings.

The other characters that the Young Man comes into contact with can equally be seen as projections of his inner world encompassing something like the seven ages of man. The First Friend is an energetic womanizer, a Don Juan figure who celebrates absolutes with no room for doubt (348; 140). Women are simply interchangeable entities, reduced to their physical attributes, and best captured in a photograph that can frame and contain them for the constant contemplation of the male gaze (337–8; 131). He

lives for and in the present and his overt hedonism stands in opposition to the more subdued Second Friend. The latter character is
in many ways an alter ego for the Young Man, correspondingly
suspended in a world that hovers liminally between dream and
wakefulness. Played by a young performer – either male or female
– he is dressed androgynously in attire that suggests an analogy
with the Dead Child. Both appear adjourned in an undetermined
time of childhood (the Dead Child) and adolescence (the Second
Friend), unable to make the transition into the adult world. The
Second Friend fears the onslaught of age embodied by the
'wrinkles and aches' of the Old Man (350; 142). Unlike the Old
Man who is 'not in the habit of remembering' (349; 141), he is
trapped by memories that prevent him acting. Positioned between
fear of the 'black pit' of death and the 'ugly' light that illuminates
his space (350–1; 142–3), he shows how both visibility and
invisibility are fraught with instability and fear.

The Old Man and the Dead Child can be seen as 'two extremes
of a spectrum of masculine subject positions' both bound by a
'shared inability to indulge in life, to live on anything other than
nostalgic yearnings for what might have been' (Wright 2000: 66).
The fear of female agency displayed by the Young Man finds
echoes in the position of the two Friends who both place women
in positions where they are the fetishized object of the male gaze.
For five years the Young Man holds an image of his fiancée in his
mind; it is the image of a passive young girl who creates herself
according to his criteria and preferences. It is an image he can
control and hold at bay because it lives only in the realms of the
fictional (335; 128).

He paints her to suit the requirements of his romantic
imagination with long golden tresses but, as both the Old Man
and the Girlfriend remind him, she never had long hair (334, 360;
127, 152). All the women in the play are, in some way, trapped
within the realms of the imaginary. They are there to service, make
legible or 'type out' the Young Man's thoughts. From the sexually
demanding Girlfriend to the demure, shy Secretary they are
mirages of the male imagination.

The Mannequin and the Mask function as projections of the
Young Man's 'fossilization' of 'the women he meets so that he

can overcome his fear of them' (Wright 2000: 77). The Mannequin, attired in his ex-fiancée's wedding gown, is a reminder of the Young Man's impotence. The truncation of the wedding finds its metaphor in the mutilated body of the Mannequin. It is as waxen, white and dry as the corpse of the Dead Child. The Servant covers the Secretary as she leaves the Young Man in Act 2, Scene 1. Here she too is 'put away' like a showroom dummy. All the female characters the Young Man comes into contact with have to be thus controlled or fixed.

The Football Player too can be positioned as a projection of the alpha male: silent, smoking, virile, brooding, dressed in the contemporary gladiatorial gear of the sportsman. He is perhaps a hologram, the empty image that the Young Man believes the Girlfriend desires, or a castrated version of the extroverted First Friend, forever silenced into the enactment of a masculine prowess that he can no longer boast of. He functions as another of the dismembered facets of a fractured masculinity presented in the play. *When Five Years Pass* has been compared to a Cubist painting, visualizing a given object from many different perspectives (Harretche 2000: 147), but the object displayed through its many shards is masculine. The Young Man's patent insecurity with regard to who he is and what he represents is tested through the play in the world of the living (the first two acts) and the dead (the scene of the Dead Child and the Dead Cat in Act 1 and Act 3, Scene 1).

Act 3, Scene 1 sees the forest invade the Young Man's consciousness. This is not however the ominous forest of *Blood Wedding* but a more ludic sphere, for a circus is in residence and its characters populate the action. The Clown and Harlequin have something of the androgyny of the Second Friend and the Dead Child – androgyny seen here as the 'full balance and command of an emotional range that includes male and female elements' (Showalter 1977: 263). Androgyny is presented as seductive and, if we use Showalter's critical framework, as a 'myth' that assists in the evasion of confrontation with the painful excesses of masculinity through a process of transcendentialism (Showalter 1977: 264). It is a further indication of the Young Man's passive abnegation.

At the end of Act 2, the Young Man questions what he will do with a future he doesn't recognize (363; 155). In Act 3, Scene 1, the resourceful Harlequin provides an answer. His two masks allow him, 'to play with and tease the various "human" characters with whom he comes into contact' (George 1995: 145). Harlequin's moves are associated with dance and he performs like a circus ringmaster. Like the Clown who addresses the audience, he functions within the realm of the extra-theatrical (370–6; 161–5). The clowning, however, has a malevolent dimension. Harlequin is not clad in his habitual attire but in green and black, colours that announce the proximity of death. The Clown too is described as having a 'powdered head' that 'looks like a skull' (373; 163).

These are Machiavellian forces that corner the Young Man, question the young Girl's search for her dead love and bring the Secretary out on cue like a puppet at the ready. The associations between the Girl, the Secretary and the Mask suggest disguised versions of the same predicament. All tell tales of unrequited love and paramours who have abandoned them in a context. All are positioned within a context that denotes loss and the impending presence of death. The open suitcases scattered across the floor of the library in the final scene suggest preparations for departure. The Young Man shows 'signs of despair and physical exhaustion' and disintegrates as the scene progresses (387; 175). By the time the three Card Players enter, he is described in ghostly terms (389; 177). His death at their hands occupies both the symbolic sphere – the Ace of Hearts projected on the wall, the pistol that fires the silent arrow – and the terrain of the real.

Delayed openings

Cipriano Rivas Cherif (1957: 1) argues that Lorca's desire to see the play staged was based in part on his own incomprehension of it. Staging not only 'makes visible' certain facets of the work that remain obscured, but also serves as a telling reminder that authorial intention is a highly precarious touchstone for analysing texts. When Lorca first read the play to Margarita Xirgu in 1930 she called it 'incomprehensible' and 'unstageable'. Years later, positioning it within the surrealist innovations in theatre she had subsequently witnessed, she expressed a desire to stage it with designs by Dalí (Rodrigo 2005: 187).

Plans to stage the play in 1936 were halted by Lorca in June for a range of reasons (see Ucelay 2003: 355–61). Rehearsals for the play were first begun in 1934 but delayed by problems over the casting of the Young Man. Germaine Montero – later to form a career in exile on the French stage – took the role of the Girlfriend. The Football Player rested her on his knee as she delivered her lengthy monologue, enveloping her in a cloud of smoke as he puffed on his cigar incessantly (Ucelay 1992: 464–5). The Mask acted out can-can steps as she reminisced about the Paris Opera in Act 3, Scene 1 (377; 166). Lorca deliberated as to whether to substitute an artificial leg under her layers of skirt to aid with these moves, further accentuating the conceptual links between the Mannequin and the Mask. He was insistent the roles of the Child and Cat be played by children (Ucelay 1992: 465). Reports of the rehearsals suggest he was keen to avoid sentimentalism, melancholy and effeminacy, deleting lines that didn't work, and pacing the action in divergent ways – with Harlequin's balletic movements contrasting with the cold certainty of the Clown. The final scene was choreographed like a silent movie, with the Players forming a circle around Young Man and gesturing as if cutting something through the air (Ucelay 1992: 465–6).

Presented first as a ballet by Merce Cunningham with music by Paul Bowles in 1943 and then premiered in English at the Provincetown Playhouse two years later, *When Five Years Pass* was not seen in Spanish until the 1954 staging at the University of Puerto Rico. The play's performance history in many ways displays the problematic dialogue between this difficult work and theatrical conventions that have languished behind experiments in the other visual arts. Reviews of Stage 73's Off-Broadway production in 1962 and Guy Suarès and Françoise Prévost's Parisian staging at the Récamier theatre in 1958 classified the piece as 'minor' and 'obscure' and in both cases bemoaned the decorative and choreographed trimmings that adorned the play (Gelb 1962; Smith 1998: 75–9). The response, in part, may be attributed to the play's positioning of an alternative Lorca to the picturesque palette of the 'known' works, but it also points to an unease at the formalist qualities of a play frequently adorned in production with iconographic elements of Jean Genet's aesthetic.

There are evident associations between Genet's dramaturgy and Lorca's 'impossible' works. While Genet never declared an affinity with Lorca, there are factors that have served to facilitate a link; both were poets and playwrights, gay, and attracted to the Arab world; both present dramatic situations that rely on mystical transformations; both envisaged a concept of theatre that drew on children's games and the mechanics and rituals of the Catholic mass (OCIII 218–21; Genet 2002: 817). Both also articulate a fascination with death, were infatuated by the vocabularies of surrealism, and present problems to actors caught between the demands of classicism's grand rhetoric and naturalism's supposed invisibility. Víctor García provided staging strategies for each that eschewed the anthropological approach favoured by more literal directors, allowing the works to negotiate a space beyond either the humanist emphasis on the degradation of social oppression or the academic sado-masochistic essay on pathological obsession.[8] Rafael Alberti sees Lorca 'doing a little that of Genet. Thirty years earlier' (Aub 1985: 312). The dramatist and scenographer Francisco Nieva (1996: 131) is less sure of the association, judging Genet a far more marginalized figure than the hugely successful Lorca. Both Genet and Lorca craft a dramaturgy that articulates 'otherness' through 'purely theatrical means of signification' (Bradby 2006: 35). The demand this places on the performers has often seen directors opt for pantomime or camp in approaches to the 'impossible' plays.

Miguel Narros's 1978 staging at Madrid's Eslava Theatre largely avoided these pitfalls. José Hernández's set opted for an abstracted environment of high cylinders positioned in configurations that suggested tombs, skyscrapers, cypress trees and chimneys (Gómez Ortiz 1978). Actors placed on them like statues on a plinth began moving as the action necessitated. They were conceived as ghostly figures as if transplanted from a Magritte canvas or suspended between worlds (López Sancho 1978). Narros avoided the literal interpretation of the stage directions in favour of a spatial world that was at once suggestive of Lorca's

New York writings and the blank laboratory-like interior of Peter Brook's *Midsummer Night's Dream* (1970). By eliminating what might be termed the culture-bound aspects of the play's setting, Narros created a spatial world unfixed within any naturalistic plane and consequently able to contain the array of loci depicted within the text – what one critic was to refer to as 'all Lorca in a work' (Llovet 1978).

When he returned to the play ten years later, at Madrid's larger Español Theatre, there was a marked shift in aesthetic. The milieu was more evidently Andalusian – from the haunting female wailing that opened the play to the flamenco guitar or *zapateado* that underscored strained elements of the action, from the bull-fighting antics of the First Friend to the local inflexions of the Manuela Vargas playing the Mask. The first act was less a library than a red walled boudoir with imposing wardrobes holding within the secrets of the Young Man's psyche, illuminated at key moments to show the figures contained within (see Figure 9). The interplay of bold, primary colours, gold leaf furniture, formalized movement and emphatic delivery to the stalls offered a more aggressive register than the earlier staging. This was also, however, a far more feminized space with Carlos Hipólito – Harlequin in the earlier staging – providing a gaunt, delicate Young Man. The transition to Act 2 was conceived through the Young Man's passage, candelabra in hand, through multiple grand arches into the Girlfriend's bedroom. This was a horizontal floating space of gauze drapes contained by a giant hovering mural referencing Dalí's many Venuses. Perhaps in classifying the spectacle 'too much', 'overloaded', 'grandiloquent and artful' (Haro Tecglen 1989; Hera 1989; López Sancho 1989), the critics demonstrated a fear of the 'performative excess' through which the play is habitually presented (Smith 1998: 101). It is as if a director cannot possibly accommodate the expectations of the reader for whom the play will forever remain suspended between its time of composition and its delayed opening.

Atalaya, the Seville-based company specializing in reverent productions of the 'impossible' plays, similarly provoked critical reserve with its 1986 reading, directed by Ricardo Iniesta, aspiring towards 'a fidelity' that trapped the play in a version of the Young

Figure 9 Décor holding the secrets of the Young Man's psyche:
When Five Years Pass, directed by Miguel Narros at
Madrid's Español Theatre, 1989. Photo: Chicho/CDT

Man conceived as Lorca in a discernibly Granadine terrain (Moya
1987). Joan Ollé's 1998 production, set on an incomplete incline
of sinewy forms and broken tiles that conceded the play's ruptured
premise, was far more successful in pointing to a fluid landscape
of coexisting idioms – referents included Murnau, Chagall, Dalí
and Miró – that recognized the play's negotiation of expressionist
and surrealist intersections. The door onto the stage suggested the
emergence from and disappearance back into a subterranean
world and the largely Catalan cast articulated the language
through inflexions that further signalled the 'otherness' of the text.

Staging surrealism: English-language productions

Parallels with *Un Chien andalou* have been comprehensively
mapped by Gwynne Edwards (1981) and have served as a

discerning reference point for directors in the English-speaking world. The British premiere directed by Robert Delamere and Maria M. Delgado for the Edinburgh Fringe Festival in 1989 was defined by a performance register located within the realms of silent cinema and underscored musically in ways that supported views of the play as structured like a musical piece with repeated motifs (Honig 1945: 136). This was a twilight world of dusty windows, discarded trunks and Daliesque melting clocks.

Charlotte Westenra's 2006 staging at London's Arcola Theatre, with clusters of clouds painted on the sky-blue back wall and red bleeding across white tablecloths, referred also to Dalí. In the absence of obvious Andalusian paradigms, directors have turned to the surrealist imagery of Buñuel and Dalí for the visual topography. Michael John Garces's 1998 production at New York's INTAR referenced the costumes of *Un Chien andalou* and suggested visual analogues between the Young Man and Lorca, the First Friend and Buñuel and the Second Friend and Dalí while playfully flirting with cultural imagery of Andalusia – as with the Young Man and his Friends' paper fans. The reinforced presence of the frame – both window and theatrical – allowed for the sense of passing through different planes.

That same year Maria Momblant Ribas's staging at London's Southwark Playhouse located the visual world of the play in the realm of fairy tales, offering a conceptual set of bare boards enclosed by a grille around which the cast sleep until called on to make their entries. Dried crumbling ashen leaves proposed mordant mortality and a compelling metaphor for the play's treatment of the concept of love as something fundamentally out of reach or ungraspable, crumbling to dust as we attempt to keep hold of it. The twenty-first century has witnessed a wave of productions of the text, including its configuration as multimedia bilingual opera by Tom Dean and David Burrows for Oakland Opera in 2002.[9] *When Five Years Pass*'s questioning of authoritative consciousness and self-reflexive meditation on its own interpretability resonates in an era where the problematic consequences of conceiving subjectivity as singular or hegemonic are ever more palpable.

The Public (1930)

Give me a glove and I'll tell you the character of its owner.
(OCIII 852)

The mystery surrounding *The Public* has impacted strongly on its critical reception. Begun in Cuba in spring 1930 and completed that summer on returning to Spain, Lorca alluded to it in an interview published in October 1930 as 'made up of six acts and an assassination' with horses in the primary roles and therefore not really performable (OCIII 372). References to the play are dropped in his correspondence and interviews over subsequent years (OCIII 418, 1171, 1182). Scenes 2 and 4 of the play were published in the Madrid journal *Los Cuatro Vientos* in June 1933 (61–78). The manuscript travelled with Lorca to Buenos Aires in October 1933 although he was firm that it wouldn't be premiered either in the city or anywhere else, 'because I don't believe there's a company who would be willing to stage it or an audience who would tolerate it without indignation. . . . My play is not for performance . . . it is a poem to be booed at' (OCIII 444). Lorca entrusted a version of the play to Rafael Martínez Nadal in July 1936 as he prepared to leave Madrid with the words: 'If anything happens to me, destroy it all. If not, you can return it to me when we next meet' (Martínez Nadal 1974: 16).

Martínez Nadal's speculation as to the whereabouts of the hypothetical 'complete' versions has been further fuelled by conjecture from other quarters. Rafael Alberti claims a version of it remained with friends, who later destroyed it in Cuba, but also ponders on the possibility that the family possessed a copy that they were not prepared to acknowledge (Aub 1985: 311). Martínez Nadal (1974: 20) initially attributed the family's hesitation in publishing the play to the expectation that a complete script might appear, but in a further interview he concurs with Alberti that the Lorca estate didn't want to see it published because of its overt homosexual subject matter (Aub 1985: 268).

The play was initially published in 1976, six years after Martínez Nadal's exhaustive study of its history, motifs and imagery first appeared in print. Critical reception has been irrevocably marked by the expectations, paradigms and observations set by Martínez Nadal. The struggle for 'ownership' of the play and its concerns points to further clashes that were to occur over subsequent decades with respect to the material possession of the manuscripts and their potential signification (see pp. 198–9).

The play lacks the cumulative structural pattern of *When Five Years Pass*. The six scenes, referred to as 'frames', dispense with spatial and temporal coherence, offering convoluted plotting and a collection of characters whose relation to each other is never concretely defined. The play opens in the Director's blue study with a large hand painted on a wall and X-ray negatives taking the place of windows (OCII 282; GL 1994 61). Here the Director – sometimes called Enrique – is told that the audience has arrived but it is four White Horses that enter. The Director associates himself with the 'theatre of the open air' but his views are increasingly questioned by the First Man – later referred to as Gonzalo – who argues for a 'theatre beneath the sand' that unsettles audience sensibilities. Shoved behind a screen, the Director reemerges as 'a boy in white satin with a white ruff' (286; 65). Pushing the Second Man behind the screen, the latter materializes as a woman 'in black pyjama pants, a crown of poppies on her head' (287; 66). Helen (of Troy?) dressed as in antiquity appears and confronts the Third Man with his homosexuality. As he accuses her of lying, the Manservant comes to her rescue.

Scene 2 involves a figure clad in Vine Leaves and a figure clad in Bells engaging in a game of seduction and refusal interrupted by the arrival of the Roman Emperor and his Centurion. The Emperor selects Vine Leaves as his new lover. Scene 3 takes place against 'a wall of sand' with 'a gelatinous translucent moon above' left and 'a huge green lanceolate leaf' centre stage (295; 73) where the Director and the Three Men debate their sexual predicaments and the constraints of masculinity. The back wall opens up to reveal Juliet's tomb in Verona. Here she is visited first by a White Horse, then a Black Horse and subsequently three further White Horses who try and seduce her. The return of the Director (dressed as Harlequin but in the English version cited here translated as Pierrot) and the First Man continues the dissection of theatre and their past amorous liaison. The Director strips off his costume and tosses it behind a column, revealing a ballerina tutu. He has now become Wilhelmina but soon strips again to reveal tights with bells and a further mutation into La Dominga de los Negritos. In the meantime the Harlequin/Pierrot costume emerges from behind the column and wanders the stage where s/he is joined by the Second and Third Man, similarly mutated and mutating. Past and present identities interact as the remains of the various characters haunt the stage.

Scene 4 opens with a Red Nude – referred to in the translation cited here as a Naked Man – adorned with a crown of thorns and crucified onto an upright bed. He is attended by a Male Nurse, who informs him of the disturbances occurring in and around the theatre following a performance of *Romeo and Juliet* where the title roles are taken by men. Four students continue discussing the riot; Four Ladies and a Boy struggle to find a way out of the theatre. Characters wander in and out through the chaos. The bed spins round and reveals that the First Man has taken the Red Nude's place. He dies as the scene ends.

A dramatic interlude of sorts titled 'The Idiot Shepherd's Solo' – sometimes placed in a different position in production – presents a recited poem delivered by a shepherd against a blue curtain decorated with shelves of white masks that he pulls away as he leaves the stage. The final scene returns to the study that opened the play only now there is a horse's head on the ground and a large eye and cluster of trees surrounded by cumuli. Here the Director meets the Magician and both argue through their positions on theatre, interrupted by Gonzalo's mother, searching for her son, and a roaming Harlequin costume. As the audience are let in the Director falls, presumably dead.

While habitually translated as *The Public* the Spanish title also signifies 'the audience' and this points to its structural conceits. The play opens and closes with lines that acknowledge the audience's presence. It situates the reader/spectator as audience members trapped in the theatre experiencing what the First Lady refers to as the horror of getting 'lost in a theatre and you can't find an exit' (315; 94). The play deploys a range of techniques – characters mutating without warning, characters functioning under different names, the entry and exit of characters for no palpable reason, a juxtaposition of signifiers from different codes, epochs and contexts, the refusal to follow a cause and effect structure, little or no exposition – to disorientate the reader. The result is a metatheatrical work that probes the role of theatre, its discontents, spectatorship and visibility in ways that intersect with concerns around the body, homoerotic desire, performative punishment and the enactment of a sexuality that moves beyond the heterosexual.

Referents for the play have been exhaustively charted and include Rivas Cherif's treatment of a lesbian relationship, *A Sleep of Reason*, presented by El Caracol while *Don Perlimplín* was being rehearsed in 1929, Cocteau's *Orphée* produced by the same company a year earlier, Azorín's *Doctor Frégoli*, adapted from Evreinov and staged in 1927, Pirandello's *Six Characters in Search of an Author* (1921) and *Each in His Own Way* (1924), the paintings of Hieronymous Bosch, Goya, Dalí, Miró, and silent cinema (see Edwards 1980: 62–5; Gibson 1989: 295; Martínez Nadal 1974: 70–82). Harlequin is, as I have outlined earlier in the book (pp. 23–4), a recurrent motif in his drawings. Shakespeare too functions as a prominent reference point through his *oeuvre* – the incomplete *Play Without a Title* features an offstage rehearsal of *A Midsummer Night's Dream*, a play whose presence also resonates through the enchanted woodland settings of *The Butterfly's Evil Spell*, *When Five Years Pass* and *Blood Wedding* (see Anderson 1985). Harretche (2000: 54–5) finds analogies between *The Public* and Buñuel's all-male *Hamlet* staged at Paris's Café Select de Montparnasse in 1927 but in many ways it is *Romeo and Juliet* that functions as the primary resource text for Lorca's play.

The decision by the Director to stage Shakespeare's play with a man of 30 and a boy of 15, who also happen to be in love, in the title roles, sparks the riot in the theatre. *Romeo and Juliet* is the quintessential play of heterosexual desire but here it is envisaged in ways that question that desire as the legitimate norm. Juliet, the exemplary ideal of constant love, is here envisaged split three ways: under the seat, as a boy actor in the role and in the tomb (Jerez Farrán 2004: 206). These splintered Juliets show how the role is appropriated to suit the requirements of the reading.

Juliet's femininity is not dependent on a woman's body, it is, rather, as articulated by the Boy when discussing Juliet's feet, 'too perfect. . . . They were a man's feet, feet invented by a man' (313; 92). The transsexual being demonstrates the modes in which all gender ontology can be reduced to the play of appearances (Butler 1990: 43–52). Representation questions the possibility that difference can be firmly marked.

The play presents a number of mechanisms that aspire to reach beyond the surface – X-ray machines, screens, beards, wigs, nudity – but surface in the play is ultimately the primary signifier. Representation is presented as a play of surfaces. Characters undergo repeated metamorphoses to the point that the reader cannot be sure where origin ends and disguise begins. Bodies are deconstructed and reconfigured as *commedia* personas, costumes, and spectres. In Scene 1, for example, the Director (alias Enrique) swaps wigs, disappears behind the screen and then emerges as a boy dressed in white satin. In Scene 3 his array of identities include a Pierrot costume and a ballerina tutu and tights with bells. Vine Leaves is one of his possible mutations; the nemesis of the First Man/Bells/Gonzalo.

Every scene has mechanisms that facilitate the process of transformation (Harretche 2000: 62–3). All masks are shown to be flexible. The characters that emerge from behind the screen in a feminized form cannot be attributed this shape as their 'truthful' state, for they frequently mutate further in ways that question an essentialist reading. In the third scene the First Man claims he has no mask, seeing himself as free of the hypocrisy that blights the Director. Deception may be seen as an unattractive vice by the Three Men but it is, as the Director articulates in the play's third scene, the cornerstone of both theatre and life: 'There's nothing but masks . . . if we mock the mask, it'll hang us from a tree' (305; 84).

Gender, sexuality, social and political interaction can all be read as imitative performance in *The Public*. The play provides no endorsed 'truth' or master narrative, rather performativity is the dominant idiom. As with Genet's *The Maids*, Lorca constructs the stage as a conscious mirror that never reflects an image with an a priori reality. This is a world where, as the White Horse tells the director, 'A lake is a surface, a superficies' and even a volume is 'a thousand surfaces' (306; 84). In *The Public*, Lorca argues for a stage practice that recognizes its own theatricality and simulacra (see Baudrillard 1983).

The debates on theatrical endeavour realized across the play – by the three Men and the Director, by the three conservative Ladies, by the five Students – can be viewed as further deflections of the central discussion between the First Man and the Director over the legitimacy of the theatre of the open air versus the theatre beneath the sand. These are not indicative of two different ideologies – the former a celebration of the trickery of theatrical duplicity and superficiality, the latter a more visceral theatrical practice that posits that revelation is paramount and nothing should remain hidden (see Edwards 1980: 69–70; Harretche 2000: 85–9). Like Smith (1989) and Jerez Farrán (2004), I would argue that the supposed separations of the two theatrical forms are not valid. The Director's experiment with *Romeo and Juliet* recognizes the dangers inherent in tampering with ideologically endorsed expectations. Revelation is ultimately unachievable when we can never be sure of the supposed original that is being masked or camouflaged. The survival of the Magician at the end of the play is perhaps the ultimate reminder that theatre is inherently dependent on the magic of transformation. The death of the Director reminds us that a subterranean theatre that prioritizes 'interiority, hermeneutic process, and the struggle for hidden essence' offers 'no real alternative: invisibility is death' (Smith 1989: 134; see also Jerez Farrán 2004: 252–8).

The male body, dressed and undressed, adorned, on display across historical epochs and mythology, is in many ways the protagonist of the play. But it is a male body tormented, beaten, wounded, maimed, marked, inscribed and transformed across multiple testing encounters: 'scattered with images of waste and excretions' – sweat, spit, saliva, mucus, tears, urine, defecation, blood (Wright 2000: 107). The emphasis is on a diseased masculinity in which pain and pleasure are irrevocably intertwined. Juliet views the conflict between the Director and First Man as antagonistic but the Black Horse reassures her that they are making love (306; 85). Desire in the play is bound up with disgust, sadism and dissatisfaction. As the dialogue between Vine Leaves and Bells in Scene 2 indicates (mirrored in the encounters between the First Man and the Director in the scenes that frame it), desire is ultimately a spiral of attraction and repulsion, compliance and disobedience, activity and passivity, abuse and affection, ecstasy and agony, visibility and invisibility.

For many years the play encouraged more commentary on Lorca's homosexuality than theatre. Theatre, however, is implicitly bound up in the enactment of sexuality. Appearance is both subject and form in the play and the regulation and control of sexuality is shown to be dependent on mechanisms of surveillance. The act of looking marks out our sexual identities and differences but in *The Public* sexual difference is not to be celebrated but instead recognized as 'man's failure, his punishment, his shame and his death' (295; 74). Jerez Farrán (2004: 25) presupposes that *The Public* offers a dramatization of a view of homosexuality that implies that gay men can only express their desires to the detriment of their masculinity. Lorca was working with stereotypes and inherited ideas. Viewing the play as a call for understanding and tolerance of homosexuality fails to recognize the contradictions raised by homoerotic desires satisfied in clandestine ways and shrouded passions that can only be articulated through sadism (Jerez Farrán 2004: 61). The play articulates a self-censoring of homosexual practices. There is a fear of feminization that leads the First Man to castrate metaphorically those who he fears will castrate him. Sacrifice is a mode of establishing authority and agency in the play but it is an authority tied to death. Identification on the part of the author lies with a dominant masculinity in a play where homosexuality is a long way from being accepted (Jerez Farrán 2004: 94–5). Guardia (1952: 308) may have viewed the superimposed imagery and dislocated dramaturgy of the play as evidence of Lorca's disorientation as a writer at the time of initial composition, but it can be read more persuasively as a commentary on documented thoughts around homosexuality and performance then in circulation.

Inscription and visibility: productions of The Public

The play's production history in many ways reflects that of its publication. Fragments were first presented in 1972 at the University of Texas where Martínez Nadal was then teaching. The first professional production took place in Poland directed by Pawel Nowicki at Lódz's Theatr Studyjny, in a double bill with *Play Without a Title* in 1984 (see Aszyk 1984). Two years later it was presented as a ballet by Óscar Aráiz at Geneva's Comédie Theatre in ways that censored its sexually explicit language within an elegant aesthetic of unspoken spectacle. The location of the body as a 'socially inscribed surface' signalling that '*surface effect is all there is*' (Wright 2000: 115) is a useful point of entry in discussing productions of the play. Pasqual's production of the play for Madrid's CDN in 1986–7 enacts a reading that materializes from a consideration of issues of visibility and invisibility performed in an arena that played on the signification of the Spanish word *arena* (meaning both sand and arena).[10]

Pasqual and his designer Fabià Puigserver removed the stage and stalls of the María Guerrero Theatre to provide a circular expansive playing area of sparkling blue sand that simultaneously evoked a circus ring, a lunar landscape, a beach and a *corral*. No attempt was made to realize the existent stage directions, the emphasis was on 'an imaginary theatre' (Pasqual 1987: 6). Upstage the stiff plush red gold, white and blue curtains, fossilized trappings of the proscenium arch stage and its reductive perspectivism, provided both a metatheatrical framing structure and a visual metaphor for a conservative theatre reduced to its decorative accoutrements (see Figure 10). Only a single row of stall seats remained, primarily occupied by actors, a dislocated remainder of a theatrical model that was inverted as the audience observed actors watching other actors, and as such denying the stability of a single field of vision.

This was a reading embedded in the interpretative and significative layers that form part of any theatrical product. The production highlighted the disparities between the theatrical and social codes of 1930 and the mid-1980s. References to Buñuel's

Figure 10 A lunar sandscape for Lorca's 'impossible' theatre: The Magician (Walter Vidarte) entering for his final entry in the closing scene of *The Public*, directed by Lluís Pasqual at Madrid's CDN, 1987. Photo: Ros Ribas

early surrealist works were positioned alongside costumes that alluded to the play's variant generic registers and were not located in any definable period or tradition. In the case of the Idiot Shepherd – part clown, part fool – differing layers of costume superimposed military insignia, signs of domesticity (an apron), profession (a sheepskin wipe), femininity (earrings) and classical antecedents (a hose, a handkerchief tied around the head). Colour coding played on the audience's expectations – Juliet was attired in sculpted white, Helen positioned on platform pedestal heels, the Emperor in white toga and red cape. Helen was thus conceived as an emblematic alluring siren evoked by the Director in celebrating the prowess of the theatre of the open air: less the alluring Death of María Casares in Cocteau's *Orphée* (1950) and more the precarious, unstable construct of a male imagination that perceives her as the carrier of loss. Juliet significantly rejected the passive role assigned to her, recognizing the theatrical discourses that have shaped her mythologization in an operatic register that contrasted with the *tanztheater* of the Horses. While the men mutated into evidently more fragile beings Juliet appeared to billow upwards, part-angel, part-spectre, part-defiant teenager.

The classical roots of the play (see Jerez Farrán 2004: 99–137; Smith 1989: 130–5) were not underlined, as in Aráiz's ballet which deployed a classical bust as the primary scenographic motif, but were played out across the rudimentary costumes of Vine Leaves, Bells, the Emperor and the Centurion. These referenced historical antecedents and classical mythology in modes that played out the multifarious ways in which the vestiges of the past impact on the theatrical present. Pasqual (1987: 6–7) has admitted that when he first read the play in 1978 he understood 'absolutely nothing'. On the eve of the production's opening he spoke of areas of the play that now appeared clearer while others remained 'in total darkness'. Beginning with white lights permeating the darkness of the playing area, the staging may have appeared to be seeking to make visible the opaque but visibility has limitations. The production negotiated different pockets of playing areas – long corridors, intimate corners, expansive arenas. Characters wandered in and out of the light – sometimes, as with the Ladies fumbling in the dark and the partially lit Students debating *Romeo and Juliet*, almost shadows flickering through the darkness. At other times, as with the Red Nude's genitalia defiantly on display, visibility appeared, as a 'trap . . . it summons surveillance and the law; it provokes voyeurism, fetishism, the colonialist/imperial appetite for possession' (Phelan 1993: 6). Pasqual's production foregrounded the gap between what is seen and unseen, pointing to the ideology of the visible's erasure of 'the power of the unmarked, unspoken and unseen' (Phelan 1993: 7). In 'revealing' an unknown play never previously staged in Spain, it simultaneously recognized that revelation is always partial and always subjective.

Jorge Lavelli used the play in 1988 to open his tenure as artistic director of France's newest national theatre, La Colline. The production again opted for a largely metaphorical playing area framed by rows of doors and stairways leading into supposed infinity. The effect was that of a labyrinth that the characters were trapped in. Conceived in distinctively Artaudian terms, Lavelli's reading presented the theatre beneath the sand as a liminal space on the border between life and death with Juliet's tomb serving as a crystal stage where key ideological battles were waged.

That same year at London's Theatre Royal, Stratford East, Ultz presented the play's British premiere. Of the triyptych of opening productions, this was the one that followed the stage directions most literally. In the opening scene, for example, X-ray plates were suspended stage right and a large imposing hand positioned at the top left corner of the pale blue backdrop. The time-consuming scene changes imposed a truncated rhythm with levers and cranes having to raise and lower backdrops. While the images created – the Roman statues of Scene 2, the grey-green backcloth with its superimposed leaf-cum-quill for Scene 3, the Oxbridge-type students dispensed through the auditorium for Scene 4 – proved striking on their own terms, the scenographic framework was so cumbersome that it governed the pacing in ways that truncated any sense of a dreamwork. While Pasqual juxtaposed different performative registers to indicate the plethora of subjectivities and desires on show and Lavelli opted for a largely realist paradigm in constructing a site of role-play, never taken as a given but instead elegantly displayed as constructed artifice, Ultz opted for pantomime – as with the bulky horse heads, a mannered camp Director, a big top drum roll to open the production – merged with a static hands-in-the-pocket actor style that involved large chunks of dialogue being delivered with largely stationary performers – as in the play's final scene. Dismissed as an 'avant-garde relic' smothered by a 'hilariously flamboyant . . . design' (Coveney 1988; McAfee 1988), it has inspired few further productions of the play in the UK.

At New York's Repertorio Español Rene Buch's 1998 production used Dalí and Buñuel as visual pointers in creating a production that pivoted knowingly around theatrical idioms. Characters struck patently actorly poses. There was no attempt to mask the extensive doubling of roles taking place. Disembodied voices echoed around the stage. The focus was on presenting an incomplete canvas. The screens were splattered with red and black. The Director and Three Men wore tuxedo jackets over their bare torsos. Characters were often presented in states of undress. The horses, partially camouflaged in masked netting and blond wigs, negotiated long samurai-like sticks. The final dialogue between the Magician and the Director was judged to forecast the 'verbal joust between Death and the Knight' in Bergman's *The Seventh Seal* (1956) (Bruckner 1998). In reimagining the look of the play in ways that referenced its incomplete form and its discussion of concerns handled subsequently by other cultural practitioners, Buch offered a reading that recognized, as had Pasqual's and Lavelli's, the evolution of theatrical language and cross-cultural vocabularies in the period between Lorca's composition of the play and its delayed stage outings.

Play Without a Title (Dream Of Life) (1936)

Play Without a Title shares a number of metatheatrical motifs with *The Public*. Again here the function of theatre is debated in a public forum and the issue of revelation occupies a central position as the Author – also referred to as Lorenzo – presents his vision for a theatre 'of truth' against the backdrop of a theatre where rehearsals are taking place for a production of *A Midsummer Night's Dream*. This is a space part-suspended between process and product, with the fixed representation located in an undefined future tense. Spectators are in the theatre watching a play but it is an act of observation that also accommodates participation, as with the First Male Spectator interruption of the Author's 'sermon' asserting the legitimacy of 'the spectator's judgement' as the 'only law in the theatre' (OCII 771; GL 1994 109). Characters veer between performers (the Actress) and roles (Bottom), but both are marked by disguise and, increasingly, the lines that demarcate them are blurred. The actress in the role of Titania comes in search of the Author with whom she appears to be involved in some type of amorous relationship but he now appears uninterested in what she represents. Actors, stagehands and aides drift in and out in search of colleagues, news and clarification on the political action enveloping them. A Worker who has succeeded in entering the theatre is shot by a Second Male Spectator who wants nothing to interrupt his evening's entertainment but his efforts appear to be in vain as the theatre's doors are broken down and the venue is bathed in symbolic red.

Unfinished at the time of Lorca's death, the play was first published in 1978 as a single act piece but we know from Margarita Xirgu, to whom he read the first act and a few scenes of Act 2 in July 1935, that he conceived it as a three-act venture with the first act set in Madrid's Español Theatre, the second in a morgue visited by the Actress and the Author and the third in heaven populated by Andalusian angels, where the Author ends his Everyman-like journey (Rodrigo 1984: 290–2). Referring to the play in an interview in early 1936, he cites it as a yet unnamed 'social drama' with interventions from the auditorium and the streets where a revolution is taking place (OCIII 626). The title *Dream of Life* appears to have been coined by mid-1936 (Anon 1936a) although it is still frequently referred to by the title with which it was first published and staged.

While the play negotiates the breaking down of the fourth wall that Pirandello was to render in the mingling of characters and author in *Six Characters in Search of an Author* its play-within-a-play format is politicized by the revolution occurring outside in the streets. The bloody Asturian revolt of 1934 has been located as a possible referent for the street skirmishes (see London 1996:

14–15; Wright 2000: 33) and in positioning the struggles within the theatre against the larger socio-political conflict without, the play suggests a radical mandate not unconnected to Lorca's vision for La Barraca. The theatre of politics appears not so distant from the politics of theatre.

The Author begins by bemoaning a theatrical culture where entertainment is the only prerogative but his aspiration to show 'truth' as a singular, infallible entity is repeatedly questioned during the play. The Author can only conceive of the Actress's protestations of love as 'artifice' because of the false qualities she bestows on Titania and because of her shifts from role to role on a daily basis (776–7; 115). She is presented as an unreliable enchantress who wants to keep the burgeoning revolution taking place outside the theatre firmly out of her sphere. Her self is seen to be as changeable as her outfits. In this sense she functions as a latter version of the title protagonist of his abandoned libretto for Falla, *Lola, the Stage Actress* (1923): a wily actress with a plethora of disguises able to manipulate both her husband and her would-be suitor, two poets, to her own artistic ends.

The Author distrusts performance but has chosen to work within it. He doesn't want to undertake 'a game of words' or conjure a show of lights (769; 107) but his mode of articulating his case presents a disparity between words and actions. For theatre, like the forest of *A Midsummer Night's Dream*, is a transformative space. He wants actors to be 'men and women of flesh and blood' (772; 110) without recognizing 'playing' is intrinsic to theatre's very being. All speech acts, as J.L. Austin (1975) reminds us, are performative. The Actress chastizes the frightened Second Female Spectator fearing for her children's safety, bemoaning her laboured inflection bestowed 'with a falseness that will never succeed in moving anyone' (785; 123). As in Valle-Inclán's *Bohemian Lights* (1920) the performative is shown to be so pervasive that the citation of authenticity is no longer a reliable measure of 'truth'.

The play repeatedly questions issues of ownership. Whose words are you speaking? Can a voice be claimed as 'authentic'? The Author positions himself as the repository of 'truth' in the play but as the First Male Spectator suggests, truth is not a definable commodity. The financial transaction of 'buying' a seat secures certain rights including that of interrupting and judging the actors' work. For the Author theatre involves simply applauding or rejecting the enacted narrative but this flies in the face of audience agency and recognition of the spectator as constructor of meanings (771–3; 110–12). 'In the theatre it's all a lie', the First Female Spectator retorts to the Author's insistence that his tale of starving children playing with their dead mother's yellow hands is 'true' (773; 110). 'Art', Adorno (1978: 222) reminds us, 'is magic delivered from the lie of being truth'. The Author conceives the doors to the outside world that he wants to see flood the theatre like a fourth wall. And while he may aspire to pull down the separation between audience and actors in the terrain of the political – 'The Theatre belongs to everyone. . . . open the doors' (779; 117) – he cannot tolerate having his judgement questioned. In theatre as in life, 'The desire for the real is impossible to realize . . . but that impossibility maintains rather than cancels the desire for it' (Phelan 1993: 14). The play thus functions as an interrogation of the pragmatics of theatremaking. What remains purely in the realms of the speculative or the impossible? How can theatre 'bring the smell of the sea to the auditorium or flood the stalls with stars?' (770; 108)? What does it mean to try and show 'reality' in a world where 'nothing is invented' (769; 107)?

The play was premiered in Spain in 1989, as a self-reflexive commentary on the construction of theatre and self. Rehearsals of Shakespeare's play, included by Pasqual in his staging, functioned as a prologue to the action. Alternative theatrical configurations undermined the spectators' sense of themselves as a cohesive group. House lights were not dimmed. The Author – conceived as a director-like figure – observed rehearsals from his stage management desk in the stalls. Unexpected noises infiltrated the auditorium. The air conditioning was switched off part-way into each performance. Actors were planted in the audience. 'Rehearsals' were disrupted by the tensions erupting outside the stage. Eventually panic set in and the boundaries between the private space of the auditorium and the undefined public space of the world beyond collapsed. Disorder enveloped the auditorium as an explosion ruptured a section of the stage. Spectators rushed out in haste, unaware that this was an illusion conjured by Pasqual and his scenographer Puigserver (see Delgado 2003: 213–17).

Harretche (2000: 185) has signalled the ways in which light is associated with the idea of 'truth' in the play. The Author and his Servant crave to see 'lights so strong they burn and destroy the hearts of those who speak' (775; 113). The Actress, on the other hand, wants red lights that cast the illusion of bloodstained hands (778; 116). Again here, however, Pasqual's reading questioned the politics of visibility. The Worker's visibility was seen to lead directly to his demise. The Actress's attempts to mark out her presence saw her progressively fall from the Author's favour. Pasqual's representational strategies indicated the modes in which those who operate in the half-light – the onstage Spectators – enjoy the most powerful positions in the play. In selecting *Play Without a Title* as his inaugural production as artistic director of the Odéon-Théâtre de l'Europe a year later, staging it in both French and Spanish and assuming the role of the Author in the latter performances, Pasqual announced a theatrical strategy that could offer a means of interrogating what the oscillating discourses of a new Europe might be and how theatre might participate in the debates raging through the shifting boundaries of the continent.

The brevity of the play has seen directors undertake multifarious framing decisions. Michael Batz's 1987 staging at London's Young Vic provided a specially written prologue and epilogue linking the action to Lorca's death and thus allocating the piece a 'prophetic' status – Lorca anticipating his own death and the outbreak of Spain's fratricidal Civil War. This was further reinforced by the Second Male Spectator shooting the Author rather than the Worker. *Cicadas* and guitar underscoring served further to ensure that for all the play's 'unknown' status, it could be placed by spectators alongside the familiar Lorca of Andalusian lore.

A production at Madrid's Teatro de la Abadía in November 2005 by Luis Miguel Cintra padded the play with *Dragon*, the final scene and solo of the Idiot Shepherd from *The Public*, fragments from lectures and interviews that allude to the responsibility and role of theatre, and the opening dialogue between the Author and the World from Calderón's *The Great*

Theatre of the World (see Breden 2006). Cristina Reis's set was a surrealist mismatch of mundane domestic objects presented in configurations that accented their distorted perspectives. The Spectators were at once presented as distant (clad in 1930s costumes) and placed in situations that stressed their proximity as audience substitutes: stepping on stage and rummaging through the onstage draws. The production was conceived as an ongoing game on theatrics where every social encounter was tainted by artifice. Even the Worker shot from his position in the dome above the lighting ring was bathed in stage blood as his body was retrieved by the lumpen sylphs-cum-stagehands, walking unemotionally off when the scene had come to an end.

Cintra's reading consciously deflected the political leanings of the piece into an affected realm that conceived the play as an evocation of the operations of theatre. Joaquin Oristrell's film *With George Bush on My Mind* (2003) used the commencement of the war in Iraq as the context for his recycling of the play as overt political drama. Here an itinerant theatre company rehearsing the play is thrown into turmoil by the death of their lead actor and the arrival of his replacement, a belligerent soap star whose seductions of the cast are conducted alongside a rallying cry for the play to be staged as an overt critique on the war and introduced by an anti-war statement at each performance. The company's actions threaten its safety however as pro-war factions confront them both inside the theatre and outside. The ghostly remnants of the play were positioned around a conceit that allowed for a discussion of issues around centralized authority (the prudish director associated with right-wing Prime Minister José María Aznar committing the country to war), cultural memory (*Play Without a Title*) and its impact on life in the present, and performance efficacy and political agitation. All theatrical and filmic productions play with our knowledges and memories of prior invocations as well as extra-theatrical materials. *With George Bush on My Mind* represents the process of staging *Play Without a Title* as a negotiation with the cultural, political, social and ethical circumstances that shape the historical moment in which a theatrical work is made and received.

Fragments and remains

The insatiable appetite for Lorca's works since the death of Franco
in 1975 has partly been due to the gaps that have been located
with the publication of his correspondence and other chronologies
of his life and work (Anderson and Maurer 1997; Gibson 1989;
Stainton 1999). While these offered a visibility to areas of his
output that had previously remained enigmatic, they also signalled
absences, fissures and cracks that have opened up considerable
academic curiosity in 'the pursuit of texts which had been lost,
censored or suppressed' (Wright 2000: 2). We know from correspondence with Dalí's sister Anna Maria in September 1925 of a
play on the sacrifice of Iphigenia, inspired by the Roman mosaic
at the port of Empúries, of which no fragments remain (OCIII
852). The following year Lorca shared ideas for a play where the
characters were 'photographic enlargements' (OCIII 882) – a
treatment remains (OCII 753; GL 1996b: 75). Mention is made
of a play on the return of Christ to Granada's Vega and a 'grand
love tragedy' called *The Beautiful Lady* but no scripts remain
(Mora Guarnido 1958: 173–4; OCIII 538). Only the first page of
The Destruction of Sodom can be consulted (OCII 765; GL
1996b: 92) although rumours of its existence in a Madrid safe-
box remain in circulation (Adams 1977: 173). What we know of
a plot Lorca once referred to as more risqué than Wilde (Gibson
1989: 396), comes from Martínez Nadal (1974: 15–16) and Luis
Sáenz de la Calzada (1976: 156–7). The latter was with Rafael
Rodríguez Rapún when Lorca read them an act of the play during
the summer of 1935. Lorca envisaged a setting that evoked both
Giotto and Piero della Francesca where the arrival of angels in
Sodom leads Lot to offer them his own virgin daughters, one of
whom he later incestuously sleeps with. The act ended with flames,
screams, wails and the harsh sound of scratching on glass or
plaster.

In an interview in early 1935, Lorca refers to an anti-war play
that he was planning to work on (OCIII 557) that Martínez Nadal
(1974: 16) fleshes out as a parable on Cain and Abel. In November
of that year, Lorca contrasts *Yerma* with a play called *Blood Has
No Voice* of such 'raw and violent passions' that it left the former

work looking as if it had 'the language of archangels' (OCIII 612). A couple of months later Lorca mentioned it again as a treatment of incest (OCIII 626–7) which holds with what we know of the play as a return to the biblical subject matter of *Gypsy Ballads*' 'Thamar and Amnon' poem (see Rivas Cherif 1957). It was likely renamed *The Taste of Blood: A Drama of Desire* and is alluded to in the list of titles and projects found among his papers (OCII 808; GL 1996b: 113).

Lorca's embrace of hyperbole leaves us unsure of how many of the 4559 projects he tantalizingly mentions in a 1935 interview might have made it to completion (OCIII 566). The speculative remains a powerful tool in Lorca scholarship. Doubt, Lacan (1988) reminds us, is a defence against the real. The putative Lorca presents the possibility of further materials that would help inscribe the 'other' Lorca of the impossible plays that have further validated the dramatist's countercultural status. While only the cast list and a single page survive of *The Black Ball* (c. 1936), the play was planned as a Linares Rivas style realist drama, opening with a son informing his pillar-of-the-community father that he's been barred from joining the local casino because he's gay (Rivas Cherif 1957).

Some projects, like *House of Maternity*, remain only as a pro-posed cast list (OCII 768), others feature established scenarios and dialogue, as with *Dreams of My Cousin Aurelia*, whose exist-ing first act was allegedly written after *The House of Bernarda Alba* for one of two actresses María Fernández Ladrón de Guevara or Carmen Díaz (OCII 878; García Lorca 1986: 233). The pitch of the dialogue is more *Doña Rosita* than *Play Without a Title* and points to the problems inherent in attempting to push the work into firm categories. While plans for the play's second act to feature the villagers in a rehearsal of Echegaray's *Stain that Cleans* (OCII 878) may point to the metatheatrical concerns of *Play Without a Title*, the lyricism of the dialogue, the provincial concerns of the characters, the playfulness of Aurelia and her complicity with the small boy point to connections with *The Shoemaker's Wonderful Wife* as well as *When Five Years Pass*.[11] The modernist dexterity of Lorca's work and his own slippery revelations ultimately render the possibility of secure groupings of plays around thematic or chronological patterns problematic (see Anderson 1986: 223). Anderson laments that Lorca's experimental drama came into the public domain too late to shape the historiographical mapping of post-war dramaturgy (Anderson 1986: 223). The Lorca canon constructed by scholars in the period up to 1976 has now mutated into a more unwieldy theatrical body that accommodates a range of myths of national, political and socio-cultural memory and points to the impossibility of ever recovering a 'truth' (either interpretative or chronological) from the textual fragments that remain.

4   Lorca's afterlives

Fredrico [*sic*] Lorca is dead and gone.
(The Clash, 'Spanish Bombs' 1979)

In 2006, on the seventieth anniversary of his death, the spectre of Federico García Lorca continues to haunt Spain's national psyche. Lying in an unmarked grave to the north-east of Granada, he functions as a potent symbol of the estimated 30,000 corpses from the Civil War and its immediate aftermath that lie buried in mass burial grounds across the country.[1] As the Fundación Federico García Lorca (FFGL), fronted by his niece Laura García-Lorca de los Ríos, pleads for his remains to rest in peace, author Ian Gibson – whose investigative works on the circumstances of his death and subsequent biographies have rendered him a persuasive spokesman for Lorca's interests – speaks for the campaign to have his corpse exhumed so that confirmation of his resting place and details of the manner of his murder can finally be verified.

Since 2000, the Association for the Recovery of Historical Memory (ARMH) has campaigned for the exhumations of civilians killed during the war and its aftermath. José Luis Rodríguez Zapatero's unanticipated victory in the 2004 general election has accorded a new profile to memory politics instituting a Law of Historical Memory that counters the collective *pacto del olvido* (pact of amnesia) that enveloped previous attempts to come to terms with the 'disremembered' traumas of the Civil War (see Davis 2005; http://www.leymemoriahistorica.com; http://www.memoriahistorica.org).

The protestations of the Lorca estate may not be able to counter the momentum this legislation will provide for those, like the families of the men assassinated alongside Lorca, who are campaigning for the disinterment of the grave's corpses. The Lorca myth was constructed in no small part through a death enveloped in mystery. Shot by nationalist troops soon after the military uprising in July 1936 that plunged Spain into civil war for three years, his name has consequently stood as a potent symbol of a liberal era brutally brought down by an illegitimate alliance of repressive right-wing forces. If the Spanish Civil War is habitually and erroneously referred to as the 'poets' war' (Cunningham 1980: 30), this is partly because it served as a rallying cry for a European intelligentsia, sufficiently perturbed at Hitler's expansionist plans and the growing profile of fascism across the continent, to take arms in support of the Spanish Republic when their own governments refused to intervene.

Lorca functioned as a figurehead for this generation, one of its own brought down by right-wing factions fearful of the power of the pen. It was a death referred to by Franco as a 'natural' accident of war (Feinstein 2004: 120); when the then President of PEN, H.G. Wells, made formal enquiries as to Lorca's whereabouts, the official reply denied all knowledge of him (Gibson 1989: 469–70). Replayed in the cultural sphere, his assassination haunts the nation's attempts to bury the scars of this fratricidal conflict. He remains a repeatedly projected image of the need to excavate the past and attempt some sense of closure on what has been referred to as 'the Spanish Holocaust' (Armengol and Belis 2004). Lorca functions as the ultimate *revenant*, the living dead that may disappear temporarily from public view but sooner or later rises again to dominate cultural discourse. Significantly, one of the few surviving reels of film footage of Lorca shows him as a spectral figure bathed in black veils performing the role of the shadow in Calderón's *Life is a Dream*. In the era of the Iraq war – from which Zapatero significantly withdrew Spanish troops on taking office – and indiscriminate terrorism – 11 March 2004 was Spain's 9/11 with 191 killed when bombs exploded on suburban trains running into Madrid's Atocha station – Lorca occupies a space between history and the imaginary. The material destruction of the body leaves behind the shadow of a corpse that returns again and again. In tracing the ways in which his life, death and poetry have been reconstructed through the performing and visual arts, this chapter examines the 'remains' of Lorca that linger in the artefacts of others. The memory of Lorca, as these 'afterlives' indicate, has refused to die.

A death replayed: poetry

The canonization of Lorca began in the immediate aftermath of his death. While Buñuel (1985: 157) disingenuously claimed that he 'never got excited about politics' and Dalí (1949: 361) reinforced this view calling him 'by essence the most a-political person on earth', his assassination and affiliation with the cultural agenda of the Second Republic marked him as 'a banner to the Spanish masses' during the Civil War (Barea 1944: 11). Illiterate *milicianos* memorized his ballads converting them into hymns for the besieged Republic and his folksongs were reset as political anthems (Barea 1944: 12–13). In 1937, Lorca's contemporary and friend, the poet Luis Cernuda, writes of the shadow of Lorca mutating into myth, concluding with the view that 'the Spanish people will never forget it' (Cernuda 1970: 153). Lorca's positioning of himself as part of an intellectual elite 'being called to sacrifice' (OCIII 545) has further fixed him within the emotionally charged terrain of martyrdom.

In his memoirs the Chilean Nobel-laureate Pablo Neruda (1977: 122) writes that 'the Spanish war, which changed my poetry, began for me with a poet's disappearance'. The unknowability of the circumstances surrounding Lorca's death was countered through attempts to make manifest that which was hidden. Antonio Machado, a further Civil War casualty who perished three years after Lorca in exile in Collioure, eulogized his death in 'The Crime Took Place in Granada', first published in October 1936, presenting those responsible as a 'platoon of executioners' who dared not face him as they pulled the triggers. Luis Cernuda's 'To a Dead Poet (F.G.L.)' celebrates Lorca as a transcendent heroic being whose existence, veiled in pain and loneliness, is liberated through the paradox of an incomprehensible death. Cernuda, like many of the other members of the Generation of 1927, mourned the death of one of their own in print. The poetic homages of Rafael Alberti, Vicente Aleixandre, José Bergamín, Jorge Guillén, Miguel Hernández, and Emilio Prados all served to reproduce 'to infinity' that which 'only occurred once' (Barthes 1982: 4).

Alberti, especially, returns repeatedly to the moment of death. The titles of the poems – 'The Coming Back of an Assassinated Poet', 'Ballad of One Who Never Went to Granada', 'I Never Went to Granada', 'Elegy for a Poet Who Never Died' and 'F.G.L' – point to their overlapping thematic concerns: a continual reinscription of the fatality of Lorca's assassination and the communist Alberti's own sense of guilt at a death that he believes should have been his. In creating a poetic 'other' body for Lorca that transcends flesh and blood, this ghost assumes a potent performative visibility that sees Alberti searching him out through the Residencia de Estudiantes in 'Federico' and conversing with Antonio Machado and Miguel Hernández in the 1942 'Funeral Eclogue to Three Voices and a Bull for the Slow Death of a Poet'. Lorca roams across the 1982 anthology 'Random Everyday Verses' like a vaporous presence, summoning Alberti, haunting the streets of New York as Alberti visits the city, a looming presence as the latter tours Granada. Alberti serializes Lorca as a Granadine martyr. Alberti becomes the ultimate custodian of the Lorca legacy: watching carefully over the international dissemination of his work in 'Chinese Song in China', and validating commemorations, as with his speech at the 1986 memorial events in Fuente Vaqueros and a high profile appearance, alongside Lorca's sister Isabel, at the premiere of *Play without a Title* in 1989.[2]

But it is not only in the poems of his Spanish-language contemporaries that the ghost of Lorca roams. The Polish poets Stanislaw Skoneczny, Stanislaw Kostka Neumann, Wlodzimierz Slobodnik, and Jan Winczakiewicz all crafted elegies to his death (Aszyk 1986: 271). The 'sudden strong repercussion of Lorca's emotive poetry on the British intellectuals who came under the sway of the Spanish War' has been mapped elsewhere (Barea 1944: 75). *The Penguin Book of Spanish Civil War Verse*, for example, features a designated section on Lorca with poems by

Geoffrey Parsons and Jacob Bronowski that conceive him as a potent metaphor for the Spanish nation and his poems a rallying anthem for Republican Spain (see Cunningham 1980: 206–8). Bronowski's 'The Death of Garcia Lorca' intertwines the imagery of picadors, matadors, Don Quixote and gypsies in a eulogy that imprisons the dead writer within prisms of Spanish exoticism.

The framing of Lorca's assassination within discourses of suffering and oppression abstracts the conditions of his death. In Greek poet Nikos Kavvadias poem 'Federico', Lorca's death is positioned alongside a massacre conducted by the Nazis during the Second World War in the Greek village of Distomo. In 'Andalusian *Casida*' the Algerian Bachir Hadj Ali binds Lorca's murder to Picasso's 'Guernica' and then further links both to the suffering of his country during the fight for independence from France.

It was not simply those who shared his political or humanitarian leanings who mapped his loss in poetic terms. In Spain, the right of centre poets Leopoldo Panero and Luis Rosales, both, like Lorca, homosexual, rendered homages that could be read by a readership who knew the discrete borders around which the public utterance of sexuality could take place. Younger poets too, not so constrained by the censorship tropes of the Franco regime, have been keen to affiliate themselves as descendants of Lorca and inheritors of a line that has no biological children. Even José María Aznar, Spain's right-of-centre Prime Minister between 1996 and 2004, recognized the political currency of affiliation with Lorca when, during the centenary celebrations of 1998, he pushed for a recognition of the latter's universalism. In stating that 'today Spain is called Federico' (Anon 1998), Aznar fabricated a unified alignment between government, playwright and state that both buried the particular historical circumstances that had led to Lorca's death and negated identity as a socially contingent construction.

A death replayed: painting

This iconography has similarly permeated representations of Lorca's death in the visual arts. Recalling their time together at the Residencia, Dalí (1949: 176) acknowledged that 'the personality of Federico García Lorca produced an immense impression upon me'. Lorca is a palpable presence – dismembered, superimposed, slyly referenced – in canvases rendered during the mid-1920s by Dalí (see pp. 22–3), but the 'impression' is arguably more powerful in death. He is cited in 'Invisible Afghan with the Apparition on the Beach of the Face of García Lorca in the Form of a Fruit Dish with Three Figs' (1938) surrounded by smouldering coals that form an eerie afghan hound, a latter day Cerberus guarding the entrance to the underworld. Lorca's face similarly dominates both 'The Endless Enigma' (1938) and 'Apparition of Face and Fruit Dish on a Beach' (1938) – in the former a hard green stone structure staring indelibly ahead, in the latter a chalk-white colossus protruding from the landscape. Here the dog who melds seamlessly into Lorca's features, may suggest a conceptual association with *Un Chien andalou*, but its optical illusions – the dog's collar may be a bridge, Lorca's face may be a bowl of fruit – suggest a mercurial, mutating Lorca unfixed in death. In 'The Three Ages' (1940), Lorca's face, positioned in eternal adolescence between that of the baby and that of the old man, contains within it the small boy who may be the young Dalí; as with 'Mysterious Mouth Appearing in the Back of My Nurse' (1941), it is a recognition of his contemporary untainted by the ravages of time.

Even in canvases where Lorca may not be immediately locatable, as with 'Metamorphosis of Narcissus' (1937), the accompanying poem by Dalí with which it was first exhibited acknowledges his presence as one of a group of revelers at the back of the painting whose sexual identity remains discretely camouflaged. If at the poem's opening the implication is that Lorca is Dalí's Narcissus, by the end Gala has taken his place as the desired other through which self is defined. The fusion of Lorca and Gala as Galsia Larca in 'Hyperxiological Sky' (1960) further conceives Gala as usurper of Lorca.[3] The subsequent doubling of the roles of Gala and Lorca in Els Joglars' theatricalized enactment of the painter's life, *Daaalí* (1999), has further served to feminize Lorca, stigmatizing him beyond androgyny into a sexual deviant seeking to entrap the younger and supposedly more vulnerable Dalí.

Dalí endorses the dominant lenses through which Lorca has been visualized in death, as martyr and Andalusian icon. Lorca is acknowledged as the point of origin for 'The Last Sacrament of the Last Supper' (1955) (Sánchez Vidal 1996: 323). Dalí also played a significant role in trapping Lorca within the iconography of the bullfight. Both Lorca and the bullfighter whose death is eulogized in 'Lament for Ignacio Sánchez Mejías' appear in 'Hallucinogenic Bullfighter' (1968–70). Engendered through the cubist Venus de Milo multiplying in the theatrical arena of the bullring, the face of the bullfighter remains masked by proliferating images of the mythical goddess. The bullfight has also proved a potent motif in affixing Lorca firmly to the Spanish psyche. References to the ring are present in a lecture delivered with Neruda where Lorca compares both to a matador fighting the bull *al alimón*, with just one cape between them (Neruda 1977: 112); a poster of a bullfight is referenced in *The Billy-Club Puppets* (OCII 53; GL 1983: 35) and Cristóbal mentions that he is on the way to a bullfight when he's made to perform in *The Puppet Play of Don Cristóbal* (OCII 400; GL 1990; 69). The *ex-libris* Dalí drew for Lorca in 1921 features a *torero* and bull. Alberti (1987: 209) refers to him as 'a kind of great poetic bullfighter'; the critic Alfredo de la Guardia (1952: 78) as a bullfighter without a suit of lights.

The circumstances of his death, shot alongside two minor bullfighters, further positioned him within an artform whose ritualistic structure is viewed as one of the few surviving remnants of the popular religious theatre festivals of Dionysian Greece (Ortega y Gasset 1958: 81). The circular enclosure of the ring, the ceremonious spectacle framing loss and success in a public manner, the focus on pose and deft movement, the dazzling costume, the division of the combat into what can be seen as *stanzas*, each to be successfully realized before the action can progress, all lend the *corrida* the air of a theatrical performance. Novelist A.L. Kennedy acknowledges Lorca as her 'way into the corrida', his imagination returning, like that of Dalí, 'again and again to the image of Saint Sebastian: a man martyred, much as the bull is – and much as the torero can be – by multiple, public penetrations' (Kennedy 2000: 37).

These penetrations are on display in the backdrop Dalí produced for La Argentinita's ballet *Café de Chinitas* in 1943, based
on the songs recorded with Lorca on the piano in 1931. Here the
bleeding crucified guitar functions as an emblematic reminder of
martyrdom. It is imagery that resounds in British artist Terry
Frost's compositions to the poet realized during 1989: 'Lament
for Lorca', 'Lament for Ignacio Sánchez Mejías' and '5 in the
Afternoon (Lorca)'. Predominantly non-figurative, these paintings
draw on a colour palette and object association that juggles shapes
from the bullfight with imagery redolent of female sexuality. The
bullfight and its incarnation as a discourse through which to read
Lorca's death fuses romantic necrology with the glamour of a
gladiatorial battle waged in the eye of a public arena. The bull's
horn, a substitute for the phallus, points to the dangers of a
sexuality where penetration and annihilation are problematically
interwoven. The juxtaposition of *toreo* with a civil conflict that
was to claim the lives of 365,000 merges both in the public
consciousness, privileging a narrative of supposed inevitable
fatality that has further been played out in the treatments of
Lorca's death realized in the cinematic and theatrical sphere.[4]

A death replayed: Lorca the movie

The redemptive features strongly in the vocabularies used to
represent Lorca's life on stage and screen (see Smith 1998:
105–13). Republican exile playwright José Antonio Rial's *The
Death of García Lorca* (1978) focuses on the final three days of
Lorca's life as the playwright comes to accept what is presented
as the inevitable imminence of his execution. The two film biopics
produced in 1987 and 1997, *Lorca, Death of a Poet* directed by
Juan Antonio Bardem and *The Disappearance of García Lorca*,
directed by Marcos Zurinaga, both begin with Lorca's death,
signalling it as the defining act in assessing both his life and work.

Lorca, Death of a Poet opens with Lorca stepping into a
spotlight as his name is called out, a figure dressed in a spotless
white suit with bow tie impeccably in place. The stage onto
which he steps, however, is no theatre but the arena of his death,
an open-topped truck in which he is driven to the site of his

assassination: a dusty track where, flanked by two bullfighters and discreetly followed by a limping schoolteacher, he takes the steps to his calvary. The iconography of the sequence alludes to the sacrificial: 'a triangular composition reminiscent of Christ framed by the two thieves' (Smith 1998: 111–12). Lorca may have spent three or four nights in dirty prison cells but he remains untainted by his sordid surroundings. At the end of the film, as the sequence is replayed, we witness Lorca animating his cellmates as they are unceremoniously told of their impending death. Lorca kneels stoically in confession, illuminated by a brilliant white light shining from the open door of the cell (see Figure 11). This is a death imbued with the religious language of redemption. His is the blood that will nourish the arid lands of Spain that feature early in the narrative and return at the film's end littered with olive groves (see also Smith 1998: 108).

Figure 11 Lorca as beatified saint: Nickolas Grace as Lorca in Bardem's *Lorca, Death of a Poet*, 1987. Photo: Suevia Films

Even in the longer six-part mini-series from which the film version was cut, each 55-minute episode is prefixed by the repeated image of Lorca's walk to his execution. All aspects of his life are ultimately reduced to the inevitability of this single act: the narrative an ongoing obituary with a predetermined and inevitable end. The myth of Lorca serves as a repository for fantasies about the symbolic body transcending death in an act of integrity that bestows on him the immortality he now enjoys as the ultimate cultural patriarch of the new Spain exemplified by film director Pedro Almodóvar. 'Bodiless' he may be but his spirit is seen to epitomize an ethereal agency; in death a *corpus* containing within it the possibility for a nation's self-reflection.

Throughout the film shots of a tormented Lorca, wandering anxiously through the garden of the Huerta de San Vicente, unable to sleep, nervously retuning the radio from a nationalist channel, contained within sallow cell walls, are juxtaposed with Republican sympathizers (often women and children) protesting on the streets, rounded up and shot by the Nationalists. He is positioned from the start as the chosen one, linked to the moon – which the camera lingers on as the white-suited Lorca heads into the family home – and the bullfight, the bull charging into the ring as Lorca attempts to sleep (Smith 1998: 109). His name is called out by the wind as the film flashes back to the boy Federico playing outdoors, suggesting an inherent and organic identification with the land. Even the casting of the English-actor Nickolas Grace as the poet underpins a conception of Lorca as the perennial outsider. Dubbed into a Spanish that bears no traces of the peculiarities of his Granadine accentuation, here Lorca becomes divorced from the context that engendered him. In appropriating him for the Spanish nation, his Granadine links are severed into tastefully composed images of Lorca framed against picture postcard backdrops of the city's oft-reproduced monuments.

Both *Lorca, Death of a Poet* and *The Disappearance of García Lorca* conceive the Nationalists who arrested Lorca as cardboard caricatures sporting the malevolent moustaches of Hollywood villains. In *Lorca, Death of a Poet* the thuggish Nationalist alliance of Falangists, the army and Civil Guard conspire clandestinely in smoke-filled rooms. Their characterizations generated complaints in the Spanish press when the TV series was first broadcast on Spanish national television's flagship channel, RTVE 1, in 1987–8, from those who could not reconcile the series' aspiration to historical accuracy with a mentality that criminalized the Nationalists, conceived Lorca's homosexuality as effeminacy, and left his poetry and plays trailing behind as secondary vehicles to his flamboyant life (e.g. Arauz de Robles 1988; Orozco 1988).

In *The Disappearance of García Lorca*, Cuban American actor Andy García refracts the poet through the 'Hispanic' imagination, denationalizing him in ways that stress his global importance and his representativeness across the international sphere. Here Lorca's Spanishness is enacted across the register of *Latinidad* with García drawing problematic generalized analogies between Lorca's predicament and those who died during the Cuban revolution (Estévez 1997: 22). This is a Lorca who speaks with a marked Cuban American accent. The opening scene sees the anguished rendition of 'Lament for Ignacio Sánchez Mejías' from Lorca in his prison cell. The recital is superimposed over images of Franco and the Civil War, fusing both biography and writings in ways that misrepresent the latter's context. 'At five in the afternoon', the repeated refrain from 'Lament for Ignacio Sánchez Mejías', is positioned as a prediction of Lorca's death rather than his comment on the death of a friend. As with the final lines from *The House of Bernarda Alba* that ring out as the guns sound out in *Lorca, Death of a Poet*, the *oeuvre* is judged a biographical hinge, a means of explaining his life.

This is a ploy appropriated by Francisco Suárez and Rafael Amargo in their respective theatrical adaptations of Lorca's best known poetic anthologies, *Gypsy Ballads* (2004) and *Poet in New York* (2003). In both, Lorca becomes a physical protagonist of the onstage drama, holding together the enacted vignettes of the individual poems. Biography becomes a way of explaining the text with key characters from the poems embodied as if they represented the author's subconscious. In *Gypsy Ballads*, the Moon and her shadow watch over Lorca – her feminine energy contrasted with the darker presence of the masculine shadow. Lorca's early appearance from a blinding light at the back of the stage introduces him as a redemptive icon that appears from the heavens to fulfil a preordained role.

The Disappearance of García Lorca was, according to one Spanish critic, 'Hollywood discovering Lorca' (Boo 1997) with a glamorous love interest for Esai Morales's investigative writer, Ricardo, piecing together the final days of Lorca's life, picturesque locations, and the shifting of events and characters into the terrain of the fictional. Luis Rosales and his brothers are recast as the Falangist Nestor González. In a smoky bohemian bar, sailors – Granada is not a port city – mingle with prostitutes, flamenco artistes, police informers and punters. The Alhambra is forever cloaked in atmospheric mist. An action-packed ending at the bullfight brings the detective writer face to face with his antagonists and the mysterious bullfighter who witnessed the assassination. Morales's writer, visiting Granada in order to complete his book on Lorca, embodies a stance where critical understanding comes solely through identification. Only by tracing Lorca's steps, suffering arrest and institutional violence from those who arrested his icon, can he hope to understand the work.

In Jaime Chávarri's *To an Unknown God* (1977), a fleeting encounter with the playwright marks José (Héctor Alterio) for life. Lorca is here a shadowy presence at the window, an emblem of a mythologized childhood in Granada. His poetry, however, is embedded into the fabric of the elder José's life as the latter listens to his 'Ode to Walt Whitman' from *Poet in New York* on a nightly basis. Lorca's photo is a prized possession clandestinely stolen from a friend's house. In *Specters of Marx*, Derrida (1994: 3–48) writes of disjunction as decisive in its interruption, a decentering and desyncronization of the unifying thinking of totalizing regimes. Ghosts need not be exorcized but they need to be acknowledged. José's disjunction, being 'out of joint', is seen as a necessity in facilitating justice. The process of self-critique undertaken in the film allows him to rethink his relationship to his individual past and that of the nation. The spectre of Lorca is seen to be a catalyst in this process.[5]

Jaime Camino's *The Open Balcony* (1984) situates Lorca as the transnational prophet of a contemporary multiculturalism that transcends geographical boundaries. His life, work and iconography are abstracted, jumbled and juxtaposed in an appreciative elegy that sees his legacy as all pervasive – from Spanish school-children to elderly African Americans, from heterosexual couples escaping the errant eye of a watchful parent to a gay pairing objectified and eroticized through their racial difference, from errant gypsies to Holy Week Penitents, he is envisaged as an authoritative voiceover who 'speaks' to the continued oppression of marginalized groups. The approach is in many ways exemplified in the closing scene of *The House of Bernarda Alba* presented in the film. It shows Adela fornicating in the stable with Pepe and then her dead body hanging from the ceiling. *The Open Balcony* is about making visible that which is reported or alluded to, that which is not manifest.

Carlos Rojas's novel *The Ingenious Gentleman and Poet Federico García Lorca Ascends to the Underworlds* (1979) speculates on the directions Lorca's life might have taken had he not been killed. Miguel Hermoso's film, *The End of a Mystery* (2003), takes this process of fetishizing the absent other to the extreme of a conceit that contemplates the possibility that Lorca was not killed but merely wounded and left for dead. Rescued by an adolescent shepherd, Joaquín, who is unaware of his identity, the brain-damaged Lorca, renamed Galápago, is left in a hospice when the young shepherd is conscripted. Forty years later Joaquín returns to Granada searching out the now homeless poet, who roams the streets of the city. The film concerns both Joaquín's attempts to find out who Galápago is (following the detective dimensions of Bardem and Zurinaga's narrative treatments) and, in the vein of *Rain Man* (1988), maps the emotive benefits of association with a savant. Adapted from Fernando Marías's 1991 novel it preaches the stability and sanctity gained from kinship and forgiveness at a time when the Association for the Recovery of Historical Memory was gaining national momentum. This is a buddy movie that sees the lonely Joaquín find a new purpose in life following the death of his wife. The film bathes Lorca/Galápago in an air of sanctity – soft-focus camerawork, hues of golden warm light that point to parallels with the birth of Jesus – here tended to in a barn by a lowly shepherd who heeds the advice of the generous doctor not to inform the authorities of the

event. The elderly Lorca/Galápago is seen at home among the
crackheads of the city protected by children and bakers who view
him as a lucky presence. He is now seen to be part of the under-
classes he commemorated – his New York poem 'King of Harlem'
is read out in the film – and the conclusion asks not that Lorca's
resurrection be announced but that he remain camouflaged among
the lower depths of the city.

A life replayed: performing Lorca

While *The End of a Mystery* pursues the familiar path of
fetishizing the playwright's murder, there has also been a move
to eschew the myth of the tortured death-driven genius that
encircles Lorca. Australian actor Trader Faulkner's one-man
show, *Lorca*, first seen at the Royal Shakespeare Company in
1970 with English actor Ben Kingsley in the title role, and then
reprised at regular intervals over the next twenty-five years, has
evolved through various mutations in ways that recognize the
shifting resonances of Lorca's life and work. In the 1994 production, at London's Lilian Baylis Theatre, sexual politics were
overtly foregrounded with political dialogues and a love letter to
Dalí juxtaposed with the more familiar setting to flamenco dance
of his poems. Lorca is framed as the pre-eminent father of modern
'multicultural' Spain in his own fusing of Gypsy, Islamic and
Jewish influences. *Lorca* was the first of a conspicuous number
of one-man shows that have appropriated the confessional forms
of live art to a treatment of authorship that recognizes the filter
of the performer and/or translator as key to the construction of
audience meaning. From Pig Iron Theatre Company's *Poet in New
York* (2000) to Emily Lewis' *Hace Federico* at London's Arcola
Theatre in 2006, the life and work of Lorca have been indelibly
fused as kernal structures for wider meditations on identity
politics, the construction of self and the processes of theatremaking.

While many tribute shows have followed the terrain of Spanish
director José Sámano's *A Short While, a Minute, a Century* (1998)
in trying to ensure that the audience left the theatre knowing
exactly who Lorca was (Sesé 1998), director Lluís Pasqual has

acknowledged this as an impossibility (Antón 1998). The approaches he has taken in such productions as *The Steps of Federico* (1988), *Doing Lorca* (1996), *The Dark Root* (1998) and *How a City Sings from November to November* (1998) have sought to construct a Lorca that recognizes the impossibility of delivering a unified or 'real' entity (see Delgado 2003: 217–21). Lorca is created through the encounter between the textual and the mythological realized by the cast, directors and audience. Lorca is as much an imagined and constructed entity as he is a bona fide referent.

This process of deconstructing the mythologization of Lorca has governed the most resonant theatrical and filmic treatments of Lorca and his legacy. Osvaldo Golijov's *Ainadamar*, directed by Peter Sellars for Santa Fe Opera in 2005, displaces Lorca as author of his work and life by mapping his professional inter-sections with actress Margarita Xirgu in ways that question a theatrical hierarchy that places individual authorship at its pinnacle. Lorca is here a mezzo-soprano, an androgynous entity that recognizes the modes in which the dramatist has functioned as a canvas on which successive generations have projected their desires and fears. Lola Guerrero's film *The Crime of a Bride* (2006) uses the preparatory research of an actress taking on the role of the Bride in *Blood Wedding* to interrogate the mythology that surrounds both play and playwright.

It is a process of interrogating the emotive associations of the playwright, much in the vein of Galician actor Pepe Rubianes's *They Were all Lorcas* (2006), which acknowledges the process of creative reconstruction that distinguishes all attempts to piece together the unknown of Lorca's final days. The play's title comes from the memorial stone placed in the mass burial ground where Lorca's remains are thought to lie. In framing his death alongside that of those who lie alongside him in Víznar, the play served as a rallying cry for the Socialist Government's Law of Historical Memory. Its thematics became emblematically interlinked with Rubianes's perceived insults on a centralized Spanish state and the play was pulled from Madrid's Español Theatre following pressure from the Partido Popular-controlled City Council which subsidizes the venue. The play's supposed ban was emphatically affiliated to Lorca's checkered trajectory under Franco and the spectres of censorship that had exerted their ugly influence on the supposedly democratic structures of the new Spain.

Beyond Spain, Peter Straughn's BBC radio play *The Ghost of Federico García Lorca Which Can Also Be Used as a Table* (2000) also conceives him as a returning ghost. In *Lorca in a Green Dress* (2003), Nilo Cruz creates multiple Lorcas suspended in a purgatory positioned between life and death; the repressed never fully effaced. Caridad Svich has traced the 'phantom memory' of Lorca's dramaturgy on her own plays and those of her Latino contemporaries and mentors – José Rivera, María Irene Fornés, Alejandro Morales and Migdalia Cruz – as a process 'whereby one is always constantly in the shadows, chasing after Lorca' (Svich 1999: 193). In the USA, the fourth-largest Spanish-speaking nation in the world, Lorca functions as emblematic of a particular linguistic dislocation, a 'meeting point' for bilingual writers who have fused their dramatic vocabularies with his in the act of translating the works (Svich 2007: 13). Nilo Cruz recognizes the ghost of Lorca that hovers over his own dramatic language by recreating him as an agony aunt to the gay painter, Emiliano, protagonist of *Beauty of the Father* (2004). Both are outsiders punished for their transgression; in Emiliano's case this has involved an enforced separation from his daughter, in Lorca's assassination. Whereas in Spain, the ghost of Lorca hangs over the nation as a painful reminder of an unresolved past, here he is an artistic muse for the gay artist, a poetic fantasy envisaged in Michael Greif's 2006 Manhattan Theatre Club production in a pristine white linen suit that corroborates his otherworldliness.

From Lindsay Kemp and Christopher Bruce's *Cruel Garden* (1977) to La Fura dels Baus's *Ombra* (1998), from Brazil's Studio Lourdes Bastos's *¡Viva Lorca!* (1986) to Cuba's Ballet de Lizt Alfonso's *Sincerely Federico García Lorca* (1998), across the cultural mainstream and the fringe, the canonization of Lorca has taken place through the realms of performance where the 'living effigy, the actor, functions as a fetishized substitute for the corpse' (Roach 1998: 27). The consistent rebirth of the poet of *Cruel Garden* explains the allure of the clichéd incarnations through which Lorca has been conceived: *matador*, gypsy, silent movie star, martyr. It points to the legacy of a myth that continues to seduce.[6]

A death replayed: sex, drugs and rock'n'roll

Because, above all, I am a musician.

(OCIII 440)

Lorca's poetry, conceived for public performance, has, posthumously, been appropriated for performative ends – from Ana Belén's easy listening pop 'Lorquiana' (1998) to Caoutchouc's jazz-infused 'Plays García Lorca' (1993). There is a musical legacy that builds on his associations with particular musical forms, like flamenco, the reverberations of his writings on *duende* and the identification with, and endorsement of, his 'outsider' status by rock icons who have sung of his martyrdom.

An accomplished pianist and arranger – the recording of Spanish folk songs made with La Argentinita remains in distribution (see Tinnell 1998: 435–64) – Lorca's fascination with popular musical forms is evident in his lectures on *cante jondo* and lullabies as well as the tempi of his dramatic works, compared to sonatas and concertos (Honig 1945: 140). Songs, ditties, ballads and references from liturgical chant and popular operettas pepper his plays; musical structures – arias, recitatives, chorales – have been located as the cornerstones of his dramatic composition (see OCIII 379; Stainton 1999: 301). There are over 200 recordings listed of his poems reworked as Gregorian chant, symphonies, concertos, operas and song cycles (Tinnell 1998: 469–503). From Paul Bowles to Simon Holt, Michael Nyman to Joni Mitchell, Robert Wyatt to Donovan, Francis Poulenc to Hans Werner Henze, Enrique Morente to Camarón de la Isla, Lorca has provided the lyrical frame for melodic strains from minimalism to flamenco rock.

One of the most persistent conceptions of Lorca is that of the gypsy poet and, like Falla, he turned to this indigenous race both as object, as in *Gypsy Ballads* and as discourse – their most visible manifestation, flamenco, provides both form and subject for *Poem of the Deep Song*. Lorca's appropriation of the codes of flamenco's *cante jondo* recognizes the social and political potency of a metaphorical performative language that 'has the potential to express the sentimental identity of the Volk, whether it be in the service of the jingoism of the Francoist regime (*nacional-flamenquismo*) or the anthropological fabulism of Falla' (Stone 2004: 14).

In turn, a range of flamenco artists have appropriated Lorca's verses in their jazz, blues, rap, acid-house and hip-hop flamenco fusions. The long list who have recorded his ballads, lullabies and poems includes Enrique Morente, Esperanza Fernández, Manolo Tena and Remedios Amaya. It is, however, those who have auto-destructed through cocktails of drugs and alcohol who have become most bound up with the Lorca myth. Pata Negra's Rafael Amador and Camarón de la Isla remain the primary exponents of a romantic dissolution 'live fast/die young' ethos.[7] The former's recording of 'Ballad of the Three Rivers' from *Poem of the Deep Song* and the latter's of *Blood Wedding*'s Act 1, Scene 2 lullaby remain landmarks in the shift of flamenco from a purist guitar and voice formula to the incorporation of wider instrumentation and orchestration. If Lorca is associated with a theatre that fuses tradition and the avant-garde so those who have commandeered his poems have similarly propelled their cultural discourses towards innovation and change.

The fascination that Lorca's persona and work continue to exert across the musical sphere indicates a craving towards modes of experiencing death vicariously, by proxy, and reliving it continuously, containing the danger by keeping it at bay. Lorca's early canonization as 'the poet of the revolution' (Anon 1936d) fixed him as a countercultural icon: the voice of the vanquished. In The Clash's 'Spanish Bombs' (1979), he is the enduring symbol of what was lost with the Republican defeat at the end of the Civil War. The Pogues' emotive 'Lorca's Novena' (1990), produced by The Clash's Joe Strummer, mourns his death as a homophobic act: 'the faggot poet they left till last/Blew his brains out with a pistol up his arse'. The alignment to Genet, another gay icon celebrated on the 1990 'Hell's Ditch' album, is also evident in the lyrics of Marc Almond, the former Soft Cell frontman, for whom homosexual affirmation has been indelibly bound up with the location of a queer sensibility that views both writers, like Wilde, Rimbaud and Cocteau, as enabling resources that allow for the articulation of 'other' voices.

Lorca's rendering of the experiential and the intangible through the iconography of the material world in such anthologies as *Poet in New York* and *Gypsy Ballads* has proved alluring to rock artists, like Tim Buckley and Nick Cave, who see music as a force for social debate, existentialist enquiry and aesthetic experimentation. *Poet in New York* confirmed Lorca as the perennial poet of urban dislocation, singing of a commercial edifice that breeds collective angst and modernist soul-searching. In a Spanish state punctured by the nationalist agendas of the different autonomous regions, the appropriation of poems from the anthology by Catalan protest singer Lluís Llach and Basque vocalist Patxi Andión indicates the continued allure of a supposedly national poet that has not been unequivocally hijacked by centrist politics.

It is worth noting the plethora of artists from across the musical sphere that have participated in the annual concerts held in the gardens of the Huerta de San Vicente Lorca museum: Patti Smith (1998), Ben Sidran Quartet (1998), Lou Reed (1998), Suzanne Vega (2000), Ali Farka Toure (2000), David Byrne (2001), and Chavela Vargas (2004). Leonard Cohen gave his daughter Lorca's name as a tribute to the poet he claims as a brother. One of Cohen's most celebrated songs, 'Take This Waltz' (1988), is based on a translation of the poem 'Little Viennese Waltz' from the posthumous *Poet in New York* anthology. Nick Cave references him in 'I'm on Fire' (2003) and Lorca's 1933 lecture on *duende* has served as referent for his own reflections on the void of loss that can be written into existence through literary and musical language (Cave, *The Secret Life of the Love Song*, 1999).

In our secular age, *duende* is located by Cave as a 'font of inspiration and guidance' (ibid.). Rather than a methodology or thought, it is the instinct that propels artistic creation, 'a power' that produces 'an almost religious enthusiasm' (OCIII 151, 155; GL 1991: 43, 46). The intangibility of *duende* has led to its dismissal as mystical nonsense but it is a reminder that destruction does have an intimate relationship with creativity, even if it is simply the destruction of the empty space that precedes it, or the necessary removal of the earlier, poorer forms that lead to a finished piece of work.

(Kennedy 2000: 39)

Duende's potency as a referent for the metaphor of artistic creation goes beyond the registers of the rational or the explainable – it is an invisible link that binds artist and audience through the thrill of the live.

The branding of Lorca: Granada, cultural tourism and the heritage industry

In Allen Ginsberg's 'A Supermarket in California' (Ginsberg 2000: 29–30), the poet's encounter with the dead Lorca in the watermelon section of the supermarket serves to position him, alongside Walt Whitman, whom he eyes by the meat counter casting furtive glances at grocery boys, as a decisive influence on his work. In positioning Lorca within the myths of consumerism, as a disposable product, hovering in the landscapes of capitalist America that the latter found so disturbing and disorientating, he points to a commodification that has seen multifarious quarters seek to 'own' their slice of Lorca and his legacy (see pp. 6–7, 173–4, 198–9).

Lorca has become as much a brand name as Picasso or Dalí and nowhere is this more apparent than in his native city of Granada. Here he is as familiar an icon as Shakespeare in Stratford-upon-Avon, a potent cultural token, appropriated and exchanged by the bourgeois society he so vehemently criticized.[8] From the moment a visitor touches down at Federico García Lorca airport to the west of the city – renamed in his honour from 19 June 2006 – he is a monumental reference point. Any number of authorized and unauthorized tourist websites and guidebooks offer heritage trails that allow the reader 'to commune with the lost Granada of Lorca and Falla' (Gibson 1992: 49).[9] Ian Gibson's *Lorca's Granada*, first published in 1992, provides ten tours of the city and the surrounding area that allows even the most diehard Lorca fan an opportunity to survey what remains of the houses in which he lived, to take in the poet Luis Rosales's house where he was arrested, and the cafés and cultural establishments he frequented. Every epoch of Lorca's time in the city is referenced against the particulars of the buildings and landscapes that shaped his consciousness. Forget the Alhambra as a military fortress of the Nasrid dynasty, rulers of the last Spanish Muslim kingdom, this is Granada enveloped with a romantic sentimentality that promotes this distinctive Moorish architectural feat as a backdrop to Lorca's adventures. Lorca now functions as part of the mystery of Granada; his homes, haunts and supposed burial ground as much part of the cityscape as the Alhambra, Albaycín and Sacromonte caves. Granada is expanding its touristic potential by positioning itself as the indispensable location to be visited in understanding the writer's work. As one taxi driver scathingly observed to me 'Here, everything begins with Lorca'.

It was not always so. In the aftermath of the Civil War, with his immediate family in exile and remaining friends maintaining a cautious silence, traces of the dramatist were wiped from the city. Few dared visit the pits where the executions of Republican sympathizers had taken place (Brenan 1951: 137–60). The ravine at Víznar, where Lorca's remains were thought to lie, became a site of unofficial pilgrimage. To gather there was a dangerous act under the Franco regime but flowers, nevertheless, appeared religiously on the night of 18 August and it remains a central site of Lorca worship to this day. The construction of a monumental garden in 1986, named in the dramatist's honour, commemorates those interred along the gully that stretches along the road from Alfacar to Víznar. Imposing iron gates enclose the garden and its centrepiece fountain surrounded by ceramic plaques carrying verses of the poet's work. A solitary olive tree close to the lower gate marks Lorca's supposed burial site.

The Fundación Federico García Lorca, arguably the clerical body of the Lorca cult, may not yet have its headquarters in Granada (see pp. 197–8) but its presence is evident across the three Lorca museums which can be visited in Granada. The first opened in 1986, in Fuente Vaqueros, at the house on 4 Calle de la Trinidad (now predictably renamed in his honour) where Lorca was born and lived for the first seven years of his life (see Figure

12). Purchased and restored by the Diputación (County Council) in 1980, under the watchful gaze of the writer's sister, Isabel, it has enjoyed more than 2 million visitors between 1986 and 2006. It houses an archive of costumes, posters, models and drawings from past productions, but the memorabilia on display in the

Figure 12 The Lorca tourist trail in Granada: left to right clockwise: T-shirts featuring Lorca's emblematic signature alongside those of bulls and Arabic insignia on sale in the city; the graffiti-marked entrance to the García Lorca park, location of the Huerta de San Vicente house museum; a bust of Lorca in the gardens of Lorca's birthplace, the Fuente Vaqueros Casa Natal museum; the Huerta de San Vicente museum. Photos: Maria M. Delgado

upstairs granary exhibition space, is largely decontextualized, a series of lone artefacts dislocated from their context of production and reception. Hourly guided tours boast of the authenticity of furniture stored lovingly by devoted servants or purchased under auction in the hope of providing a trip back in time to a house untouched by the forces of history. Cultural weight is further attributed to the venture by the signed comments and clipboard of photographs of visiting cultural, political and regal dignitaries (including Salman Rushdie, Leonard Cohen and the King and Queen of Spain) that testify to the lasting 'greatness' of the authorial voice. Projections of the only surviving film footage of Lorca to the accompanying soundtrack of musical arrangement of folksongs for La Argentinita forge together the dismembered remains of the author in a single sound and light show. Even if you can not visit in person, the tour provided by the museum's website familiarizes the virtual tourist with the museum's artifacts and events.[10] Physical distance is no impediment to the Lorca experience.

In the neighbouring village of Valderrubio, the family summer house from 1907 to 1925, offers a less self-regarding Lorca museum. With no official website, no printed tickets, allowing inside photography and a consideration of the locations that surround the edifice, it is positioned more as cultural amenity than monument, with the makeshift theatre in the stables at the back of the house betraying a space in use. That historical reconstruction is never neutral or transparent is evident from the description of objects stressing that what has been selected for display does not necessarily reflect what might have been in place when Lorca lived in the house. The narrative presented by tour guide José Pérez Rodríguez is one of acknowledging the selection of evidence based on availability and financial limitations. There is at present no provision for the sale of souvenirs.

While there is a small stall selling postcards, posters and in-house editions of the works funded by Granada's county council at the museum in Fuente Vaqueros, relic worship is more prevalent at the Huerta de San Vicente. The summer house of the García Lorca family from 1926, the Huerta, is situated to the south of Granada in what was the Vega but is now residential suburbs carved up by a giant ring road that runs across the periphery of the city. Bought by the City Council from the García Lorca family in 1985 and opened ten years later, it has been converted into a museum located within a park that takes the poet's name (see Figure 12). Much is made of the historical reconstruction of an original whose sepia images adorn the accompanying publicity leaflet. Nevertheless we are constantly reminded of the manifest process of recovery and appropriation that marks the trans-formation of the abode: the closed off areas that provide storage space for archive material, the construction work that knocked his parents' and sisters' rooms into a single exhibition space, the rumble of the motorway in the distance, the graffiti that refuses to be wiped off the facade of the house. Granada may aspire to offer the retracing of Lorca's routes and routines unimpaired by the forces of historical change, but these cannot easily be erased.

Paradoxically, these are also capitalized on when appropriate: as with the interactive science museum, Parque de las Ciencias' 'Lorca's Universe', a multimedia animation extravaganza that presents Lorca as speaking subject collaborating with the Moon in a poetic guide to the Cosmos. The cultural cachet of the son of Granada providing a link to the world beyond has not been lost on the marketplace of the city's newest museum. The Lorca myth may trade on the past but it can be harnessed towards the understanding of scientific phenomena and the possibilities of the future when necessary.[11]

Nowhere is Lorca's status as registered cultural trademark more evident, however, than at the Huerta. On entry or exit the visitor can acquire any number of trinkets and souvenirs. In-house editions feature the Huerta's brand logo. Fans imprinted with the famed Lorca signature offer an icon of Andalusia authen-ticated by the playwright's brand association. Mugs and espresso cups facilitate material consumption. Pencils, rubbers, notebooks and bookmarks provide discerning artefacts for the budding writer. Earrings, broaches and T-shirts adorned with the poet's illustrations allow us to 'wear' Lorca and not just on our sleeve.

The symbolic function of a souvenir or photograph is partly acquisitive – you exhibit it to show that you've been there, done that place – but it also operates, like the medieval relic, as the embodiment of an experience: a trigger for memory, with a magical capacity to release recollection: a mnemonic device designed to preserve memory from the wastage of time.

(Holderness 1988: 7)

The Huerta is the ultimate site of worship with pilgrims arriving sporting tattoos bearing Lorca's emblematic signature and dressed in his trademark white linen suit with hair groomed in deference. These are the *enlorquecidos*, an adjective that reworks the Spanish for 'going out of your mind' to the particularities of Lorca adoration that the shrine attracts and the contemporary stigmata that the faithful display with due pride.

This is not to denigrate the educational work conducted by these institutions or the valuable archival resources housed there. The Huerta's 'Poetry for beginners' programme works with local schools to facilitate group visits and interactive workshops.[12] It is however important to position these initiatives as part of the appropriation of Lorca into the ideological apparatus of both the city and the nation. Arts enterprises are inseparable from business imperatives: 'the stability of the market society depends crucially on a matrix of cultural traditions which at once legitimate it and find expression in it' (Gray 1993: 43). Lorca functions as such a potent symbol within democratic Spain for this very reason: he allows for the articulation of particular ideologies and their discontents. His impregnable status within the school and university curriculum renders him a powerful hegemonic instrument. That Lorca remains a site of ideological struggle is discernible in the Huerta's temporary closure in 1996, seven months after the Socialist PSOE lost control of the City Council, when a cut in funding rendered it impossible to pay the guides (García 1998: 38). The proposed move of the Madrid-based Fundación Federico García Lorca in late 2009 to a newly constructed temple in central Granada, the Centro García Lorca, looks to embed the Lorca myth even more firmly within the cityscape. The vested financial interest of a range of local and national institutions, including the Ministry of Culture, the Fundación Federico García Lorca, Granada City Council, and the Andalusian Government, in the construction and operation of the 18.5 million euro building complete with multipurpose theatre space, administrative offices, exhibition halls, a library, bar and shop, looks to ensure the centring of Lorca as a national symbol controlled from a city that demonstrates the possibilities of regional autonomy.

Lorca as commodity

Ownership of Lorca has proved a fraught issue in contemporary Spain. Gibson, Lorca's biographer, now enjoys something of the role of custodian: widely consulted and quoted on matters pertaining to the poet's inheritance and visibility. It is not insignificant that one critic labelled 1998 not Lorca's year but Gibson's, with Gibson's commentary exhaustively sought on declarations made by both politicians and the family members who front the Fundación Federico García Lorca (Castillo Gallego 1998). In print, academics and translators endorse the legitimacy of *their* Lorca: proximity to Lorca lending them by association something of the aura that envelops him (see Edwards 1988; Johnston 1998b). When 1989 Nobel Prizewinner, Camilo José Cela, publicly criticized the appropriation of the dramatist's centenary events by 'homosexual elements' it provoked nation-wide indignation (see Moix 1998; Rosetti et al. 1998). The auctioning of manuscripts and drawings through the 1980s and 1990s has further whet the appetites of the riches that might yet emerge (Pulido 1995). The Lorca estate, fronted initially by his nephew Manuel Fernández-Montesinos and, since 2005, by his niece Laura García-Lorca de los Ríos, are the ultimate arbitrators of the Lorca corpus, authorizing translations for staging and publication, approving or otherwise uses of the writer's words for advertising, film and television. The family's refusal to comment on *Lorca, Death of a Poet* in 1988, claiming not to have yet seen it, and its denigration of *The Disappearance of García Lorca* were viewed as a public delegitimization of both projects (Sánchez Bardón 1988: 111; Tapia 1997).

The battle for ownership of the writer's work saw the Lorca heirs take out a court injunction to prevent the sale of the surviving manuscript of *Poet in New York*. The subsequent trial in 2002 at the Royal Courts of Justice in London pitted Fernández-Montesinos against the then owner of the manuscript Manola Saavedra de Aldama, a Mexican actress who had performed in two of Lorca's works. The sale went ahead and while the Fundación Federico García Lorca was to secure the manuscript through auction on 4 June 2003 at a price of £120,000, they were also to incur, as losers, legal costs thought to be in excess of £400,000 (Lennon 2002). This was 'Lorca the Soap Opera', a *culebrón* that was to be played out beyond the stage of the High Courts of Justice in both the Spanish and UK press (see Hart 2003: 283; Ruiz Mantilla 2003). With allegations that the estate had duplicitously used an intermediary to try to secure the manuscript in 1997–8 and sought to manipulate the sale price of the manuscript (Hart 2003: 279, 283), the Lorca heirs were presented as wily schemers not beyond utilizing underhand means to secure what they perceived as legitimately theirs.

The case indicates the ways in which Lorca's authorial body is now perceived as public property. Lorca's anniversaries are national celebrations with the dramatist paraded across the pages of Spain's established broadsheets and celebrity magazines like *¡Hola!* and *Semana*. The centenary celebrations in 1998 opened with King Juan Carlos and Queen Sofía's public blessing of the Lorca year with a pilgrimage across Granada's Lorca landmarks (see Delgado 2003: 220; El Khattat 1998). Both were keen to endorse the author as the sublime, mystical locus of contemporary Spain, with King Juan Carlos stressing his authority to profess such judgements in having read all Lorca's poetry (Calleja 1998).

Beyond the governmental sphere, association with Lorca lends artistic credibility and kudos. Rafael Alberti and Nuria Espert's poetry recitals of Lorca in the 1980s toured extensively with the former, longenitor of the Generation of 1927, viewed as arbiter of Lorca's corpus, and the latter as the inheritor of Xirgu's mantle as the primary interpreter of his work. Referenced in Carlos Ruiz Zafón's bestseller *Shadow in the Wind* (2002) and Alberto Miralles's play *Squatters at the Prado Museum* (2000), Lorca's influence can be traced beyond the literary sphere to embrace all aspects of the country's performative culture. Both La Barraca and the amateur Anfistora theatre club Lorca was associated with have often been judged prototypes for the student companies and touring theatrical troupes, like Els Joglars and Tábano, that emerged during the latter years of the Franco era (Byrd 1975: 99–113; Sáenz de la Calzada 1976: 46–7). The approaches to stagecraft introduced by Lorca with La Barraca were also appropriated by directors of the right like Luis Escobar in his religious *autos sacramentales* staged in the cathedral atriums during the 1940s. As early as 1932 La Barraca was cited as the model for a Spanish national theatre (Espina 1932), serving as a mock-up for Escobar's Teatro Nacional de la Falange Española set up during the Civil War (Byrd 1975: 16). If Lluís Pasqual proved so keen to grant Lorca's work a central position during his time as director of Spain's national theatre, the CDN, this may have been as much to do with Lorca's symbolic status as artistic director of La Barraca as with the resonance of the plays. For Calixto Bieito he is a Spanish Brecht, Spain's first dramaturg, providing concrete examples of how canonical plays from the past might be reshaped to speak more directly to the theatrical present. Beyond Spain, he has been viewed as the model for practitioners in Chile and Argentina who responded to the political crisis of the dictatorships in which they were trapped with strategies that reflected the concerns of the age (Boyle 2006: 163; Svich 1999: 201–5).

The remains of Lorca traced in this book function as 'a montage of bodies *and* texts' across opera, dance, film, theatre and the visual arts, a locus of 'resilient remainders' that undermine 'totalizing interpretations' and 'resist total deconstruction' (Lehmann 2002: 16). From the opening of Dmitri Shostakovich's Symphony no. 14 (1969), with its musical setting of 'De Profundis' and 'Malagueña', to the iconography of Sam Shepard's *Curse of the Starving Class* (1978) and *Fool for Love* (1983) and Buñuel's *Viridiana* (1961) and *The Exterminating Angel* (1962), the residues of Lorca's authorial function haunt the cultural landscape (see Bigsby 2002: 12–16; Sánchez Vidal 1996: 196, 202, 311, 322–3). Derrida's call to learn to live with the ghosts of history rather than repress them, argues for a recognition of both the paradoxical state of the spectre – a being and not-being, both present and absent, alive and dead – and the need for justice with responsibility to the ghosts of our past and, by association, our inheritance (Derrida 1994: xviii–ix, 37–48). While Alberti refers to Lorca's 'immortality' (Sánchez Bardón 1988: 111), I prefer to conclude with his 'hauntology', a speaking to the spectre across the visual and performing arts as mapped in this book.

List of play titles and English translations

The 'known' Lorcas

Amor de don Perlimplín con Belisa en su jardín
The Love of Don Perlimplín and Belisa in the Garden

Bodas de sangre
Blood Wedding

Doña Rosita la soltera o El lenguaje de las flores
Doña Rosita the Spinster or The Language of Flowers

El maleficio de la mariposa
The Butterfly's Evil Spell

La casa de Bernarda Alba
The House of Bernarda Alba

La niña que riega la albahaca y el príncipe preguntón
The Basil-Watering Girl and the Prying Prince

La zapatera prodigiosa
The Shoemaker's Wonderful Wife

Los títeres de Cachiporra. Tragicomedia de don Cristóbal y la señá Rosita
The Billy-Club Puppets: Tragicomedy of Don Cristóbal and Miss Rosita

Mariana Pineda

Retablillo de don Cristóbal
The Puppet Play of Don Cristóbal

Yerma

The 'unknown' Lorcas

Ampliación fotográfica
Photographic Enlargement

Así que pasen cinco años
When Five Years Pass

Casa de maternidad
House of Maternity

Comedia de la Carbonerita
The Play of the Young Girl Who Sells Coal

Comedia sin título or *El sueño de la vida*
Play Without a Title or The Dream of Life

Comedieta ideal
A Perfect Little Play

Cristo. Tragedia religiosa
Christ: A Religious Tragedy

Del amor. Teatro de animales
Of Love. Theatre of Animals

Diálogo con Luís Buñuel
Dialogue with Luís Buñuel

Diálogo del Amargo
Dialogue of Amargo, the Bitter One

Diálogo del dios Pan
Dialogue of the god Pan

Diálogo mudo de los cartujos
Silent Dialogue of the Carthusians

Dios, el Mal y el Hombre
God, Evil and Man

Dragón
Dragon

El paseo de Buster Keaton
Buster Keaton Takes a Walk

El primitivo auto sacramental
The Primitive Auto Sacramental

El público
The Public

El sabor de la sangre. Drama del deseo
The Taste of Blood. A Drama of Desire

Escena del Teniente Coronel de la Guardia Civil
Scene of the Lieutanant Colonel of the Civil Guard

La bola negra
The Black Ball

La destrucción de Sodoma
The Destruction of Sodom

La doncella, el marinero y el estudiante
The Maiden, the Sailor and the Student

La sangre no tiene voz
Blood Has No Voice

La hermosa. Poema de una mujer deseada
The Beautiful Lady. Poem of a Desired Woman

La viudita que se quería casar. Poema trágico
The Little Widow Who Longed to Marry. A Tragic Poem

Lola la comedianta
Lola, the Stage Actress

Los sueños de mi prima Aurelia
Dreams of My Cousin Aurelia

Quimera
Chimera

Sombras
Shadows

Teatro de almas. Paisajes de una vida espiritual
Theatre of Souls. Landscapes of a Spiritual Life

Viaje a la luna
Trip to the Moon

Notes

Overview

1 Studies of Lorca's trajectory on the Polish, German and French stages are provided elsewhere; see Aszyk 1986; Gorman 1973; Zatlin 1994: 49–56.

2 On translations of Lorca, see also Anderman 2005: 292–316; Doggart and Thompson 1999: 225–59; Svich 2007.

3 On the reworking of *Blood Wedding* in *All About My Mother*, see Delgado 2003: 224. The 2007 stage adaptation of *All About My Mother* presented at London's Old Vic Theatre overtly weaves *Blood Wedding* into the fabric of the play – as a metatheatrical text commenting on the thematics of motherhood that underpin both the film and Samuel Adamson's theatrical version of it. Diana Rigg's Huma Rojo views the character of the Mother as a role to 'kill' for (Adamson 2007a: 95). The parallels between Almodóvar's film and Lorca's play are further inscribed by Adamson in Huma Rojo's recital of two speeches from *Blood Wedding* at Lola's funeral in the closing moments of the play. The Mother's words to the Father in Act 2, Scene 2 and her rebuttal to the Neighbour in *Blood Wedding*'s final scene are spliced together in a mode that merges the texts of Almodóvar and Lorca into a single image of the tragedy of lost male youth and the pain of the mothers left behind to mourn (Adamson 2007a: 114–15; OCII 447, 471; GL 1987: 65, 88–9).

4 See also OCIII 438, 509, 513, 686–90; Gibson 1989: 12, 155; Stainton 1999: 53.

1 Life, politics and mythology

1 For Lorca's views on the folklore of Valle-Inclán and the Álvarez Quinteros, see OCIII 423.

2 Since 1994 the Fundación Federico García Lorca (FFGL) has been housed in the complex of the Residencia buildings; see http://www.garcía-lorca.org/

3 The images can be found on http://www.salvador-dali.org.eng. cat1104/finici.htm. For details of Lorca's impact on Dalí's work post-1936, see pp. 177–80.
4 Lorca's drawings are collected in Hernández 1998. While Alberti (1984: 285) may have referred to Lorca's art as a hobby, it was to play a crucial role in the development of his visual language.
5 For Dalí's Saint Sebastian, see Dalí 1927a; for Lorca's, see Hernández 1998: 102, 199.
6 See Emilio Ruiz Barrachina's film, *Lorca: The Sea Stops Still* (2006).
7 For the lectures and speeches, see OCIII 33–290; GL 1991.
8 For details on the audition processes, see OCIII 495; Aub 1985: 279–80; Sáenz de la Calzada 1976: 66–7.
9 The women in the company wore a skirt and blue blouse.
10 On Lorca as director, see OCIII 542, 563, 572, 614; Auclair 1968: 257–99; Byrd 1975: 39, 73; Sáenz de la Calzada 1976: 49–60, 109–22, 155. The programme presented by the company on tour was usually made up of a short comic interlude followed by a full-length play.
11 Putrefaction and rotting flesh are similarly potent motifs in the work of Dalí and Buñuel, see Sánchez Vidal 1996: 81–6. Worth noting here also is Joseph Roach's (1998: 23) consideration of performance as 'the desire to communicate physically with the past, a desire that roots itself in the ambivalent love of the dead'.
12 Alberti argues that the family was keen to stop the gay Lorca emerging (Aub 1985: 311). On Lorca's supposed affairs with the sculptor Emilio Aladrén and his La Barraca collaborator Rafael Rodríguez Rapún, see Gibson 1989: 209–13; Rivas Cherif 1957: 4.

2 The 'known' Lorcas

1 On Shakespearian resonances in Lorca's dramaturgy, see Anderson 1985.
2 On Barbara Forst's 1974 and Tony Mata's 1997 New York stagings, see, for example, Sainer 1974; Wasserman 1974; Bruckner 1997; Russo 1997.
3 The premiere, directed by María Teresa León and Felipe Lluch Garín, took place at Madrid's Zarzuela Theatre on 10 September 1937; see Anon 1937. On the different treatments, see OCII 37–79, 395–411, 707–31; García Lorca 1986: 147–54.
4 For details of operatic reworkings, see Tinnell 1998: 241.
5 On the impact of the ballad form on Lorca's dramaturgy, see Sánchez 1950: 123–33.
6 On the two different manuscripts, see Anderson 1991: 11–17; García Lorca 1986: 171–80. The English quotations are from the translation of the composite earlier draft. The second version can be found in OCII 645–706.

7 This is just a fraction of the twenty-six operatic, balletic and symphonic treatments of the play referenced in Tinnell 1998: 11–14.

8 On *Blood Wedding*'s debt to Lorca's earlier poetry and Valle-Inclán, see Edwards 1980: 127–31; to Greek tragedy, see Anderson 1987; to *Riders to the Sea*, *Peer Gynt*, Lenormand and D'Annunzio, see Guardia 1952: 316–23; to Lope de Vega, see Sánchez 1950: 109–15; to O'Neill, see Binding 1985: 168; to Benavente, see Higginbotham 1976: 122–7; to Guimerà, see Fernández Cifuentes 1986: 145.

9 On stagings of the play, see Delgado 1995; Edwards 1988; 1997; 2003: 118–25; 2005; Smith 1998: 44–70; Stainton 1986; Yarmus 1988.

10 For Lorca's assertions that he had received letters from gynaecologists and neurologists who verified Yerma as a legitimate case study, see OCIII 613.

11 Escobar was then artistic director of the Eslava; from 1940 to 1952 he had served as director of the María Guerrero National Theatre.

12 Tinnell (1998: 289–92) cites twenty-three ballet and six operatic versions of the play. Dramatic reworkings include Tarell Alvin McCraney's Louisiana-set *In the Red and Brown Water*. For further information on stagings of *Yerma*, see Anderman 2005: 294–303; Delgado 2003: 42–5, 146–51; Edwards 1999; 2003: 150–5; Higuera Estremera 1999; Vilches de Frutos and Dougherty 1992b: 96–104; Yarmus 1988: 40.

13 See García Lorca 1986: 66–7, 223–4; Gibson 1989: 40–2, 406–7; Higuera Rojas 1980: 189; Stainton 1998: 393–5.

14 On further sources and influences on the play from Ibsen to Pirandello, see Anderson 1994.

15 Hunter later took the title role in Helena Kaut-Howson's 2006 staging of *Yerma*; see p. 94.

16 Only a fragment remains of *The Destruction of Sodom*, initially marked as the concluding part of the triptych (OCII 765; OCIII 419). By 1934 Lorca had either renamed the play *The Daughters of Lot* or envisioned an altogether different work completing the trilogy (OCIII 548).

17 On colour imagery and the function of sound in the play, see Edwards 1980: 241–76; Vilches de Frutos 2005: 77–89.

18 On transgression, imprisonment and anxieties around female sexuality, see Gilbert and Gubar 1979. On gender and *The House of Bernarda Alba*, see Gabriele 1993; Knapp 1984. My reading of the house through the mechanics of Foucault's panopticon is greatly indebted to Smith 1989: 105–37.

19 Tinnell (1998: 88–91) cites twenty-six ballets of the play and three operatic versions prior to Reimann's. On stagings of the play, see Anderman 2005: 297–303; Delgado 2003: 50–2, 172–3, 219–20;

Edwards 2000; 2003: 204–13; 2005; Podol 1995; Yarmus 1988: 40–2.

3 The 'unknown' Lorcas

1 Plays from this early period also include the verse drama, *The Little Widow Who Longed to Marry* (1919) and *The Play of the Young Girl Who Sells Coal* (1921). The plays are collected in OCIV 877–1047; see also Soria Olmedo 1996.
2 The works are collected alongside further sketches and dialogues in OCII 177–92, 637–44 and GL 2002: 152–7, 158–65.
3 The filmscript can be found in OC II 265–78 and GL 2002: 746–55.
4 The drawings are collected in Hernández 1998: 107, 156, 199, 200, 201, 202, 210.
5 On the Harlequin drawings, see also pp. 23–4.
6 On Lorca's work as a director, see pp. 28–32, 131–8 and Vilches de Frutos and Dougherty 1992a.
7 The drawings referred to can be seen in Hernández 1998: 165, 168. It is worth noting here that even a more ostensibly realist work, like *Blood Wedding*, features a reference to the man whose hands were cut off by the machine (OCII 419; GL 1987: 37).
8 On Víctor García's production of *Yerma*, see pp. 91–3.
9 On the play's production history, see also Edwards 2003: 79–83; Mora Guarnido 1958: 174–5; Smith 1998: 71–104.
10 The staging opened at the Piccolo Theatre Milan on 12 December 1986 but did not commence its run at the María Guerrero until January 1987. Further readings of this production and others mentioned in the chapter are offered by Delgado 2003: 205–13; Delgado and Edwards 1990; Edwards 2003: 55–60; Smith 1998: 118–38.
11 For details of Lorca's further ideas and plans for plays, see Anderson 1986: 219.

4 Lorca's afterlives

1 The figure of 30,000 is a conservative estimate. Some organizations believe the number is closer to 150,000.
2 These elegies (and others) are collected in Clúa 2006; see also Alberti 1984: 47–104. On Lorca's time at Madrid's Residencia de Estudiantes, see pp. 21–6.
3 For Lorca's presence on Dalí's canvases, see Gibson 2003: 297–333; Sánchez Vidal 1996: 269–82.
4 Described as 'an artist's poet' by curator Hans Ulrich Obrist (Luke 2007), Lorca's writings are traceable in the canvases of Douglas Gordon; his drawings have inspired Rivane Neuenschwander; his

relationship with Dalí has been reframed by Tacita Dean; Gilbert and George have photographed themselves replete in their distinctive suits on Lorca's bed in the Huerta de San Vicente. For further details, see Luke 2007; http://www.huertadesanvicente.com.

5 In Carlos Saura's *Buñuel and King Solomon's Table* (2001), Lorca (Adrià Collado) similarly functions as a ghost (slightly vacant and always clad in unspoilt shades of beige), hovering between past and present and forever bound up with the youthful Dalí (Ernesto Alterio) and Buñuel (Pere Arquillué).

6 *Cruel Garden* was revived during the 1980s, televised in 1984 and remounted with a new generation of dancers for the Lorca centenary celebrations in 1998. *Lorca, Death of a Poet* made RTVE almost 100 million pesetas in international sales (Anon 1988).

7 Camarón de la Isla died aged 42 in 1992. Amador is still alive but rarely performs.

8 This section is greatly indebted to the cultural framework established by Graham Holderness in his study of Bardolatry and the Shakespeare myth; see Holderness 1988: 2–15.

9 See http://www.turismodegranada.org/Lorca/Lorca-nivel1.php?PHPSESSID=a0ef3eb2d71bd190c177a3c965849439 (accessed 9 October 2006); Garvey and Ellingham 2006: 552–4; *Time Out* 2007: 264–5.

10 See http://www.museogarcialorca.org (accessed 9 October 2006). Across the way from the museum is a purpose-built theatre named after Lorca that now houses the University of Granada's theatre activities.

11 See http://www.parqueciencias.com/exposiciones/planetario/lorca/ (accessed 10 October 2006).

12 See http://www.huertadesanvicente.com/ (accessed 10 October 2006).

Bibliography

Primary

Anderson, Andrew and Christopher Maurer (eds) (1997) *Federico García Lorca: epistolario completo*, Madrid: Cátedra.

García Lorca, Federico (1927) 'Reyerta de gitanos', *L'Amic de les Arts*, 15 (30 June): 45.

—— (1983a) *Selected Letters*, ed. and trans. David Gershator, New York: New Directions.

—— (1983b) *Five Plays: Comedies and Tragicomedies*, trans. James Graham-Luján and Richard L. O'Connell, Harmondsworth: Penguin.

—— (1984a) 'La niña que riega la albahaca y el príncipe preguntón', *ALEC*, 9(1–3): 295–306.

—— (1984b) *La casa de Bernarda Alba*, cuaderno de dirección del montaje de José Carlos Plaza (Los libros del Teatro Español 4), Madrid: Teatro Español.

—— (1987) *Three Plays*, trans. Gwynne Edwards and Peter Luke, London: Methuen.

—— (1990) *Plays: Two*, ed. and trans. Gwynne Edwards, London: Methuen.

—— (1991) *Deep Song and Other Prose*, ed. and trans. Christopher Maurer, London: Marion Boyars.

—— (1994) *Plays: Three*, ed. Gwynne Edwards, London: Methuen.

—— (1996a) *Obras completas*, 4 vols, ed. Miguel García-Posada, Barcelona: Galaxia Gutenberg/Círculo de Lectores.

—— (1996b) *The Unknown Federico García Lorca*, ed. and trans. John London, London: Atlas Press.

—— (2000) *Impossible Theatre*, ed and trans. Caridad Svich, Hanover: Smith & Kraus.

—— (2002) *Collected Poems*, ed. Christopher Maurer, New York: Farrar, Straus, Giroux.

—— (2007) *Major Plays*, vol. 1, ed. and trans. Caridad Svich, Southgate, CA: NoPassport Press.

Secondary

Abril, Manuel (1926) 'Los pintores de Eslava', in Gregorio Martínez Sierra (ed.) *Un Teatro de Arte en España 1917–1925*, Madrid: Esfinge: 19–36.

Adams, Mildred (1932) 'The Theatre in the Spanish Republic', *Theatre Arts Monthly*, March: 237–9.

—— (1977) *García Lorca: Playwright and Poet*, New York: George Braziller.

Adamson, Samuel (2007a) *All About My Mother, based on the film by Pedro Almodóvar*, London: Faber & Faber.

—— (2007b) 'Where the Power Lives', Essay in the programme for *All About My Mother*, London: Old Vic Theatre.

Adorno, Theodor W. (1973) *Negative Dialectics*, trans. E.B. Ashton, London: Routledge.

—— (1978) *Minima Moralia: Reflections from Damaged Life*, trans. E.F.N. Jephcott, London: Verso.

Aguilera Sastre, Juan and Manuel Aznar Soler (1999) *Cipriano de Rivas Cherif y el teatro español de su época (1891–1967)* (Teoría y práctica del teatro, 16), Madrid: ADE.

Alberti, Rafael (1984) *Federico García Lorca: poeta y amigo*, Granada: Biblioteca de la Cultura Andaluza.

—— (1987) *La arboleda perdida: libros III y IV de memorias*, Barcelona: Seix Barral.

—— (1988 [1959]) *La arboleda perdida: libros I y II de memorias*, 7th edn, Barcelona: Seix Barral.

Aleixandre, Vicente (1978 [1968]), 'Evocación de Federico García Lorca', in *Obras Completas*, II, 2nd edn, Madrid: Aguilar: 287–90.

Allen, R.C. (1974) *Psyche and Symbol in the Theater of Federico García Lorca: Perlimplín, Yerma, Blood Wedding*, Austin, TX: University of Texas Press.

Alonso, José Luis (1991) *Teatro de cada día: escritos sobre teatro*, ed. Juan Antonio Hormigón (Teoría y práctica del teatro 4), Madrid: ADE.

Álvarez, Olga (1980) 'Reflexiones del director argentino sobre su montaje de *Doña Rosita la soltera*, de García Lorca. Jorge Lavelli, "profundamente satisfecho" de su trabajo en España', *El País* [Artes], 27 September: 1.

Álvarez-Ossorio, Pedro (1998) '*El público*', paper presented at the 'Lorca y la cultura árabe' Conference, Gran Cairo Library, Egypt, 10 November.

Álvaro, Francisco (ed.) (1965) *El espectador y la crítica (El teatro en España en 1965)*, Valladolid: Edición del Autor.

—— (1972) *El espectador y la crítica (El teatro en España en 1971)*, Madrid: Editorial Prensa Española.

—— (1983) *El espectador y la crítica (El teatro en España en 1982)*, Valladolid: Edición del Autor.

Anderman, Gunilla (2005) *Europe on Stage: Translations and Theatre*, London: Oberon.

Anderson, Andrew A. (1985) 'Some Shakespearean Reminiscences in Federico García Lorca's Drama', *Comparative Literature Studies*, 22: 187–210.

—— (1986) 'The Strategy of García Lorca's Dramatic Composition 1930–1936', *Romance Quarterly*, 33(2): 211–29.

—— (1987) 'García Lorca's *Bodas de sangre*: The Logic and Necessity of Act Three', *Hispanofila*, 90: 21–37.

—— (1991) *García Lorca: La zapatera prodigiosa* (Critical Guides to Spanish Texts, 53), London: Grant & Cutler/Tamesis.

—— (1992) '*El público, Así que pasen cinco años*, y *El sueño de la vida*: tres dramas expresionistas de García Lorca', in D. Dougherty and M.F. Vilches de Frutos (eds) *El teatro en España*, Madrid: CSIC/FFGL/Tabacalera: 215–26.

—— (1993) 'On Broadway, Off Broadway: García Lorca and the New York Theatre 1929–30', *Gestos*, 16: 135–48.

—— (1994) 'More Sources for García Lorca's *Doña Rosita la soltera*', in Nigel Griffin, Clive Griffin, Eric Southworth and Colin Thompson (eds) *The Discerning Eye: Studies Presented to Robert Pring Mill on his Seventieth Birthday*, Llangrannog: Dolphin.

—— (1999) 'Was García Lorca Dyslexic (Like W.B.Yeats)?', *Modern Language Review*, 94: 700–17.

Anderson, Reed (1984) *Federico García Lorca* (Macmillan Modern Dramatists), London: Macmillan.

Anon (1932) 'La silueta de la semana. Federico García Loca (1) o cualquiera se equivoca', *Gracia y Justicia*, 47 (23 July): 10.

—— (1936a) 'Sección de rumores. Se dice', *Heraldo de Madrid*, 29 May: 9.

—— (1936b) 'Viva la España antifascista', *El Diluvio*, 1 September: 1.

—— (1936c) 'Los fascistas han fusilado a Federico García Lorca', *Solidaridad Obrera*, 5 September: 2.

—— (1936d) 'Otra protesta por el vil asesinato de García Lorca', *El Sol*, 12 September: 2.

—— (1988) 'Cien millones por *Lorca, muerte de un poeta*', *Deia*, 28 September, unpaginated cutting from FFGL file on *Lorca, muerte de un poeta*.

—— (1998) '"Hoy España se llama Federico", afirmó Aznar en homenaje al poeta andaluz', *Diario de Navarra*, 6 June: 20.

Antón, Jacinto (1998) 'Lluís Pasqual: "¡Quién sabe cómo era Lorca!"', *El País*, 12 May: 36.

Arauz de Robles, Santiago (1988) 'Lorca: un serial para el odio', *Ideal*, 15 January, unpaginated cutting from FFGL file on *Lorca, muerte de un poeta*.

Armengol, Montse and Ricard Belis (2004) *Las fosas del silencio: ¿hay un holocausto español?*, Barcelona: Plaza y Janés.

Astles, Cariad (1999) 'Lorca, Don Cristóbal and the Carnivalesque', in S. Doggart and M. Thompson (eds) *Fire, Blood and the Alphabet*, Durham: Durham Modern Languages Series: 107–21.

Aszyk, Urszula (1984) 'El último Lorca, privilegio polaco', *El Público*, 14 (November): 24–5.

—— (1986) 'Federico García Lorca y su teatro en Polonia', *Cuadernos Hispanoamericanos*, 433–6 (July–August): 270–80.

Aub, Max (1985) *Conversaciones con Buñuel seguidas de 45 entrevistas con familiares, amigos y colaboradores del cineasta aragonés*, Madrid: Aguilar.

Auclair, Marcelle (1968) *Enfances et mort de García Lorca*, Paris: Seuil.

Austin, J.L. (1975 [1955]) *How To Do Things with Words*, 2nd edn, Oxford: Clarendon Press.

Barea, Arturo (1944) *Lorca: The Poet and his People*, trans. Ilsa Barea, London: Faber & Faber.

Barthes, Roland (1982) *Camera Lucida: Reflections on Photography*, trans. Richard Howard, London: Vintage.

Baudrillard, Jean (1983) *Simulations*, trans. Paul Foss, Paul Patton and Philip Beitchman, New York: Semiotext(e).

Bigsby, Christopher (2002) 'Born Injured: The Theatre of Sam Shepard', in Matthew Roudané (ed.) *The Cambridge Companion to Sam Shepard*, Cambridge: Cambridge University Press: 7–33.

Binding, Paul (1985) *Lorca: The Gay Imagination*, London: GMP.

Bonaddio, Federico (ed.) (2007) *A Companion to Federico García Lorca*, Woodbridge, UK: Tamesis.

Boo, Juan Vicente (1997) 'Hollywood descubre a Lorca de la mano de Andy García y Marcos Zurinaga', *ABC*, 31 January: 80.

Borrás, Tomás (1926) 'Compañía Cómico-Dramática G. Martínez Sierra', in Gregorio Martínez Sierra (ed.) *Un Teatro de Arte en España 1917–1925*, Madrid: Esfinge: 9–16.

Bosquet, Alain (1966) *Entretiens avec Salvador Dalí*, Paris: Pierre Belfond.

Boyle, Catherine (2006) 'A Reflection on Crisis and Meaning in Federico García Lorca's Dramatic Languages', *Bulletin of Spanish Studies*, 83(1): 161–72.

Bradby, David (2006) 'From Theatricality to Performance Theory: *The Screens*', in Clare Finburgh, Carl Lavery and Maria Shevtsova (eds) *Jean Genet: Performance and Politics*, Basingstoke: Palgrave Macmillan: 34–43.

Brenan, Gerald (1951) *The Face of Spain*, New York: Grove Press.

Buñuel, Luis (1926) 'Tarjeta postal de Luis Buñuel a Federico García Lorca', 18 June, FFGL M.Lorca COA-146.

—— (1985) *My Last Breath*, trans. Abigail Israel, London: Fontana.

Burgín, Richard (1973) *Conversations with Jorge Luis Borges*, London: Souvenir Press.

Butler, Judith (1990) *Gender Trouble: Feminism and the Subversion of Identity*, London: Routledge.

Byrd, Suzanne Wade (1975) *García Lorca: 'La Barraca' and the Spanish National Theater*, New York: Abra.

Caballero, José (1984) 'Con Federico en los ensayos de *Yerma*', *ABC* [Cultural], 29 December: I.

Calleja, Álvaro (1998) 'He leído todos los poemas de Federico', *El Correo de Andalucía*, 17 January: 48.

Campbell, Roy (1952) *Lorca: An Appreciation of his Poetry* (Studies in Modern European Literature and Thought), Cambridge: Bowes & Bowes.

Cano, José Luis (1966) 'Biografía acelerada de Federico', *ABC*, 6 November: n.p.

Cao, Antonio F. (1984) *Federico García Lorca y las vanguardias: hacia el teatro*, London: Tamesis.

Carr, Raymond (1980) *Modern Spain 1875–1980*, Oxford: Oxford University Press.

Castillo Gallego, Rubén (1998) 'El año de Gibson', *La Verdad*, 8 June, unpaginated clipping from the Lorca centenary file, FFGL.

Cernuda, Luis (1970) *Crítica, ensayos y evocaciones*, ed. Luis Maristany, Barcelona: Seix Barral.

Clements, Andrew (1998) 'A Parallel Life', *The Nightingale's to Blame* programme, Opera North: 13–14.

Clúa, Isabel (ed.) (2006) *Elegías a la muerte de García Lorca: el crimen fue en Granada*, Barcelona: Lumen.

Cornago Bernal, Óscar (2001) *Discurso teórico y puesta en escena en los años sesenta: la encrucijada de los 'realismos'*, Madrid: CSIC.

Cunningham, Valentine (ed.) (1980) *The Penguin Book of Spanish Civil War Verse*, Harmondsworth: Penguin.

Dalí, Salvador (1927a) 'Sant Sebastià', *L'Amic de les Arts*, 16 (31 July): 52–4.

—— (1927b) 'Federico García Lorca: exposició de dibuixos colorits (Galeries Dalmau)', *La Nova Revista*, 3(9): 84–5.

—— (1949) *The Secret Life of Salvador Dalí*, trans. Haakon M. Chevalier, London: Vision Press.

—— (1950) 'To Spain, Guided by Dalí', *Vogue*, 15 May: 54–7, 94.

—— (1976) *The Unspeakable Confessions of Salvador Dalí as told to André Parinaud*, trans. Harold J. Salemson, London: W.H. Allen.

—— (1986) 'Matización de Dalí', *El País*, 30 January: 11.

—— (1987) *Salvador Dalí escribe a Federico García Lorca (1925–1936)*, ed. Rafael Santos Torroella, *Poesía: Revista ilustrada de información poética*, 27–28 (April).

Davis, Madeleine (2005) 'Is Spain Recovering its Memory? Breaking the *Pacto del Olvido*', *Human Rights Quarterly*, 27: 858–80.

Delgado, Maria M. (1995) 'Marketing Lorca in Britain: Lawrence Till's *Blood Wedding*', *Estreno* 21(2): 45–8.

—— (1998) 'Redefining Spanish Theatre: Lluís Pasqual on Directing, Fabià Puigserver and the Lliure', *Contemporary Theatre Review*, 7(4): 81–109.

—— (2003) *'Other' Spanish Theatres: Erasure and Inscription on the Twentieth-Century Spanish Stage*, Manchester: Manchester University Press.

Delgado, Maria M. and Gwynne Edwards (1990) 'From Madrid to Stratford East: *The Public* in Performance', *Estreno*, 16(2): 11–18, 6.

Derrida, Jacques (1994) *Specters of Marx: The State of the Debt, the Work of Mourning and the New International*, trans. Peggy Kamuf, London: Routledge.

Díaz-Plaja, Guillermo (1954) *Federico García Lorca: su obra e influencia en la poesía española* (Colección Austral no 1221), Buenos Aires: Espasa-Calpe.

Doggart, Sebastian and Michael Thompson (eds) (1999) *Fire, Blood and the Alphabet: One Hundred Years of Lorca*, Durham: Durham Modern Languages Series.

Domenech, Ricardo (1992) 'Valle-Inclán y García Lorca: una perspectiva del teatro español', in D. Dougherty and M.F. Vilches de Frutos (eds) *El teatro en España*, Madrid: CSIC/FFGL/Tabacalera: 333–43.

Dougherty, Dru and María Francisca Vilches de Frutos (eds) (1992) *El teatro en España: entre la tradición y la vanguardia 1918–1939*, Madrid: CSIC/FFGL/Tabacalera.

Edwards, Gwynne (1980) *Lorca: The Theatre Beneath the Sand*, London: Marion Boyars.

—— (1981) 'Lorca and Buñuel: *Así que pasen cinco años* and *Un Chien andalou*', *García Lorca Review*, 9(2): 128–42.

—— (1988) 'Lorca on the English Stage: Problems of Production and Translation', *New Theatre Quarterly* 4(16): 344–55.

—— (1997) '*Bodas de sangre* in Performance', *ALEC*, 22(3): 469–91.

—— (1998) 'Lorca in the United Kingdom', *Donaire*, 10: 23–30.

—— (1999) '*Yerma* on Stage', *ALEC*, 24(3): 433–51.

—— (2000) 'Productions of *La casa de Bernarda Alba*', *ALEC*, 25(3): 699–728.

—— (2003) *Lorca: Living in the Theatre*, London: Peter Owen.

—— (2005) 'Lorca on the London Stage: Problems of Translation and Adaptation', *New Theatre Quarterly*, 21(4): 382–94.

El Khattat, Mohamed (1998) 'Los Reyes siguen las huellas de Lorca en su centenario', *El Mundo*, 17 January: 41.

Espina, Antonio (1932) 'Nuevo régimen: El teatro dramático nacional', *Luz*, 27 May: 3.

Estévez, María (1997) 'Andy García "Trato de identificarme profundamente con Lorca:"', *La Vanguardia* [Magazine], 16 February: 20–3.

Feal Deibe, Carlos (1989) *Lorca: tragedia y mito* (Ottowa Hispanic Studies 4), Ottawa: Dovehouse.

Feinstein, Adam (2004) *Pablo Neruda: A Passion for Life*, London: Bloomsbury.

Feldman, Sharon (1991) '*Perlimplín*: Lorca's Drama about Theatre', *Estreno*, 17(2): 34–8.

Fernández, Julio (1986) '*La casa de Bernarda Alba* inicia su rodaje en Antequera', *El Periódico*, 23 November: 69.

Fernández Cifuentes, Luis (1986) *García Lorca en el teatro: la norma y la diferencia*, Zaragoza: Universidad de Zaragoza.

—— (1988) 'La verdad de la vida: Gibson versus Lorca', *Boletín de la Fundación Federico García Lorca*, 4: 87–101.

—— (1992) 'El viejo y la niña: tradicción y modernidad en el teatro de García Lorca', in D. Dougherty and M.F. Vilches de Frutos (eds) *El teatro en España*, Madrid: CSIC/FFGL/Tabacalera: 89–102.

Foucault, Michel (1985) *Discipline and Punish*, trans. Alan Sheridan, Harmondsworth: Penguin.

—— (2001) 'What is an Author?', in V.B. Leitch et al. (eds) *The Norton Anthology of Theory and Criticism*, New York: Norton: 1622–36.

Fraser, Angus (1992) *The Gypsies* (The Peoples of Europe), Oxford: Blackwell.

Freud, Sigmund (2001) 'The "Uncanny"', in V.B. Leitch et al. (eds) *The Norton Anthology of Theory and Criticism*, New York: Norton: 929–52.

Gabriele, John (1993) 'Of Mothers and Freedom: Adela's Struggle for Selfhood in *La casa de Bernarda Alba*', *Symposium*, 47(3): 188–99.

García, Alejandro V. (1998) 'Los escenarios de su memoria', *El País* [Semanal], 1 February: 36–9.

García Lorca, Francisco (1980) *Federico y su mundo*, ed. and intro. Mario Hernández, Madrid: Alianza.

—— (1983) 'Introduction', in Federico García Lorca (1983b) *Five Plays*, Harmondsworth: Penguin: 9–20.

—— (1986) *In the Green Morning: Memories of Federico*, trans. Christopher Maurer, New York: New Directions.

Garvey, Geoff and Mark Ellingham (2006 [1994]) *The Rough Guide to Andalucía*, 5th edn, London: Rough Guides.

Gaskell, Ronald (1972) *Drama and Reality: The European Theatre since Ibsen*, London: Routledge & Kegan Paul.

Genet, Jean (2002) *Théâtre complet*, eds Michel Corvin and Albert Dichy, Paris: Gallimard.

George, David (1995) *The History of the Commedia dell'arte in Modern Hispanic Literature with Special Attention to the Work of García Lorca*, Lewiston, NY: Edwin Mellen Press.

Gibson, Ian (1974) *The Death of Lorca*, 2nd edn, Frogmore: Paladin.

—— (1986a) 'Con Dalí y Lorca en Figueres', *El País* [Revista], 26 January: 10–11.

—— (1986b) *Granada en 1936 y el asesinato de Federico García Lorca*, Barcelona: Cítica.

—— (1989) *Federico García Lorca: A Life*, New York: Pantheon.

—— (1992) *Lorca's Granada: A Practical Guide*, London: Faber & Faber.

—— (1998) 'García Lorca: la breve vida de un poeta genial', *El País* [Semanal], 1 February: 28–35.

—— (2003) *Lorca-Dalí. El amor que no pudo ser*, Barcelona: DeBols!llo.

Gilbert, Sandra M. and Susan Gubar (1979) *The Madwoman in the Attic: The Woman Writer and the Nineteenth-Century Literary Imagination*, New Haven, CT: Yale University Press.

Ginsberg, Allen (2000) *Howl and Other Poems*, San Francisco, CA: City Lights.

Gorman, John (1973) *The Reception of Federico García Lorca in Germany*, Göppingen: Alfred Kümmerle.

Gray, John (1993) *Beyond the New Right: Markets, Government and the Common Environment*, London: Routledge.

Guardia, Alfredo de la (1952 [1941]) *García Lorca, persona y creación*, 3rd edn, Buenos Aires: Schapire.

Guerenabarrena, Juanjo (1989) 'Margarita Ucelay: recuerdos de la profesora y de la actriz', *El Público*, 68 (May): 8–9.

Guillén, Claudio (1990) 'El misterio evidente: en torno a *Así que pasen cinco años*', *Boletín de la Fundación Federico García Lorca*, 4(7–8): 215–32.

Handley, Sharon (1996) 'Federico García Lorca and the 98 Generation: The *Andalucismo* Debate', *ALEC*, 21(1–2): 41–58.

Harretche, María Estela (2000) *Federico García Lorca: análisis de una revolución teatral* (Biblioteca Románica Hispánica), Madrid: Gredos.

Harrison, Joseph and Alan Hoyle (eds) (2000) *Spain's 1898 Crisis: Regeneration, Modernism, Post-Colonialism*, Manchester: Manchester University Press.

Hart, Stephen (1989) 'The Bear and the Dawn: Versions of *La casa de Bernarda Alba*', *Neophilologus*, 73: 62–8.

—— (2003) 'Poetry on Trial: The Strange Case of Lorca's *Poeta en Nueva York*', *Hispanic Research Journal*, 4(3): 271–84.

Havard, Robert (2001) *The Crucified Mind: Rafael Alberti and the Surrealist Ethos in Spain*, London: Tamesis.

Hernández, Mario (1979) 'Cronología y estreno de *Yerma*, poema trágico, de García Lorca', *Revista de Archivos, Bibliotecas y Museos*, 82(2): 289–315.

—— (1984) 'Introducción', in Federico García Lorca, *La casa de Bernarda Alba*, Madrid: Alianza: 9–46.

—— (1998) *Libro de los dibujos de Federico García Lorca*, Madrid: Comares/FFGL.

Higginbotham, Virginia (1976) *The Comic Spirit of Federico García Lorca*, Austin, TX: University of Texas Press.

Higuera Estremera, Luis Felipe (1999) 'El primer estreno comercial de García Lorca en la posguerra española (*Yerma*, Teatro Eslava 1960)', *ALEC*, 24: 571–92.

Higuera Rojas, Eulalia-Dolores de la (1980) *Mujeres en la vida de García Lorca*, Granada: Editora Nacional, Excma. Diputación Provincial de Granada.

Holderness, Graham (1988) 'Bardolatry: or, The Cultural Materialist's Guide to Stratford-upon-Avon', in G. Holderness (ed.) *The Shakespeare Myth*, Manchester: Manchester University Press: 2–15.

Holguín, Sandie (2002) *Creating Spaniards: Culture and Identity in Republican Spain*, Madison, WI: University of Wisconsin Press.

Honig, Edwin (1945) *García Lorca*, London: Editions Poetry.

Hopewell, John (1986) *Out of the Past: Spanish Cinema after Franco*, London: British Film Institute.

Jerez Farrán, Carlos (2004) *Un Lorca desconocido: análisis de un teatro 'irrepresentable'* (Estudios críticos de literatura), Madrid: Biblioteca Nueva.

Johnston, David (1993) 'Las terribes aduanas: The Fortunes of Spanish Theatre in English', *Donaire*, 1: 18–24.

—— (1998a) *Federico García Lorca*, Bath: Absolute Press.

—— (1998b) 'Translating García Lorca: The Importance of Voice', *Donaire*, 11: 54–60.

—— (1999) 'García Lorca: After New York', in S. Doggart and M. Thompson (eds) *Fire, Blood and the Alphabet*, Durham: Durham Modern Languages Series: 57–66.

Kennedy, A.L. (2000) *On Bullfighting*, London: Yellow Jersey Press.

Knapp, Bettina (1984) 'Federico García Lorca's *The House of Bernarda Alba*: A Hermaphrodite Matriarchate', *Modern Drama*, 26(3): 382–94.

Lacan, Jacques (1988) *The Ego in Freud's Theory and in the Technique of Psychoanalysis, 1954–1955*, ed. Jacques Alain Miller, trans. Silvana Tomaselli, New York: Norton.

LeFanu, Nicola (1994) 'b. 1947', *Contemporary Music Review*, 11(1–2): 183–7.

Lehmann, Courtney (2002) *Shakespeare Remains: Theater to Film, Early Modern to Postmodern*, Ithaca, NY: Cornell University Press.

Leitch, Vincent B. et al. (eds) (2001) *The Norton Anthology of Theory and Criticism*, New York: Norton.

Lennon, Peter (2002) 'Tussle for a Treasure', *Guardian*, 19 November: http://books.guardian.co.uk/poetry/features/0,,902846,00.html (accessed 12 December 2006).

León, María Teresa (1977) Memoria de una melancolía, Madrid: Laia.

Lima, Robert (1963) The Theatre of García Lorca, New York: Las Américas.

London, John (1996) 'Introduction', in Federico García Lorca (1996b) The Unknown Federico García Lorca, London: Atlas Press: 7–22.

—— (1997) Reception and Renewal in Modern Spanish Theatre: 1939–1963, London: W.S. Maney and Son for the MHRA.

López Castellón, Enrique (1981) F. García Lorca: el poeta ante la muerte, Madrid: Felmar.

Luke, Ben (2007) 'In Bed with Lorca', Guardian [Review], 15 December: 14.

McDermid, Paul (2007) Love, Desire and Identity in the Theatre of Federico García Lorca, Woodbridge, UK: Tamesis.

McDermott, Patricia (1996) 'Lorca's Viaje a la luna: The Cinema as Sacrilegious Art', in Derek Harris (ed.) Changing Times in Hispanic Culture, Aberdeen: University of Aberdeen Press: 121–32.

Marinello, Juan (1965) García Lorca en Cuba, Havana: Belic.

Martínez Nadal, Rafael (1974) Lorca's The Public: A Study of his Unfinished Play (El Público) and of Love and Death in the Work of Federico García Lorca, London: Calder & Boyars.

—— (1980) Cuatro lecciones sobre Federico García Lorca, Madrid: Fundación Juan March/Cátedra.

Martínez Sierra, Gregorio (ed.) (1926) Un Teatro de Arte en España 1917–1925, Madrid: Esfinge.

Moix, Terenci (1998) 'El Nobel, en la letrina', El País, 15 June: 36.

Monleón, José (1971) 'Con Víctor García y Nuria Espert', Primer Acto, 137 (October): 14–21.

—— (1986) 'Cinco imágines de la historia política española a través de otros tantos montajes de La casa de Bernarda Alba', Cuadernos Hispanoamericanos, 433–6 (July–August): 371–83.

Mora Guarnido, José (1958) Federico García Lorca y su mundo: testimonio para una biografía, Buenos Aires: Losada.

Moreno, Pedro (1984) 'Vestuario', in Federico García Lorca (1984b) La casa de Bernarda Alba, Madrid: Teatro Español: 239–49.

Morla Lynch, Carlos (1957) En España con Federico García Lorca (páginas de un diario íntimo. 1928–1936), Madrid: Aguilar.

Morris, C. Brian (1972) Surrealism and Spain 1920–1936, Cambridge: Cambridge University Press.

—— (1990) García Lorca: La casa de Bernarda Alba (Critical Guides to Spanish Texts, 50), London: Grant & Cutler/Tamesis.

—— (1997) Son of Andalusia: The Lyrical Landscapes of Federico García Lorca, Liverpool: Liverpool University Press.

Neruda, Pablo (1977) *Memoirs*, trans. Hardie St. Martin, London: Souvenir Press.

—— (1984) *Passions and Impressions*, eds Matilde Neruda and Miguel Otero Silva, trans. Margaret Sayars Peden, New York: Farrar, Straus, Giroux.

Neville, Edgar (1966) 'La obra de Federico, bien nacional', *ABC*, 6 November: n.p.

Newberry, Wilma (1976) 'Patterns of Negation in *La casa de Bernarda Alba*', *Hispania* 59(4): 802–9.

Nieva, Francisco (1996) *El reino de nadie*, Madrid: Espasa-Calpe.

Oppenheimer, Helen (1986) *Lorca: The Drawings. Their Relationship to the Poet's Life and Work*, London: Herbert Press.

Orozco, Manuel (1988) 'Diálogo: el último asesinato de Federico, por Bardem', *Ideal*, 9 January, unpaginated clipping from the FFGL file on *Lorca, muerte de un poeta*.

Ortega y Gasset, José (1957 [1946]) *Obras completas*, 1 (1902–1916), 4th edn, Madrid: Revista de Occidente.

—— (1958) *Idea del teatro*, Madrid: Revista de Occidente.

Ortiz, Lourdes (1998) 'El local de Bernardeta A.', *Acotaciones* 11(1): 63–101.

Pasqual, Lluís (1987) 'La verdad del amor y del teatro', *El Público*, 40 (January): 6–9.

Phelan, Peggy (1993) *Unmarked: The Politics of Performance*, London: Routledge.

Plaza, José Carlos (1984) 'Cuaderno de dirección, Montaje 1984', in Federico García Lorca (1984b) *La casa de Bernarda Alba*, Madrid: Teatro Español: 183–230.

Podol, Peter (1995) '*La casa de Bernarda Alba* in Performance: Three Productions in Three Media', *Estreno*, 21(2): 42–4.

Preston, Paul (1983) *The Coming of the Spanish Civil War: Reform, Reaction and Revolution in the Second Republic*, London: Methuen.

Pulido, Natividad (1995) 'Durán subasta varios textos inéditos y autógrafos de Federico García Lorca', *ABC*, 6 February: 73.

Río, Ángel del (1952) *Vida y obras de Federico García Lorca* (Colección Estudios Literarios, III), Zaragoza: Heraldo de Aragón.

Rivas Cherif, Cipriano (1957) 'Poesía y drama del gran Federico. La muerte y la pasión de García Lorca', *Excelsior* [Dioramana de la cultura], 13 January: 1, 4.

Roach, Joseph R. (1992) 'Introduction', in Janelle G. Reinelt and Joseph R. Roach (eds) *Critical Theory and Performance*, Ann Arbor, MI: The University of Michigan Press: 293–8.

—— (1998), 'History, Memory, Necrophilia', in Peggy Phelan and Jill

Lane (eds) *The Ends of Performance*, New York: New York University Press: 23–30.

Rodrigo, Antonina (1984) *García Lorca: el amigo de Catalunya*, Barcelona: Edhasa.

—— (2005) *Margarita Xirgu: una biografía*. Barcelona: Flor del Viento.

Rosetti, Ana et al. (1998) 'Contra los exabruptos de Cela', *El País*, 23 July: 13.

Ruiz Mantilla, Jesús (2003) 'Los Lorca advierten de que lo que Christie's subasta hoy es sólo una copia de *Poeta en Nueva York*', *El País*, 4 June: 38.

Sáenz de la Calzada, Luis (1976) *'La Barraca' Teatro Universitario*, Madrid: Biblioteca de la Revista de Occidente.

Sánchez, Roberto G. (1950) *García Lorca: estudio sobre su teatro*, Madrid: Jura.

Sánchez Bardón, Luis (1988) 'Los amigos de García Lorca no le reconocen en la serie de Bardem', *Tiempo*, 18–24 January: 110–13.

Sánchez Vidal, Agustín (1996) *Buñuel, Lorca, Dalí: el enigma sin fín*, Barcelona: Planeta.

Santos Torroella, Rafael (1984) *La miel es más dulce que la sangre. Las épocas lorquiana y freudiana de Salvador Dalí*, Barcelona: Planeta.

—— (1995) *Los putrefactos de Dalí y Lorca: historia y antología de un libro que no pudo ser*, Madrid: Publicaciones de la Residencia de Estudiantes.

Sesé, Teresa (1998) 'Lola Herrera y Carmen Linares evocan la figura de Lorca en el Tívoli', *La Vanguardia*, 17 March: 45.

Showalter, Elaine (1977) *A Literature of their Own: British Women Novelists from Brontë to Lessing*, Princeton, NJ: Princeton University Press.

Smith, Paul Julian (1989) *The Body Hispanic: Gender and Sexuality in Spanish and Spanish American Literature*, Oxford: Clarendon Press.

—— (1996) *Vision Machines: Cinema, Literature and Sexuality in Spain and Cuba, 1983–1993*, London: Verso.

—— (1998) *The Theatre of García Lorca: Text, Performance, Psychoanalysis*, Cambridge: Cambridge University Press.

Soria Olmedo, Andrés (1996) 'Introducción', in Federico García Lorca, *Teatro inédito de juventud*, Madrid: Cátedra: 9–68.

Soufas, C. Christopher (1996) *Audience and Authority in the Modernist Theater of Federico García Lorca*, Tuscaloosa, AL: University of Alabama Press.

Stainton, Leslie (1986) 'A Concept of the Land: José Luis Gómez, Lorca and *Bodas de sangre*', *ALEC*, 11: 205–13.

—— (1999) *Lorca: A Dream of Life*, New York: Farrar, Straus, Giroux.

Stallybrass, Peter and Allon White (1986) *The Politics and Poetics of Transgression*, Ithaca, NY: Cornell University Press.

Stone, Rob (2004) *The Flamenco Tradition in the Works of Federico García Lorca and Carlos Saura: The Wounded Throat*, Lewiston, NY: Edwin Mellen Press.

Sullivan, Henry W. (1983) *Calderón in the German Lands and the Low Countries: His Reception and Influence, 1654–1980*, Cambridge: Cambridge University Press.

Svich, Caridad (1999) 'Looking for Lorca: A Legacy in the Americas', in S. Doggart and M. Thompson (eds) *Fire, Blood and the Alphabet*, Durham: Durham Modern Languages Series: 191–205.

—— (2000) 'Towards an Impossible Theater: An Introduction and Imagined Manifesto', in Federico García Lorca, *Impossible Theatre*, Hanover: Smith & Kraus: xv–xix.

—— (2007) 'On the Art of Translation', in Federico García Lorca, *Major Plays*, Vol. 1, Southgate, CA: No Passport Press: 13–18.

Tapia, J.L. (1997) 'La familia Lorca, ausente', *Ideal*, 13 February: 47.

Teevan, Colin (1999) 'Irish ReLorcations', in S. Doggart and M. Thompson (eds) *Fire, Blood and the Alphabet*, Durham: Durham Modern Languages Series: 175–90.

Time Out (2007 [2002]) *Seville and Andalucia*, 3rd edn, London: *Time Out*.

Tinnell, Roger D. (1998 [1993]) *Federico García Lorca y la música: catálogo y discografía anotados*, 2nd edn, Madrid: Fundación Juan March.

Trend, J.B. (1956) *Lorca and the Spanish Poetic Tradition*, Oxford: Basil Blackwell.

Ucelay, Margarita (1990) 'Introducción', in Federico García Lorca, *Amor de Don Perlimplín con Belisa en su jardín*, ed. M. Ucelay, Madrid: Cátedra: 9–231.

—— (1992) 'El Club Teatral Anfistora', in D. Dougherty and M.F. Vilches de Frutos (eds) *El teatro en España*, Madrid: CSIC/FFGL/Tabacalera: 453–67.

—— (2003 [1995]) 'Introducción' and 'Apéndice', in Federico García Lorca, *Así que pasen cinco años: Leyenda del Tiempo*, 3rd edn, ed. M. Ucelay, Madrid: Cátedra: 9–145, 355–61.

Vilches de Frutos, María Francisca (1998) 'El teatro de Federico García Lorca en el contexto internacional: la dirección de escena', *Acotaciones*, 2(1): 11–21.

—— (2005) 'Introducción', in Federico García Lorca, *La casa de Bernarda Alba*, ed. M.F. Vilches de Frutos, Madrid: Cátedra: 9–133.

Vilches de Frutos, María Francisca and Dru Dougherty (1992a) 'Federico García Lorca como director de escena', in D. Dougherty and M.F.

Vilches de Frutos (eds) *El teatro en España*, Madrid: CSIC/FFGL/ Tabacalera: 241–51.

—— (1992b) *Los estrenos teatrales de Federico García Lorca (1920–1945)*, Madrid: Tabapress.

Wesker, Arnold (1986) 'Nuria Espert abre para Lorca las puertas de la escena británica', *El Público*, 37 (October): 3.

Wright, Sarah (2000) *The Trickster-Function in the Theatre of García Lorca*, London: Tamesis.

Yarmus, Marcia D. (1988) 'New York City Theatrical Productions of Federico García Lorca's Three Tragedies: *Blood Wedding, Yerma,* and *The House of Bernarda Alba*', *Estreno*, 14: 38–42.

Zatlin, Phyllis (1994) *Cross-Cultural Approaches to Theatre: The Spanish–French Connection*, Metuchen, NJ: Scarecrow Press.

Press reviews of productions

Blood Wedding

Agustí, Ignasi (1933) *Mirador*, 8 June: 5.

Anon (1935a) *New York Sun*, 16 February [*Blood Wedding* clippings file, NYPL].

—— (1935b) *New York Herald Tribune*, 24 February [*Blood Wedding* clippings file, NYPL].

Atkinson, Brooks (1935) *New York Times*, 12 February [*Blood Wedding* clippings file, NYPL].

Brown, John Mason (1935) *New York Evening Post*, 12 February [*Blood Wedding* clippings file, NYPL].

Clem (1954) n.p., n.d. [*Blood Wedding* clippings file, NYPL].

Fernández Almagro, Melchor (1933) *El Sol*, 9 March: 8.

Gussow, Mel (1992) *New York Times*, 15 May:
http://www.nytimes.com/books/99/09/12/specials/lorca-blood2.html (accessed 11 August 2005).

Mori, Arturo (1933) *El Liberal*, 9 March: 6.

Nuñez de Arenas, M. (1933) *La Voz*, 9 March: 3.

Porter, Andrew (1992) *Observer*, 8 November: 54.

Sobel, Bernard (1935) *Daily Mirror*, 18 February: 24.

Buster Keaton Takes a Walk

Gray, Emma (1990) *What's On*, 25 April, collected in *Theatre Record*, 10(8) (9–22 April): 524.

Don Perlimplín

Anon (1949) *Scotsman*, 23 August: 4.
Chabás, Juan (1933) *Luz*, 6 April: 3.
Cueva, Jorge de la (1933) *El Debate*, 6 April: 6.
Fernández Almagro, Melchor (1933) *El Sol*, 6 April: 7.
Finch, Hilary (1999) *The Times*, 27 April [ON Archive].
Maddocks, Fiona (1998) *Observer* [Review], 22 November: 7.
Marín Alcalde, Alberto (1933) *Ahora*, 6 April: 19.
Nuñez de Arenas, M. (1933) *La Voz*, 6 April: 3.
Page, Tim (1984) *New York Times*, 4 August: http://www.nytimes.com/books/99/09/12/specials/lorca-don.html (accessed 22 January 2006).

Doña Rosita

Agustí, Ignasi (1935) *L'Instant*, 16 December: 6.
Artis, Andreu A. (1935) *Última Hora*, 13 December: 7.
Billington, Michael (1983) *Guardian*, 31 August: 9.
Brennan, Mary (1983) *Glasgow Herald*, 31 August: 4.
Cruz Salido (1935) *Política*, 15 December: 2.
Díez Crespo, M. (1980) *El Alcázar*, 14 September: 35.
Espina, Antonio (1935) *El Sol*, 16 December: 4.
García Osuna, Carlos (1980) *El Imparcial*, 17 September: 23.
Guansé, Domènec (1935) *La Publicitat*, 14 December: 9.
Hanks, Robert (1997) *Independent on Sunday*, 4 May, collected in *Theatre Record*, 12(9) (23 April–6 May): 542–6.
Haro, Eduardo (1935) *La Libertad*, 19 December: 1–2.
Marín Alcalde, Alberto (1935) *Ahora*, 14 December: 29.
Morales, María-Luz (1935) *La Vanguardia*, 14 December: 9.
Olmedilla, Juan G. (1935) *El Heraldo de Madrid*, 13 December: 8.
Sánchez-Boxa, G. (1935) *El Día Gráfico*, 14 December: 15.
T. B., G. (1935) *Crónica*, 22 December: 36–7.

Mariana Pineda

Ayala, Francisco (1927) *La Gaceta Literaria*, 15 October: 5.
Bernat i Durán (1927) *El Noticiero Universal*, 25 June: 4.
Díez-Canedo, Enrique (1927) *El Sol*, 13 October: 5.
Fernández Almagro, Melchor (1927) *La Voz*, 13 October: 2.
G.C., E. (1927) *El Diluvio*, 26 June: 30.
Machado, M. (1927) *La Libertad*, 13 October: 3.
Madrid, Francisco (1927) *La Noche*, 25 June: 3.
Moragas, Valentín (1927) *Diario de Barcelona*, 26 June: 11.
R.C., M. (1927) *La Vanguardia*, 26 June: 15.
R.S., C. (1927) *El Liberal*, 25 June: 1.
Vicuña, Andrés de (1927) *El Correo Catalán*, 26 June: 4.

Play Without a Title

Breden, Simon (2006) *Western European Stages*, 18(1): 45–50.

The Billy-Club Puppets

Anon (1937) *El Sol*, 11 September: 3.

The Butterfly's Evil Spell

Alsina, José (1920) *El Sol*, 23 March: 11.
Andrenio (1920) *La Época*, 23 March: 1.
Bruckner, D.J.R. (1997) *New York Times*, 10 September: C14.
Floridor (1920) *ABC*, 23 March: 21.
Machado, M. (1920) *La Libertad*, 23 March: 2.
Russo, Francine (1997) *Village Voice*, 9 September: 93.
Sainer, Arthur (1974) *Village Voice*, 14 March: 66.
Wasserman, Debbi (1974) uncredited clipping, dated 28 February: 8
    [collected in Federico García Lorca clippings file, NYPL].

The House of Bernarda Alba

Atkinson, Brooks (1951) *New York Times*, 8 January: http://www.
    nytimes.com/books/99/09/12/specials/lorca-alba.html (accessed 8
    November 2005).
Brantley, Ben (2006) *New York Times*, 7 March: http://theater2.nytimes.
    com/2006/03/07/theater/reviews/07alba.html (accessed 10 November
    2006).
Brustein, Robert (1973) *Observer* [Review], 25 March: 35.

Clapp, Susannah (2005) *Observer* [Review], 20 March, collected in *Theatre Record*, 25(6) (12–25 March): 339–44.
Hoyle, Martin (1987) *Financial Times*, 19 January: 10.
Preston, Paul (1986) *Times Literary Supplement*, 26 September: 1064.
Shorter, Eric (1987) *Daily Telegraph*, 19 January: 9.
Taylor, Paul (1999) *Independent*, 21 May, collected in *Theatre Record*, (19/10) (7–20 May): 624–6.
Wardle, Irving (1973) *The Times*, 23 March [*The House of Bernarda Alba* clippings file, NYPL].

The Public

Bruckner, D.J.R. (1998) *New York Times*, 21 May: E5.
Coveney, Michael (1988) *Financial Times*, 4 October [Collection of TRSE].
McAfee, Annalena (1988) *Evening Standard*, 4 October [Collection of TRSE].

The Shoemaker's Wonderful Wife

Díez-Canedo, Enrique (1930) *El Sol*, 26 December: 4.
Espina, Antonio (1935) *El Sol*, 19 March: 2.
Fernández Almagro, Melchor (1930) *La Voz*, 25 December: 2.
—— (1933) *El Sol*, 6 April: 7.
Floridor (1930) *ABC*, 25 December: 38.
Marín Alcalde, Alberto (1933) *Ahora*, 6 April: 19.
Mori, Arturo (1935) *El Liberal*, 19 March: 7.
Ojeda, José (1935) *La Libertad*, 19 March: 4.
Olmedilla, Juan G. (1930) *Heraldo de Madrid*, 25 December: 7.

When Five Years Pass

Gelb, Arthur (1962) *New York Times*, 11 May: http://www.nytimes.com/books/99/09/12/specials/lorca-pass.html (accessed 11 August 2005).
Gómez Ortiz, Manuel (1978) *Ya*, 22 September: 44.
Haro Teclen, Eduardo (1989) *El País*, 30 April: 27.
Hera, Alberto de la (1989) *Ya*, 3 May: 44.
Llovet, Enrique (1978) *El País*, 21 September: 33.
López Sancho, Lorenzo (1978) *ABC*, 22 September: 47.
—— (1989) *ABC*, 30 April: 93.
Moya, Mabel (1987) *Sur*, 17 December: 10.

Yerma

Anon (1935) *La Publicitat*, 15 September: 5.

Araujo Costa, Luis (1934) *La Época*, 31 December: 5.

Bargas, Corpus (pseud. of Andrés García de la Barga y Gómez de la Serna) (1935) *Diario de Madrid*, 6 January: 1–2.

Billington, Michael (1987) *Guardian*, 28 March [NT Archive].

C., A. (1934) *ABC*, 30 December: 54.

Cortés, Joan (1935) *Mirador*, 26 September: 5.

Cueva, Jorge de la (1934) *El Debate*, 30 December: 4.

Díez-Canedo, Enrique (1934) *La Voz*, 31 December: 3.

Escalpelroff, Dimitri (1935) *Gracia y Justicia*, 5 January: 8.

Fernández Almagro, Melchor (1934) *El Sol*, 30 December: 8.

Haro, Eduardo (1934) *La Libertad*, 30 December: 7.

Hassell, Graham (1993) *What's On*, 6 October, collected in *Theatre Record*, 13(20) (24 September–7 October): 1116.

Kerr, Walter (1966) *New York Times*, 9 December: 60.

Laín Entralgo, Pedro (1972) *La Gaceta Ilustrada*, 17(798) (23 January): 3.

Marlowe, Sam (2006) *The Times*, 30 August, collected in *Theatre Record*, 26(16–17) (30 July–26 August): 928–30.

Marqueríe, Alfredo (1971) *Pueblo*, 30 November: 48.

Martínez Tomás, A. (1973) *La Vanguardia Española*, 16 February: 56.

Moragas, Valentín (1935) *Diario de Barcelona*, 19 September: 5–6.

Morales, María-Luz (1935) *La Vanguardia*, 19 September: 10.

Peter, John (1987) *Sunday Times*, 29 March [NT Archive].

Prego, Adolfo (1971) *ABC*, 1 December: 81.

Romero, Enrique (1972) *Triunfo*, 5 February: 42.

Sánchez-Boxa, G. (1935) *El Día Gráfico*, 19 September: 17.

Sherman, Robert (1971) *New York Times*, 14 August [*Yerma* clippings file, NYPL].

Walker, Tim (2006) *Daily Telegraph*, 3 September, collected in *Theatre Record*, 26(16–17) (30 July–26 August): 928–30.

Films and DVDs

A un dios desconocido/To an Unknown God, dir. Jaime Chávarri (Spain 1977). Manga Films. B46209–2004.

Bodas de sangre/Blood Wedding, dir. Carlos Saura (Spain 1981). Suevia Films. MND 1003.

Bodas de sangre/Blood Wedding, dir. Souhel Ben Barka (Morocco, 1976). Divisa Ediciones. M-15641-2002.

Buñuel y la mesa del Rey Salomón/Buñuel and King Solomon's Table, dir. Carlos Saura (Spain, Mexico, Germany 2001). Filmax. B-13416/02.

Doña Rosita, dir. Jorge Lavelli, 1981. CDT 118.

El balcón abierto/The Open Balcony, dir. Jaime Camino (Spain 1984). Tibidabo Films. 14095.

El crimen de una novia/The Crime of a Bride, dir. Lola Guerrero (Spain 2006). Cameo Media. B-34922-2006.

Feast of Ashes, based on *The House of Bernarda Alba,* choreog. Alvin Alley, 1976. NYPL. MGZIC 9-5315.

La casa de Bernarda Alba/The House of Bernarda Alba, dir. Mario Camus (Spain 1987). Cinemateca Literaria. B0006GAOJ.

La luz prodigiosa/The End of a Mystery dir. Miguel Hermoso (Spain-Italy 2003). Manga Films S.L.B.9086-2003.

Las desenamoradas, based on *The House of Bernarda Alba,* choreog. Eleo Pomare, 1983. NYPL. MGZIA 4-5124.

Las hermanas, based on *The House of Bernarda Alba,* choreog. Kenneth MacMillan, 1976. NYPL. MGZ1C 9-1497.

Lorca: el mar deja de moverse/Lorca: The Sea Stops Still, dir. Emilio Ruiz Barrachina (Spain 2006). Impacto Films. M.44978-2006.

Lorca, muerte de un poeta/Lorca Death of a Poet, RTVE series dir. Juan Antonio Bardem. Divisa Ediciones. M-2496-2002.

Lorca, muerte de un poeta/Lorca Death of a Poet, dir. Juan Antonio Bardem (Spain-France-Germany-UK, 1987). Suevia Films. MND 1018.

Los abajo firmantes/With George Bush on My Mind, dir. Joaquín Oristrell (Spain 2003). Cameo Media S.L. B-50529-2004.

Mariana Pineda (Sara Baras Company. Music and Orchestration: Manolo Sanlúcar), dir. Lluís Pasqual, 2003. Sony Music Entertainment Spain. SMM 2022809000.

Passion of the Blood, based on *Blood Wedding,* choreog. Augustus van Heerden, 2001. NYPL. MGZIA 4-5435.

The Disappearance of García Lorca (Death in Granada), dir. Marcos Zurinaga (USA 1997). Sony Pictures. B00004S5PV.

The House of Bernarda Alba, choreog. J. Marks, undated. NYPL. MGZIA 4-4998.

The House of Bernarda Alba, choreog. Mats Ek, 1986. NYPL. MGZIC 9-2550.

The House of Bernarda Alba by Federico García Lorca, trans. and dir. Emily Mann, 1997. NYPL, NCOV 2098.

The Love of Don Perlimplín, composer: Conrad Susa, libretto: Conrad Susa and Richard Street, dir. David Alden, 1984. NYPL. NCOV 360.

The Shoemaker's Prodigious Wife, trans. Michael Dewell and Carmen Zapata, dir. Max Ferra, 1988. NYPL. NCOV 2261.
Yerma, dir. David Stivel (Argentina 1963). FFGL.
Yerma, choreog. J. Marks, 1965. NYPL. MGZIC 9-1091.
Yerma dir. Imre Gyöngyössy and Barna Kabay (Canada, Germany, Hungary 1985). Starfilm, Macropus Film, Ma Film, Hungarian Television, Sefel Pictures International.
Yerma, dir. Pilar Távora (Spain 1999). Manga Films. DO966.

CDs and scores

Ainadamar, composed by Osvaldo Golijov, Deutsche Grammophon, 2006. 028947761655.
Amor [t], composed and produced by Karel Goeyvaerts, Megadisc Classics, 2000. 7829–30.
Bernarda Alba, composed by Michael John LaChiusa. Ghostlight, 2006. 79155844122.
Clash on Broadway, Epic/Legacy, 2000. E3K 63521.
Coleción de Canciones Populares Españolas, Federico García Lorca, La Argentinita, Sonifolk, 1994. M-28429-1994.
Camarón 'Autoretrato', Camarón de la Isla, Universal Music Spain, 1990. 0042284670823.
Cantando a Federico García Lorca, Manzanita et al. (La palabra más tuya), Iberautor Promociones Culturales, 2006. SA01137.
Caoutchouc Plays García Lorca, RN Discs, 1993. SJP399.
Lorca, Tim Buckley, Elektra Entertainment, 1970. 7559-61339-2.
Don Perlimplín/Serenata per un Satellite, composed by Bruno Maderna, conducted by Mauro Ceccanti, Contemporartensemble, Arts Music, 2005. B0007N48IA.
Hell's Ditch, The Pogues, WEA Records Ltd, 1990. 5046759622.
Lorquiana, poemas de Federico García Lorca, Ana Belén, BMG Music Spain, 1998. 74321626102.
Los gitanos cantan a Federico García Lorca, Diego Carrasco et al., Polygram Ibérica, 1993. 536 195–2.
Nocturama, Nick Cave and the Bad Seeds, Mute Records Ltd, 2003. 0724354300424.
Omega, Enrique Morente and Lagartija Nick, El Europeo Música, 1996. EEM 001.
Poetas en Nueva York, Leonard Cohen et al, Sony Music 1998. 477773 2.
The Concert for García Lorca, Ben Sidran. GoJazz Records, 2000. 9596160332.

The Secret Life of the Love Song, The Flesh Made Word, Two Lectures by Nick Cave, King Mob, 1999. KMob7.

Vérnász, an adaptation of *Blood Wedding* composed by Sándor Szokolay, conducted by Andras Korodi, Hungarian State Opera Orchestra, 1994. B00000303R.

Yerma, music by Heitor Villa-Lobos. Score, 1955. NYPL. JOB 04-1.

Yerma, music by Raymond Wilding-White. Vocal Score, 1962. NYPL. AMC M1503W673 Y4.

Index

Works by Federico García Lorca are listed in bold. Play texts by other authors are only listed when they deal with Lorca or when they are referred to on numerous occasions within the manuscript. Films are listed, in most cases, initially by their English-language titles. Directors, composers and performers mentioned in the book who have had an association with Lorca's work are also listed.

234   *Index*

242   *Index*

Related titles from Routledge

Routledge Modern and Contemporary Dramatists:

J.B. Priestley

J.B. Priestley is the first book to provide a detailed and up to date analysis of the enormous contribution made by this playwright, novelist, journalist and critic to twentieth century British theatre.

Priestley was often criticised for being either too populist or too experimental and this study unpicks the contradictions of a playwright and theatre theorist popular with audiences but too often dismissed by critics; describing and analysing in detail not only his plays but also their specific historical and contemporary productions.

Using a combination of archive, review and critical materials, the book relocates Priestley as a theatre theorist of substance as well as a playwright who challenged theatre conventions and assumptions about audience expectations, at a time when theatre was considered both conservative and lacking in innovation.

Professor Maggie B. Gale is Chair of Drama at the University of Manchester, England. Her published works include *British Theatre Between the Wars* and *The Cambridge Companion to the Actress*.

Hbk: 978–0–415–40242–2
Pbk: 978–0–415–40243–9

Available at all good bookshops
For ordering and further information please visit:
www.routledge.com

Related titles from Routledge

Routledge Modern and Contemporary Dramatists:

Susan Glaspell and Sophie Treadwell

Susan Glaspell and Sophie Treadwell presents critical introductions to two of the most significant American dramatists of the early twentieth century. Glaspell and Treadwell led American Theatre from outdated melodrama to the experimentation of great European playwrights like Ibsen, Strindberg and Shaw.

This is the first book to deal with Glaspell and Treadwell's plays from a theatrical, rather than literary, perspective, and presents a comprehensive overview of their work from lesser known plays to seminal productions of *Trifles* and *Machinal*.

Although each woman pursued her own themes, subjects and manner of stage production, this shared volume underscores the theatrical and cultural conditions influencing female playwrights in modern America.

Barbara Ozieblo teaches American Literature at the University of Málaga, Spain. She is the author of *Susan Glaspell: A Critical Biography*, editor of *The Provincetown Players: A Choice of the Shorter Plays* and co-editor of *Disclosing Intertextualities: The Stories, Plays, and Novels of Susan Glaspell*. She is co-founder and President of the Susan Glaspell Society.

Jerry Dickey is Associate Professor of Theatre Arts at the University of Arizona. He is the author of *Sophie Treadwell: a Research and Production Sourcebook* and co-editor of *Broadway's Bravest Woman: Selected Writings of Sophie Treadwell*. His essays on Treadwell have appeared in *A Companion to Twentieth-Century American Drama* and the *Cambridge Companion to American Women Playwrights*.

Hbk: 978–0–415–40485–3
Pbk: 978–0–415–40484–6

Available at all good bookshops
For ordering and further information please visit:
www.routledge.com

Related titles from Routledge

Twentieth Century Theatre: A Sourcebook

Edited by Richard Drain

Twentieth Century Theatre: A Sourcebook is an inspired handbook of ideas and arguments on theatre. Richard Drain gathers together a uniquely wide-ranging selection of original writings on theatre by its most creative practitioners – directors, playwrights, performers and designers, from Jarry to Grotowski and Craig. These key texts span the twentieth century, from the onset of modernism to the present, providing direct access to the thinking behind much of the most stimulating theatre the century has had to offer, as well as guidelines to its present most adventurous developments.

Setting theory beside practice, these writings bring alive a number of vital and continuing concerns, each of which is given full scope in five sections which explore the Modernist, Political, Inner and Global dimensions of twentieth century theatre. *Twentieth Century Theatre: A Sourcebook* provides illuminating perspectives on past history, and throws fresh light on the sources and development of theatre today. This sourcebook is an essential and versatile collection for students at all levels.

Richard Drain is a playwright and director whose plays have been performed on stage and radio, and his devised works have toured to theatres, festivals, schools, community centres and prisons.

Hb: 978–0–415–09619–5
Pb: 978–0–415–09620–1

Available at all good bookshops
For ordering and further information please visit:
www.routledge.com

Related titles from Routledge

History of European Drama and Theatre

by Erika Fischer-Lichte

This major study reconstructs the vast history of European drama from Greek tragedy through to twentieth-century theatre, focusing on the subject of identity. Throughout history, drama has performed and represented political, religious, national, ethnic, class-related, gendered, and individual concepts of identity. Erika Fischer-Lichte's topics include:

- ancient Greek theatre
- Shakespeare and Elizabethan theatre by Corneille, Racine, Molière
- the Italian commedia dell'arte and its transformations into eighteenth-century drama
- the German Enlightenment – Lessing, Schiller, Goethe, and Lenz
- romanticism by Kleist, Byron, Shelley, Hugo, de Vigny, Musset, Büchner, and Nestroy
- the turn of the century – Ibsen, Strindberg, Chekhov, Stanislavski
- the twentieth century – Craig, Meyerhold, Artaud, O'Neill, Pirandello, Brecht, Beckett, Müller.

Anyone interested in theatre throughout history and today will find this an invaluable source of information.

Hb: 978–0–415–18059–7
Pb: 978–0–415–18060–3

Available at all good bookshops
For ordering and further information please visit:
www.routledge.com